ANTONY FISHER

Gerald Frost

ANTONY FISHER
Champion of Liberty

P

PROFILE BOOKS

LONDON

First published in Great Britain in 2002 by
Profile Books Ltd
58A Hatton Garden
London ECIN 8LX
www.profilebooks.co.uk

10 9 8 7 6 5 4 3 2 1

Typeset in Bembo by MacGuru
info@macguru.org.uk

Printed and bound in Great Britain by
Clays, Bungay, Suffolk

A CIP catalogue record for this book is available from the British Library.

ISBN 1 86197 505 8

For Mark, Linda, Mike and Lucy

Contents

Illustrations

All photographs reproduced by permission of the Fisher family

Antony's mother, c.1914.

Antony's father during World War I.

Antony with his mother and younger brother Basil.

Basil and Antony at Eton College in 1931.

Antony at RAF Central Gunnery School, December 1942.

Antony and Tony Pendry, his partner in Buxted Chicken. *(The Farmer & Stockbreeder magazine)*

Antony beside one of the Buxted Chicken Company's broiler sheds in 1956.

Newplace, Antony's home in Sussex.

Antony and his first wife, Eve, in the 1960s.

Antony with his eldest son Mark in the Cayman Islands in 1972, holding a turtle.

Antony with Milton Friedman, Pascal Salin, Jean Pavlevski and Rose Friedman in Paris in October 1980. *(Association pour la Liberté Economique et le Progrès Social)*

Antony with Arthur Seldon, Ralph Harris and his mentor Friedrich Hayek at the Institute of Economic Affairs in London in the early 1980s.

Antony and Margaret Thatcher celebrating the IEA's 30th anniversary in 1987. *(Institute of Economic Affairs)*

Antony and members of his family celebrating his 70th birthday.

Antony on his last family holiday in 1987, with second wife Dorian and his children and grandchildren.

Antony's widow Dorian being given Antony's knighthood insignia in September 1988.

Acknowledgements

The initial research on which this book is based was undertaken by Barney Towns. I am indebted to him for the compilation of a detailed, meticulous and painstaking timeline. I have also drawn on transcripts of interviews carried out by Russell Lewis with Antony Fisher's former colleagues and family members.

I am grateful to Lord Harris of High Cross for a great number of helpful comments and improvements to the text, and to Edith Hastings for enhancing the quality of my prose by rescuing me from various infelicities of phraseology.

My greatest intellectual debt is to Richard Cockett, whose book, *Thinking the Unthinkable*, provides the best account of how the climate of political ideas underwent a profound change during the post-Second World War era and of the part played in that process by the Institute of Economic Affairs and by the other think tanks with which Antony Fisher was associated.

Antony's children, Linda Whetstone, Lucy Giles, and Mark and Mike Fisher, all shared their recollections of him. I owe a similar debt to Antony's widow, Dorian Adams. All gave generously of their time and made many helpful suggestions. I am also indebted to Linda Whetstone for the prodigious organisational task underlying the compilation of an appendix listing details of the numerous think tanks with which her father assisted, or was in some way associated with.

Tony Pendry, Antony Fisher's partner at Buxted Chickens, provided a first-hand account of Fisher's role in the transformation of an important branch of British agriculture. John Hall, DFC, QC, who served under Antony as a young flying instructor, offered extremely helpful insights into his war service.

From John Blundell, General Director of the Institute of Economic Affairs, and Alejandro Chafuen, President of the Atlas Economic Research Foundation, I learned much about the background and record of the think tanks which Antony Fisher started or assisted. Much of John Blundell's written work on the subject is collected in *Waging the War of Ideas* (Occasional Paper 119, IEA, 2001). Teresa Brown, Director of Publications at the Atlas Foundation's headquarters in Fairfax, Virginia displayed diligence beyond the call of duty in sifting manuscripts and in drawing my attention to letters and documents of which I was previously unaware.

Others who added significantly to my knowledge of Antony Fisher's life include: Dr Digby Anderson, Robert Boyd, Dr Eamonn Butler, Joycie Coke, Commander and Mrs John Davey, Sue Lee Emery, Dr Edwin J. Feulner Jnr, Dr John C. Goodman, Dr Jo Ann Kwong, Professor Leonard Liggio, Greg Lindsay, Terry Martens, Dr Madsen Pirie, Randolph Richardson, Sally Pipes, John Raybould, Dr Arthur Seldon CBE, Dr Michael Walker and Francis Whetsone.

Not least, I am grateful to my wife, Meg, for her constant encouragement and for tolerating my neglect of family responsibilities as I struggled with the text, a pattern of behaviour which became more extreme as the copy deadline approached.

I am grateful for permission to quote from the following published works:

Battle of Britain: The Jubilee History by Richard Hough and
    Denis Richards (Hodder & Stoughton), copyright ©
    Richard Hough and Denis Richards 1989
Capitalism by Arthur Seldon (Blackwell), copyright © Arthur
    Seldon 1990
The Commanding Heights by Daniel Yergin & Joseph Stanislaw

(Simon & Schuster), copyright © Daniel Yergin & Joseph Stanislaw, 1998

Eton Renewed by Tim Card (John Murray), copyright © Tim Card 1994: by kind permission of John Murray (Publishers) Ltd

Keith Joseph – A Single Mind by Morrison Halcrow (Macmillan), copyright © Morrison Halcrow 1989; by kind permission of Curtis Brown on behalf of Morrison Halcrow

Last Chance Lost by Peggy and Sam Fosdick (Irvin Naylor), copyright © Irvin Naylor 1994

Margaret Thatcher: The Path to Power by Margaret Thatcher (HarperCollins Publishers Ltd), copyright © Margaret Thatcher 1995

Thatcher's People by John Ranelagh (HarperCollins Publishers Ltd), copyright © John Ranelagh 1991

Thinking the Unthinkable by Richard Cockett (HarperCollins Publishers Ltd), copyright © Richard Cockett 1994

Every effort has been made to obtain copyright permission for quoted extracts. Any omissions or errors of attribution are unintentional and will, if brought to the publisher's attention, be corrected in future printings.

Foreword

It is hard today to reconstruct the intellectual atmosphere in 1945, when Antony Fisher, the subject of this book, was completing his wartime service as a fighter pilot and gunnery instructor. It was taken for granted that socialism, government control of the means of production, was the way of the future – a view supported by all decent, progressive individuals. Those of us who were deeply concerned about the danger to freedom and prosperity from the growth of government, from the triumph of the welfare state and Keynesian ideas, were a small, beleaguered minority regarded as reactionaries by the great majority of our fellow intellectuals.

F. A. Hayek's famous tract, *The Road to Serfdom*, published in March 1944, was dedicated to 'the socialists of all parties'. An eloquent and passionate statement of the dangers to freedom from state control of the means to production, it is now regarded as one of the most important books of the twentieth century. Yet it was turned down for publication in the United States by three publishers, in one case because it was considered 'unfit for publication by a reputable house', before it was submitted to the University of Chicago Press, which accepted it on the urging of a leading faculty member. Hayek himself believed that the negative reception of this book destroyed his reputation as an economist.

Antony Fisher came across *The Road to Serfdom* through a *Reader's Digest* condensation. For him, as for many other young men and women who had been in the armed forces, Hayek's predictions about the consequences of collectivism were not simply hypothetical possibilities but visible realities that they had themselves experienced in the military. His first reaction was to enter elective politics to fight for freedom. He was dissuaded from this course when he visited Hayek at the London School of Economics in 1945. Hayek told him that the ideas of the intellectuals would ultimately determine the ideas of politicians and the course of events. The real task was to change those ideas.

Ten years later, in 1955, Antony was able to act on Hayek's advice thanks to the commercial success of a venture in breeding chickens. With some of his first profits from that venture he set up the Institute of Economic Affairs, and shortly thereafter persuaded Ralph Harris to serve as its director. When Arthur Seldon joined, completing the critical trio essential to its success, the Institute was off and running and played a major role in changing the climate of opinion in Britain.

If Antony had done no more in the think-tank world, it would have been enough to put all believers in freedom in his debt. But after a digression to breeding green turtles, scientifically successful but commercially disastrous, he returned to breeding think tanks, at first on a retail basis, and then, with the establishment of the Atlas Economic Research Foundation, on a wholesale basis.

I first met Antony in the fall of 1957 at a meeting in St Moritz of the Mont Pélerin Society – an international society of free-market intellectuals that had been founded a decade earlier by Hayek. I saw him thereafter at the IEA on my occasional trips to Britain. I got to know Antony better and to appreciate his strengths after 1977, when my wife and I moved into the apartment house in which he and his second wife, Dorian, were living. It was from here that he set up the Atlas Foundation and achieved a degree of success that passed my – and perhaps even his – fondest expectations. His death in 1988 was a great loss to us personally as it was to the world.

His remarkable story is well told in the pages that follow.

MILTON FRIEDMAN
Stanford, California

Introduction

With characteristic modesty, Antony Fisher wrote to a friend, 'I suppose what I do is unusual. Some say it is unique.' But when Fisher died in San Francisco on 8 July 1988 aged 73, four weeks after being knighted in the Queen's birthday honours list, the world was largely unaware of him or his influence. He was not listed in *Who's Who*; he was not well known to the British or American media; and he had never held major elected office. Although he had made – and lost – a considerable fortune he relied during his latter years on the financial support of a rich and devoted second wife. The belated knighthood, which fitted the tall, spare, handsome Englishman like a glove, was almost the sole public recognition he received during his lifetime, and this did not come until he was terminally ill.

Only two politicians, Enoch Powell and Keith Joseph, both respected friends, attended his memorial service held at St Lawrence Jewry in the City of London later that year. That, however, would probably have been more a matter of satisfaction than of regret, since throughout his life the former businessman and decorated World War II pilot displayed an ill-concealed contempt for the generality of politicians. He believed that their capacity for harm far outweighed their ability to do good. He consequently took very little interest in the political process, of which he was in many respects quite ignorant. Among MPs generally, probably only a small handful were aware of Fisher's remarkable influence. Yet in founding the Institute of Economic Affairs, the London-based free-market think tank, he had played a crucial role in helping to reverse economic trends that many had judged to be irreversible, thereby changing the direction of British post-war politics. In creating and nurturing many similar bodies in other countries he also helped spread the ideas underlying the Thatcher revolution of the 1980s worldwide. But his influence did not end there. The retreat of governments from the market place under the impact of those ideas in turn made possible the wider process of globalisation, with its vast potential for transforming economic conditions and expanding human liberty. And as the political agenda of the world's rich nations has increasingly focused on social rather than economic issues, it has been the think tanks that Fisher founded, or assisted, which have laid the intellectual foundations of new and distinctive responses to the problems of crime, juvenile delinquency, welfare dependency, and poor educational standards. The following tribute from a politician – Oliver Letwin, a brilliant young Conservative politician who showed a rare understanding of Fisher's role – may actually have underestimated the extent of his influence: 'Without Fisher, no IEA; without the IEA and its clones, no Thatcher and quite possibly no Reagan; without Reagan, no Star Wars; without Star Wars, no economic collapse of the Soviet Union. Quite a chain of consequences for a chicken farmer!'

Other businessmen – some vastly richer than Fisher – have used their wealth and influence to pursue political goals, often through ownership of the media, sometimes by seeking a direct impact on the programmes of political parties, or, like James Goldsmith and Ross Perot, by starting their own. Some of these were blessed with more penetrating intellectual gifts – though Fisher was an intelligent and able man – or with greater powers of persuasion or personal magnetism. It is difficult to think of any whose influence has been as pervasive or who pursued his task more single-mindedly, more persistently over 40 years, and with such scant regard to personal fame or advantage.

This book tells the story of a life that was marked by adversity and personal tragedy as well as great achievement. In so doing it also describes how the intellectual resources underlying the Thatcher revolution were organised, a process in which coincidence played a large part, and it seeks to assess the impact of the think tanks which Fisher founded or helped bring to maturity. I believe that it illustrates not only the power of ideas – something in which Fisher believed passionately – but also the decisive role of an essentially private individual. For at a time when it was widely asserted that history was determined by huge impersonal forces, Fisher and those he recruited showed that the individual still counted. Perhaps because he was a reserved and modest man, Antony periodically disappears from the action in this account of his achievements, or remains barely visible in the background, while those he motivated or helped take centre stage. Nevertheless, it will be evident that major changes in the direction of events in Britain, and elsewhere in the world, would not have occurred in the way they did without his influence, and some, indeed, might not have happened at all.

In writing this book, I have increasingly come to believe that, although he may well have been oblivious to the fact, Antony Fisher's gentlemanly virtues were crucial to the success of his endeavours – as were the moral qualities of key individuals who gave intellectual substance to his dream. The task could not have been accomplished by those whose lives were regulated *only* by a narrow ideology. A favourite and oft-repeated Fisher phrase was, 'Ideas have consequences.' No less do the personal qualities of those who advance them.

A defining moment

The fifteenth of August 1940 began as a fine, bright day, but as the afternoon sunshine grew hazy it was to witness the fiercest fighting so far in the Battle of Britain. While the first air skirmishes were taking place, the Cabinet met at 10 Downing Street. All returned to their respective ministries at the conclusion of business, except for the Prime Minister, Winston Churchill, and Anthony Eden, the Secretary for War, who later recorded:

> Squadron after squadron of the RAF went up to engage the enemy and still the Luftwaffe kept coming. The news was scrappy at first and still more squadrons were called for, until it seemed that they had all been committed. As we listened and conjectured, things looked very stern, with the odds heavily against us. At last Churchill announced that he would drive to Fighter Command HQ and I went back to the War Office, neither of us yet knowing that this was to be one of the critical days of the war.[1]

The Luftwaffe flew more sorties that day than on any other during the entire battle; and it was the only day during the battle on which the German air force used all of the operational warplanes available. But honours went decisively to the RAF, with the Luftwaffe recording the loss of 75 warplanes – the biggest such loss to have been suffered by either side – compared to the loss of 34 British fighters. In conversation with his private secretary that evening, Churchill described it as 'one of the greatest days in history'. Hitler responded to German losses by ordering that the air campaign be intensified still further; and the American Ambassador to London, Joseph P. Kennedy, instructed the US Embassy staff to flee Britain prior to what he was certain would be the German invasion.

That day was also a turning point in the life of Antony Fisher, a young pilot officer with RAF 111 Squadron, which was scrambled from Croydon as German planes crossed the Channel at Dungeness. The squadron, which had been engaged in fierce fighting during two earlier missions, comprised ten Hurricane fighters, including that flown by Antony's younger brother, Basil. As it flew to engage the enemy, the view of London in the late afternoon sunshine was uninterrupted: 'To the north lay the great urban sprawl of London, the dome of St Paul's, the tower of the Roman Catholic Cathedral beyond the Palace of Westminster and the white splash of the Savoy Hotel between them, all identifiable beneath the silver-grey floating sea of barrage balloons.'[2]

The task of 111 Squadron was to engage *Erpro* 210, a German Messerschmitt squadron of fifteen 110s and eight 109s, which earlier that afternoon had destroyed RAF Martelsham Heath. The mission of German fighter bombers was now to attack RAF Kenley in Sussex, but Walter Rubensdoerffer, the German commander, mistook the Croydon RAF base, situated 15 miles north of Kenley, for his target. The Messerchmitts came in low, climbing at the last minute: 'Rubensdoerffer now led his fighter bombers down on to the target, confident that this would be the second airfield Erpro 210 would write off on this day. No anti-aircraft fire. How could they miss? Then suddenly, at the most critical moment as they were selecting targets, left thumb on the bomb release, right thumb on gun button, they found unfamiliar aircraft, behind, at their side and above.' Number III Squadron was waiting.[3]

In the intense fighting that followed, seven Messerschmitts were brought down, including that flown by Rubensdoerffer, but as the Hurricanes pursued the German fighter-bombers back towards the Channel, Antony saw his brother leave a dog-fight over the village of Sidlesham in Sussex trailing smoke and flames. The aircraft headed west but then turned sharply to port and Basil was seen to bale out. His parachute, when it opened, was on fire and his fall accelerated as the pilotless Hurricane dived, swooped and turned erratically before crashing into a barn, setting fire to an adjacent farm building.

When Antony landed safely at RAF Croydon shortly after-wards, palls of smoke were rising above the bomb-damaged hangars, armoury and airport terminal. Around the perimeter of the airfield firemen could be seen tackling at least a dozen other fires while ambulances raced through suburban streets. The scene of devastation was the consequence of III Squadron's success: because of its intervention many of the German bombs had fallen wide on private houses, killing 70 people and injur-ing many more. But RAF Croydon remained defiantly opera-tional.

Later that evening Antony learned that his brother's body had been recovered from a pond near Sidlesham. Basil had fallen free of his parachute, its harness having burned through.

The brothers had been constant companions at school and university. Neither had known their father, George Fisher, who had been killed by a Turkish sniper's bullet in Gaza during World War I when Antony was two years old. In the absence of a close senior male relation, he had come to regard his more gregarious and extrovert younger brother with an almost paternal pride and care, often regaling friends and relatives with stories of Basil's achievements and exploits with obvious pleasure. Their privileged and carefree pre-war days had been characterised by an almost Wodehousian innocence. At Cambridge, they ap-peared largely indifferent to the political and ideological debates which absorbed many of their contemporaries. As befitted Old Etonians, they had taken their studies seriously, but not so seriously as to blight their social lives. They drove smart sports cars, learned to fly and jointly purchased their own aircraft. They enjoyed parties, dancing, and the blandishments of the London social scene. For Antony, the brief period between university and war brought a promising start to a career in the City and marriage to a beautiful and vivacious girl – Eve Naylor – to whom he had been introduced at a dance. It remained a life that was privileged, fulfilling, and unusually free of material care.

Like that of many others, it was a life transformed by war. The loss of Basil had a profound effect upon Antony. Their mother, Janet, had died shortly before the war's outbreak after a long and painful illness. David Berry, also a member of III Squadron and Antony's best friend, had died over France in May 1940. During the same month, a cousin, Michael Fisher, with whom Antony had often played cricket at the family home in Norfolk, was killed in the Battle of Flanders. Later, another cousin, Peregrine Young, with whom both Antony and Basil had formed a firm friendship during family holidays, was to die during the fall of Tobruk. Their deaths added to Antony's isolation and grief caused by the loss of Basil.

Antony emerged gradually from the trauma of his brother's death a more serious man and ultimately a more determined one, but in the immediate aftermath his nerve was shattered and it was many months before he flew again. Grounded by his commanding officer, he very quickly found a new role as an RAF instructor. He knew from his brief but intense experience as a Battle of Britain pilot that young fliers were being sent into battle with insufficient gunnery skills and that such ignorance could be fatal. He therefore set about using the engineering knowledge he had acquired at Cambridge to devise and build a ground-based trainer that would enhance shooting accuracy and thus improve a pilot's prospects of survival. His clear-sighted analysis of the practical problems faced by frightened and inexperienced young fliers and his single-minded application in finding a solution to them were to typify his approach to a range of subsequent problems. Although he found his wartime experiences were too painful to speak of, even to his family, he drew lessons about human behaviour from them that were to shape his views and guide his future life. In a book dedicated to Basil's memory and published some 30 years after his brother's death, Antony wrote:

> I survived, but no thanks to my own efforts, for it was some time before I was to learn that the main ability for which I and my squadron existed, to destroy enemy aircraft, I did not possess. Unaware of my inability, and maybe with less than average inclination for violent aggression, I was no credit in that particular occupation. Later I was to learn the great difficulty, even with eight machine guns, of hitting an enemy plane. Yet as soon as I became aware of that difficulty, I became a more useful Royal Air Force officer ... From that moment I became an asset and no longer a liability ... I learned that good intentions were not enough.[4]

Failure to identify a problem and the tendency to proceed naively on the basis of good intentions alone, were accusations he was later to level repeatedly at those politicians he held responsible for Britain's deepening post-war economic malaise. Earlier generations of his family had devoted themselves to public service, and it is probable Antony would have followed their example. But his brother's death appears to have strengthened his desire to do so, while deepening an inner resolve that enabled him to concentrate on a problem to the exclusion of almost everything else – a trait which could make him seem boring and obsessional to those who did not share his concerns. In the aftermath of war these centred increasingly on Britain's relative economic decline and the growing restrictions placed on liberty as a result of socialist policies. In the words of his daughter, Linda Whetstone: 'After the war he realised that both his father and his brother had given their lives for the freedom of their fellow countrymen, yet he saw freedom diminishing, not increasing. Ration books, endless restrictions such as exchange control, and such petty regulations as to which colour you could paint your front door all seemed irrational and unnecessary ... he felt alone and depressed.'[5] The enemies of freedom had now changed, but out of this sense of isolation came an ambition to continue the fight waged on its behalf by George Fisher in Gaza and Basil Fisher in the skies over England.

Antony was born on 28 June 1915 at 23 Launceston Place, Kensington, into a prosperous upper-middle-class family. His father, a captain in the Fourth Norfolk Regiment, had been at home on leave but was unable to wait for the birth of his first son and had returned to his battalion at Chelmsford.

Antony's parents at first seemed unsure of what to call their first-born. He is referred to as Torvald or 'T' in letters between them, but eventually they decided on Antony, then George after his father, and Anson after his mother, who was descended from William Anson of Shugborough through the younger sister of Vice-Admiral George Anson, First Lord of the Admiralty and later Lord Anson – best remembered for his four-year voyage around the world during which he captured a Spanish treasure ship whose priceless contents were escorted under guard from Portsmouth to the Tower of London on his triumphant return. The story of the voyage is one of the epic tales of British naval history and, along with the record of Anson's defeat of the French fleet off Cape Finisterre in 1747, was one on which Antony was brought up. Anson had earlier distinguished himself through conscientious and humane command of a vessel which protected the coasts of North and South Carolina from the French. He seems to have been equally popular with the colonists, who named Anson County in North Carolina after him, as with his crew. Writing to her sister in London, a Carolina lady declared that she could 'say nothing worse of him than that it was averred that he loved his bottle and was far from being a woman hater; whilst on the other hand he was handsome, good natured, polite, well bred, generous, and humane; passionately fond of music and so old fashioned to make a profession of religion'.[6] Unlike the distinguished sea lord, Antony Fisher was teetotal, but otherwise the description fits him in all respects. Moreover, in Antony's determination to improve the training given to young RAF fliers it is possible to see traces of Anson's measures as First Sea Lord to improve naval equipment and dockyards – to which more than one naval historian has attributed Britain's success in the Seven Years' War.

The family of Antony's paternal grandmother, the Thompsons, had prospered as mine owners in Durham. Like a number of others from rich north-country families during the mid-nineteenth century, Thomas Charles Thompson wished to move south to be near the centres of art, culture and politics. Although he continued to maintain a home in Durham he also wished to live the life of a country squire and chose one of the more attractive corners of Ashdown Forest in East Sussex – an otherwise bleak expanse of heathland long since bereft of trees – to settle his family. In his *Rural Rides,* William Cobbett describes the forest as 'verily the most villainously ugly spot I ever saw in England. There may be Englishmen who wish to see the coast of Nova Scotia. They need not go to sea; for here it is to the life. If I had been in a long trance … and had been waked up here, I should have begun to look about for the Indians and the squaws, and to have heaved a sigh at the thought of being so far from England.'

Thompson, who was to represent Durham City as MP from 1875 until 1880, obviously thought more highly of the area, for it was here in 1867 that he purchased a house and 3,563 acres from the widow of a retired admiral. Thompson razed the existing mansion and built a substantial if slightly smaller house in the Victorian gothic style. It was here that Antony and Basil were to spend the early part of their childhood.

What distinguished Thompson as a member of the English gentry was not only his unusual generosity but his ability to form friendships that cut across divisions of class and rank, without in any way calling them into question. This was a trait shared by successive generations of his family. Thompson was also remembered for another trait: the readiness to spend freely in order to ensure that family events went off in style. When he died in 1892, he left in his will a black suit to each of his employees so that they might be properly attired at his funeral. His cherished plans for turning Ashdown into the family seat for future generations of Thompsons, however, were sadly frustrated: in the absence of surviving male offspring, the house and land were bequeathed to his daughter Mary, the wife of George Carnac Fisher, Antony's grandfather.

Fisher, a curate from the neighbouring parish of Forest Row who, like Thompson, had been active in the temperance movement, was to rise steadily through the church to become successively Suffragan Bishop of Southampton and of Ipswich. Although a man of simple tastes and few affectations, Bishop Fisher was a rich man when he died in 1921, having inherited the family home at Burgh in Norfolk. He left an estate amounting to £178, 455, the equivalent of many millions today.

Fisher's eldest son, George Kenneth Thompson Fisher – Antony's father – was born in Barrow in 1879, the first of eight children who were brought up at the Fisher family home at Burgh and at Ashdown Park. After Harrow, George read history at New College, Oxford, and through university connections later met and fell in love with Janet Katherine Mary Anson, a striking, lively and independent-minded girl. Her father, Frederick, had been sent to make his fortune in New Zealand, and had begun to prosper in the tiny settlement of Piraki, Akaroa in South Island but returned home on hearing that his eldest brother, Sir William Anson – Warden of All Souls, MP for the university seat in the 1890s, and briefly Vice-Chancellor of Oxford – was terminally ill. Since Sir William was childless the title would pass to Frederick and subsequently to his son, Denis. Consequently, Frederick settled his family – including Antony's mother – outside Oxford.

By a bizarre turn of events, however, five Ansons were to die in quick succession. First, William's young brother, Rear-Admiral Algernon Anson, died on 12 November 1912. A few weeks later Frederick died before he could claim the title for which he had yearned and for which he had returned home. He was followed six months later by Sir William, whose title then passed to Denis. But less than one month later Denis drowned after the society beauty Diana Manners (later Lady Diana Cooper), then aged 21, encouraged him to dive into the Thames so that she might win a £10 bet. The title then passed to John Anson, who died four years later while on active service with the Royal Navy in March 1918. He was succeeded by his brother, Sir Edward Anson, who survived both world wars – the first as a midshipman in the Royal Navy and the second as a lieutenant-colonel in the Royal Artillery. Thus chance and circumstance, which were to play a prominent role in Antony's life, determined the succession of the Anson baronetcy, just as it was to play a crucial role in bringing Antony's parents together.

George Kenneth Thompson Fisher was a man of largely conventional views and habits: modest, decent, unassuming, anxious to play a useful role in society but unwilling to use his connections to secure his own advancement. His passion was for painting and after university he studied under a succession of noteworthy artists of the day. His surviving landscapes and portraiture suggest a distinct talent but he believed himself to lack the necessary imagination to be truly successful. After coming down from Oxford, where he took a fourth in history, he travelled widely in the Balkans and the Middle East, painting and collecting plant specimens for Ashdown Park, before opting for a civil-service career at the Board of Trade, where he made steady if unspectacular progress. In 1909, as a major European war looked increasingly possible, George was commissioned into the army, as a second lieutenant in a Territorial battalion of the Norfolk Regiment.

In contrast to her future husband, Janet Fisher was a non-conformist both in religion – she was a devout, lifelong

Christian Scientist – and in outlook. Her non-conformism was allied to a considerable independence of thought and a presumption that problems existed to be solved, qualities which she bequeathed in full measure to her eldest son. On 23 August 1914, three weeks after the outbreak of World War I and the mobilisation of his regiment, George and Janet were married at St Bartholomew's Church in the City of London.

George was to prove a conscientious and popular officer, and one who was not unaware of the comic aspect of military life. In a letter to Janet from a training camp he wrote: 'We are to have a review on Saturday for the benefit of his Lordship of Leicester, who is our colonel-in-chief and a few other things. I wish you could come to it. It will be funny. If you knew the people who, disguised as men of war, will take part in it, you would realise how funny … A little soldier veterinary who has apparently travelled everywhere is discussing the Balkan question …'[7]

After spending the initial year of the war in training and home duties, the regiment departed for the Dardanelles and landed at Suvla Bay, where the incompetence of the high command prevented the British force from exploiting the element of surprise. The campaign, which involved heavy British and Australian losses as the allied forces were pinned down on the coast, was to end in failure and humiliation. But Fisher, who was mentioned in dispatches, was elated by finally having encountered the enemy. He was also justifiably proud of his company's performance under fire:

> We've had hard work of all sorts since we landed, and I am now sitting in a comfortable dug-out with our guns blazing away over me. It's a satisfactory sound. I am extraordinarily well; never really felt better in my life, in spite of almost no sleep for two or three days – up to last night when I had several hours; and very little food, an occasional biscuit and a little marmalade. I don't seem to want any more. I am wonderfully happy, which is odd,

perhaps; but the fact that the men are doing so well is most encouraging, and gives one a sense of contentment in spite of very considerable discomfort.[8]

After a little more than three weeks, Fisher was suffering from severe dysentery, and returned home via a series of hospital ships. Even after a year the illness was judged to be sufficiently serious for Fisher to be considered for a medical discharge, but after turning down the opportunity to appear before a medical board, he chose to return to his former battalion, then in Palestine.

The following months were spent on desert patrol. He kept busy with the needs and problems of his company, wrote almost daily to Janet, and occupied the interminable hours of waiting by painting and sketching. His letters to his wife reflect a soldier's longing for home and family, but also a resignation to the deprivations and hardships of active service. There are few complaints; most concern his loyal and devoted servant, Private Fred Hawes, whose usefulness was limited by a poor memory and modest intelligence. Fisher felt guilty at his own exasperation with him, alternating between deciding to sack him and finding him a safer posting behind the lines, and a resolution to be more patient. [9] Most letters show evidence of a father's concern for his sons. The fact that George's wartime billets – a series of dug-outs in the desert – were regularly under fire from Turkish positions does not seem to have diminished his interest in Basil's teething difficulties or Antony's first attempts at speech. Given the latter's subsequent career, one of them reveals a prophetic awareness of his eldest son's interests: 'I love your stories of the precious T. I should enjoy seeing him feeding and chasing the chickens. I'm so glad he's fond of animals …'[10]

No less prophetically, the last letter written by George Fisher to his wife concerned his will and the division of his estate, explaining that Ashdown Park and the family home would pass to Antony under the terms of the family trust. Shortly after completing the letter, Fisher asked Fred – to the latter's considerable surprise – to accompany him to Holy Communion, and in the evening sent a note of thanks to him for cooking a fine dinner, before taking a patrol out beyond the line. Moving ahead of the patrol in order to see over a ridge, he began to sketch the ground that lay beyond when he was hit through the shoulder by a Turkish sniper concealed among a grove of fig trees. Members of the patrol immediately returned fire, but the sniper then hurled a bomb, fragments of which struck Fisher, mortally wounding him. He died at a field hospital about an hour later, his only recorded words being an apology for making a fuss.

In a letter to his widow on behalf of the company's NCOs, Company Sergeant Major Blyth, who was with him on his last patrol, wrote: 'Although he was my captain and I, his sergeant major he treated me like a chum, and I was his constant companion. He was an officer whom the Company had confidence in, for the men recognised that he never asked them to do anything he would not do himself. I have not only lost a good company officer, but a friend I can never replace.'[11]

His words were echoed not only by Fisher's commanding officer, who regretted the loss of an irreplaceable officer and a friend who had taught him the rudiments of sketching, but also by the incomparable Fred, who wrote to Janet: 'It is a real grief to me to lose so good and kind a master. He was more than a master to me, if I be allowed to say it, he was a comrade.' Writing in his diary, Lieutenant Jewison, a young subaltern in the company, revealed that Fisher had escaped death by the narrowest of margins shortly before, when shells landed either side of his dug-out. 'Fisher was the most courageous and fearless officer we had left; he was a soldier I much admired.'[12]

Fisher was buried at Sampson Ridge Military Cemetery following a brief service; two months later his body was exhumed and reburied at the Gaza Military Cemetery, Palestine. In England his death was marked by a crowded memorial service for family and friends at the Church of Sir Richard de Wych – the church built by his grandfather at Ashdown. Buglers from Hobbs Barracks were meant to sound the Last Post but arrived too late to do so, explaining they had got lost in the woods. Villagers suspected them of dallying in order to gather chestnuts — an excuse which would have caused wry amusement to the soldier in whose memory the buglers were intended to sound a final farewell.

Antony was not yet two years old at the time of his father's death, Basil not yet one. Neither could remember their father as adults, and although not given to expressions of regret, Antony was later to explain to his own children how keenly he felt the absence of a senior male relative to whom he could turn as a boy. It was not that Janet Fisher was weak or inadequate; on the contrary, her strong character, her deep religious beliefs and her practical upbringing enabled her to cope with her loss with courage and determination. Indeed, her confidence in her ability to do so may have discouraged family and friends from doing more to help in the upbringing of her sons. The boys' early years were spent between the Fishers' London home in Kensington, Burgh in Norfolk, and Ashdown Park. In 1916, however, Lady Brassey approached the family with a request that the Sussex house be turned into a convalescent home for injured Belgian officers. (Lady Brassey's own home, Chelwood House, had already been opened for convalescent English officers, one of whom, Siegfried Sassoon, described his stay there in *Memories of an Infantry Officer*.) The formidable Lady Brassey prevailed, and as a consequence the Fishers' main family home became the former ale house – The Roebuck – at Wych Cross, in its chequered career alternately the scene of inebriation and sobriety. Later the family were to move to a cottage next door, and the Roebuck again became a pub.

Brought up in the country by an unconventional mother, the boys enjoyed considerable freedom, but religion also played a central part. Each day began with one hour's reading from the works of Mary Baker Eddy, the founder of Christian Science, and selected texts from the Bible. Janet's earlier attempts to convert her husband by sending Christian Science texts to him on the front appear to have failed. But Antony remained a

Christian Scientist until his death, attended Christian Science services throughout his life and accepted teachings uncritically, without seeking to force his convictions on others. Following the example of his mother, for the remainder of his life, whatever worldly distractions there might be, the first hour of his day was spent reading the Bible and Mrs Baker Eddy's texts.

In 1923, at the age of eight, Antony was sent to St Michael's School, Uckfield. The headmaster, the Revd Harold Herbert Hubert Hockey, was for some unrecorded reason known to the boys as 'Mr Bean'. Earlier, when showing the family around on their initial visit, the matron, keen to demonstrate that pupils would be well looked after, vigorously plunged a hot-water bottle into a bed already being warmed by one placed there by the deputy matron. Her embarrassment as the bottles exploded and water cascaded from the bed was one of Antony's favourite memories of his early schooldays.

Although not sporting, Antony's boyhood enthusiasms were for outdoor activities, for sketching and painting and for model trains, the first indication of a lifelong fascination with machines and gadgets. Janet Fisher was firm in her views but anxious that her sons should widen their experience of life, so to teach them something of the world at an early age, she purchased a Buick for the purpose of driving them round Europe.

Antony's father and paternal grandfather had gone to Harrow and then Oxford. Antony chose Cambridge by way of Eton, where he arrived in 1928. Eton was probably his mother's choice and it proved to be an apt one. Though he was never to shine either academically or on the sports field, Antony enjoyed the freedom which the school allowed and was to send both of his own sons there. School records show that he won the Geoffrey Gunther Memorial Prize for art during his first year, but that appears to have been the limit of his achievements. Jo Grimond, later the leader of the Liberal Party and for whom Antony fagged, recalled him 'as not only being clever but also a very nice character', remarking that this was 'a fatal combination' which led others to get him to do their homework.

Grimond's judgement of Fisher's academic abilities was probably on the generous side: Antony seems to have been a pupil of
average abilities, but a modest and unassuming boy who maintained lasting friendships, among them with Rex Fripp, later his
accountant and business adviser. Beatings – by a prefect wield-
ing a cane – and fagging were normal practices at Eton during
this period, but do not seem to have troubled him. Describing
the school regime during this period, one observer recalled that
both beating and fagging were regarded as open and acceptable
matters, requiring no justification: 'Boys regarded such hardships
as were to be undergone as matters of passage and, although
abuses did occur, normally both fagging and beating were regarded as tolerable initiations to the roughness of life.'[13]

What Antony seems to have enjoyed most was the spirit of
independence that allowed boys to pursue their own interests –
in his case engineering – provided that the rules were observed.
This aspect of Eton life had not changed when, many years later,
his eldest son, Mark, followed in his father's footsteps: 'It was a
school that allowed you to do your own thing … It did encourage individualism. At the age of 12 you went there and had your
own tailor, your own bank account, found your own clothes and
had to keep your personal accounts, so you had to take responsibility for yourself and live what was quite a rough life in many
ways – in school at 7.30 in the morning. It certainly was not a
pampered existence, as many people thought it was.'[14]

A year later Antony was followed to Eton by Basil, whose superior sporting prowess and more extrovert personality quickly
brought him reputation and popularity. Within a short time
Basil had established himself as a promising cricketer, leading
Eton to a resounding success against Harrow at Lords in 1934 in
which he kept wicket. He was chosen to play in the Eton Wall
Game and for Fives and was elected to Pop, of which he subsequently became chairman.

Among adolescent males of his class and background, few
privileges were so delicious as membership of the mysterious
self-governing world of Pop – or so fiercely envied by those

who failed to be admitted: 'They alone can wear sumptuous clothes; can sit on the Long Wall; can walk arm in arm; can keep their change coat and great collars turned down; can use a certain room in the school stores; can wear buff shorts instead of grey. Even when a member of Pop wishes to tan some one, there is a special kind of cane sacred to his use. And they alone can stop any Lower boy and fag him, no matter where he boards.'[15] Basil's membership of this unique and privileged world, however, was not resented or envied by his brother; nor was the fact that Basil was regarded as more academically gifted. In fact, Basil's progress and achievements were reported by Antony to aunts and cousins with evident pride and no trace of envy. Throughout their days at Eton and subsequently at Trinity College, Cambridge, they remained the constant companions they had been at 'Mr Bean's' school in Uckfield.

When Antony arrived at Cambridge in October 1934, rising unemployment and a worsening political climate in Europe dominated discussion at the High Table and in the university's political forums. Some of his contemporaries were to spend much of their time railing against the iniquities of international capital, and by the time they left Cambridge a select few, we now know, had been recruited by the intelligence services of the Soviet Union (and a greater number had joined the Communist Party). There is no record or anecdotal evidence that either brother took part in the great ideological contest which raged in the debating chambers and political clubs, or even took much interest in it. By contrast, the Fisher brothers lived a life that had more in common with those of well-born young men prior to World War I. While others engaged in political activity or earnest discourse, Antony sped through the country lanes of Cambridgeshire in his Speed 20 Alvis sports car, and Basil in his MG. The latter played cricket for his college, but did not win the hoped-for Blue. Both liked dancing, at which Antony excelled, but unlike the more gregarious Basil, he was often content with his own company. According to contemporaries, it was Basil who usually dragged Antony along to parties and social events, a pattern which was to be repeated when they moved to a flat in Mayfair. The brothers lived in some style in a comfortable flat near King's College. A favourite pastime on Sunday mornings was to drop sugar lumps from their first-floor window into the hats of ladies on their way to and from the College Chapel, a jape which typified the innocence and carefree quality of their undergraduate days.

Excitement came in the form of flying lessons with the University Flying Squadron based at Duxford, and the purchase of their own Vega Gull aeroplane, partly to impress girlfriends. This, however, was rented out three weeks out of four to help pay for their extravagance. Their jaunts to Europe appear to have been imbued with a kind of *Boys' Own* spirit of adventure. 'What's that?' cried Basil as a huge metal structure loomed through the clouds above and in front of them during a flight to France. Several moments passed before they realised that it was the Eiffel Tower. On another occasion, flying from Cambridge to a family gathering at Burgh, Antony announced his arrival by clipping the top branches of the cedars that grew at the end of the garden. His uncle, William Fisher, prepared a suitable rebuke, but was disarmed by Antony's beaming smile and instead joined in the gales of laughter which his antic had prompted among the younger members of the family.

So Antony's Cambridge days contained some elements of a playboy existence, but in other ways his life was in direct contrast to the spoiled and decadent bright things of the 1920s. Both Fishers seem to have taken their studies seriously. Antony, who studied engineering, was already contemplating a career in business. Basil, who read modern history and languages, looked forward to a career as a diplomat. As always, each day began with readings from the Bible. Antony attended church unfailingly and in accordance with his religion did not drink, smoke or swear. Although no great scholar, and extremely modest about his academic abilities, he was proud of the third-class degree he was awarded in 1938. He took satisfaction in owning a car and aeroplane and other possessions far beyond the reach of many of his friends, but never flaunted them. He remembered aunts and uncles, being a special favourite with the former, to whom he later offered investment advice. The fact that it was offered by a tall, dark and handsome young man with impeccable manners no doubt made his attention all the more welcome. But in the main his advice seems to have been shrewd; investment tips which he gave during the 1950s enabled two of them to exchange their places at convents for rooms at good hotels.

Antony also began to think about business not just as a career, but its role and the conditions for its success. If he took no interest in the debates over the 'crisis of capitalism' then raging around him it was presumably because he was unimpressed by what he heard. Later he was to conclude that the economic problems of the 1930s were the result of a crisis of government intervention rather than of capitalism. At that stage, however, he was more interested in understanding how capitalism worked and in playing a practical role in the capitalist process through entrepreneurship than in contributing to public debate.

Some of his early thoughts about economics were imparted to Gerald Palmer, a young engineer and motor designer to whom he was introduced in 1934 by a fellow Christian Scientist, F. J. Cleeland. Antony was especially anxious to learn more about small businesses, while Palmer was looking for capital to develop and build a sports car incorporating his own original ideas about suspension. Palmer, who was later to design and build the popular Jowett Javelin, described his plans in detail and with enthusiasm to his new acquaintance. Fisher responded by investing £1,000 (around £30,000 today), which enabled the two men to set up the Deroy Car Company. Fisher probably played a role in the financial and legal arrangements for the new company, but allowed Palmer to get on with the management of the business – to 'sink or swim', as Palmer put it. This was an approach that characterised all of his subsequent business ventures and was to be repeated years later when he founded the IEA. 'Pick a good man, and let him get on with it,' was how Fisher told John Blundell he did things when, some fifty years later, Fisher appointed him director of his Atlas Economic Research Foundation, then in San Francisco.

Palmer, a designer and engineer of brilliance, clearly fulfilled this basic requirement. But, like Fisher, he was inexperienced. When a prototype car was completed, its styling was considered to be the equal of many of the trend-setting European companies of the day, incorporating many novel design features. In many respects its mechanical specification was ahead of its day, but the side-valve, 1-litre engine lacked power, so the performance of the car proved woefully inadequate. Many years later, Palmer told Antony's son Mike about the one occasion that his father had accepted a lift in the car: 'I think the last and only time Antony had a ride in my creation ... the poor old Deroy was so slow, your father said, "I can't bear this any longer – take me back." Anyway, that was the end.' Bearing in mind that Antony loved cars and possessed a degree in engineering it seems remarkable that this was the only spin in the ill-fated Deroy and that he never took the wheel himself. But this was to typify his hands-off approach to business.

Later, Palmer considered fitting the car with a more powerful engine, but with a European war looming no one was prepared to risk further capital – not even Antony – and the company was closed in 1938. Palmer was given the prototype in compensation. Antony lost his money – but, as with subsequent ventures that failed, he was not in any way discouraged from further risk-taking. In any case, Palmer believed that Antony's desire for understanding how an economy functioned greatly exceeded his interest in the Deroy Car Company. 'He was greatly interested in how the country's economics were going ... The Deroy Car Company was his practical means of finding out how firms are born and run,' Palmer told Mike Fisher.

In 1935, the same year that witnessed the creation of the Deroy Car Company, Antony joined the merchant bank Close Brothers, the nearest to a conventional job he was ever to hold. Although he was keen to learn, Antony knew little of

commerce. His task and that of another recent recruit, Terry
Martens, was to create the Lombard Trust, one of the first unit
trusts to be established in Britain. Since both were largely ignorant of the stock market and were uncertain how to assess
the future performance of stocks, the two devised a strategy
which was simple but effective. The two men, who became
firm friends, approached stockbrokers and asked them for a
list of best-performing equities. Having built up a potential
portfolio of stocks, the two then retired to the nearest public
library, where they spent the next months researching the performance of their chosen companies over a 20-year period.
Since the pocket calculator had not been invented, and few of
the tools for such analysis then existed, this was a laborious
process, but one that yielded results. The value of the trust's
assets gradually rose and the venture was regarded as a significant if not spectacular success by the time the two men left
the company to volunteer for war service in 1939.

Antony's social life during the pre-war years included jaunts
to Europe in his plane, and dancing and dinner with Basil or
Terry Martens at the Berkeley Buttery, his favourite restaurant.
He did not seek out company and seldom if ever made close
friendships. But the combination of good looks, wealth, excellent manners, not to mention the ownership of a private plane
and a succession of expensive cars, ensured that he was high on
the invitation lists of London's hostesses, especially those with
unmarried daughters. At about this time, probably in 1937,
Antony met Eve Naylor at a dance. She made an immediate impression. 'She's the sweetest girl,' Antony reported to Terry
Martens, with such obvious enthusiasm that Martens could
recall their conversation more than fifty years later. To a cousin,
he declared: 'She really is the most wonderful dancer.'

Dancing was a favourite pastime of both Eve and Antony.
Sometimes the couple took cousins or friends who might otherwise be left by themselves. At a dance at Maidenhead, Joycie
Coke – a pretty cousin of eighteen who had accompanied them
– observed Antony talking on friendly terms to a young Amer-

ican of striking looks. Anxious to meet him, Joycie asked whether she might be introduced. Antony explained that the young man was John Kennedy, the son of the US Ambassador – but sensibly declined her request with a knowing smile.

By the time the Deroy Car Company had been established, Antony had also opened what may have been Britain's first car-rental business, at Hatfield in Hertfordshire, with Rex Fripp, his old friend from Eton. The business, which also included a petrol station, prospered sufficiently for the owners to purchase a new Ford every eight weeks. (Antony was thus able to contemplate with equanimity the loss of one car, swept away by the tide after being left on the beach at Blackpool.) Originally named the Hatfield Car Company, it was renamed 'Charles Anson' after his mother's family, but Antony invariably referred to it as 'Charlie Anson', or just 'Charlie'. Antony may well have got the idea for the company from reading about successful car-rental firms in the US. Characteristically, he seems to have been responsible for the basic business plan and to have borne all of the financial risk while leaving the day-to-day management largely to others. The company, whose pre-war growth suggests that it might have developed into one of Britain's biggest car-rental operators, ceased to trade at the outbreak of the war as its principal partners entered military service.

2

Marriage and war

Antony was married to Eve Lilian Naylor at the Parish Church, Sunninghill, Berkshire, on 29 July 1939. The marriage took place against the background of a steadily worsening international climate and a widespread belief that war was imminent. Antony, who seems to have been in little doubt about the matter, took it for granted that it was his duty to fight when war came, as his father had done in World War I. Accordingly, he volunteered for the Royal Air Force Volunteer Reserve on 10 July 1939, less than three weeks before his wedding, and two months before Chamberlain's formal declaration of war. Basil, who was bestman, also volunteered for the RAFVR about the same time. Notification that Antony had been commissioned as a pilot officer arrived on 1 August, two days after his marriage to Eve; Basil received his commission a few days later.

Pilot Officer Fisher proved an above-average flier and a competent and highly conscientious officer. As a keen amateur flier and a member of his university's air squadron he already had more than 200 hours of flying experience, but like many young men who were asked to turn themselves into fighter pilots within a matter of weeks, he found air warfare a terrifying and bewildering experience and believed himself to lack the instinctive aggression that characterised the most successful fighter pilots. His natural reserve set him aside from more extrovert

RAF officers who responded to the risks of war by living life to the full. Indeed, in many respects he was the antithesis of the boisterous, moustachioed, beer-drinking Battle of Britain pilot depicted in newspapers and films. His reserved, reflective temperament and serious demeanour meant that he did not join easily in the badinage of his fellow officers, while his religious convictions denied him the solace of alcohol and the camaraderie of Mess and pub – where, during the climatic summer of 1940, licensing hours and the landlord's indulgence could usually be stretched.

After training at the Cranwell Air School both Fishers were assigned to 111 Hurricane Squadron based at Croydon, where Antony and Eve established a routine which they were to follow for the remainder of the war. On completion of duties Antony would meet Eve (who was to follow him to each of his numerous postings) who would be usually at the airbase waiting for his return. Until Basil's death they would ensure that he was also safe, and then drive home for dinner.

The brothers' posting to Croydon in April 1940 was quickly followed by tragic news. In May, their cousin Michael Fisher was killed in the Battle of Flanders. Described by his commanding officer as being 'magnificent almost to the point of rashness', he died at Nieuport while visiting the scattered and rapidly diminishing posts under his command during intense shell and mortar fire. A few days later, David Berry, Antony's closest friend and a member of their squadron, was killed when his Hurricane was brought down over Flanders during the evacuation from Dunkirk.

Their squadron had played a prominent part in the Battle of France, where fighting had been especially intense. During this period its commanding officer, John Thompson, a particularly daring and enterprising leader, devised his own individual method of attack which was intended to surprise and intimidate the enemy. It was one that required rare nerve – head-on, with the entire squadron flying abreast – which he was to repeat during the Battle of Britain. The squadron's arrival over Dover on 10 July, when a particularly heavy build-up of German bombers was coming under fire from ground batteries, had just the effect that its commanding officer had hoped for:

> Through this lethal barrage nine of John Thompson's Hurricanes came roaring in as if this was no more than a Hendon airshow display, their line abreast attack proving as fearful to the bomber crews as the British CO had predicted. A number of Hurricanes latched on to one of them and gave it short deflection bursts until it broke up and fell away. The Dornier formation broke up before the Hurricanes cut through the bombers, and then Thompson and his pilots turned, climbed sharply and began snapping like terriers at the rearmost sections of the demoralised Dorniers.[1]

Among the RAF fliers snapping at the heels of the Dorniers were Antony and Basil. The younger Fisher narrowly escaped death when he came under 'friendly fire' from a Spitfire as he returned to base. His fuel tank and tailplane were riddled with .303 bullets, but against the odds he somehow managed to get back safely. Four days later, Antony's Hurricane crashed on take-off, but he stepped unscathed from the plane.

Antony's career as a fighter-pilot came to an abrupt end four weeks later with Basil's death on 15 August 1940. Although he seldom talked about it, the experience of observing Basil in near free-fall from his stricken fighter plane had a traumatic effect upon him, shattering his nerve and destroying the love of flying which he had shown during his carefree pre-war days. It seems also to have exacerbated the bouts of depression from which he suffered, a family trait shared by two uncles. At their most acute these could last weeks or even months and could render him in-active and silent, miserable but apologetic.

Basil was buried at St John's at Eton, where only a few years earlier he had shown such promise. Until his own death more than fifty years later Antony continued to pay for a local gardener to maintain Basil's grave. He attributed his preference for cremation to his anxieties that the grave was not being adequately tended. An obituary in *The Times*, written by a former school friend and bearing the signature 'C.A.E' gives some clue to Basil's popularity:

> It is difficult to write with restraint about the death of Basil Fisher. Perhaps his most salient characteristics were an extreme modesty and an almost childlike integrity which survived the buffetings of youth and early manhood. His attitude was never influenced by the affection he inspired ...Yet he inspired a respect which was all the greater because he never laid claim to it. Once he had made up his mind he was hard to move and the doggedness with which he stuck to his examination work, which was often uncongenial, is witness to his tenacity and sense of duty. But beyond this there was about him a simplicity and an unworldly charm that will remain a perdurable memory with all who knew him. As ever war takes the best.[2]

RAF records give no indication of the severity of the depression triggered by Basil's death or how much time Antony was given to recover. Later in his life, the down cycle of his mood-swings was sufficiently severe to prevent an unusually active and energetic man from doing any kind of meaningful work. On this occasion, however, it is clear that the devastating impact of Basil's death actually helped him to find a new role and sense of purpose.

Although withdrawn from active duty, Antony was recruited as a flight instructor by Squadron Leader A. G. 'Sailor' Malan, the South African Battle of Britain air ace whose ice-cold nerve and natural competitiveness made him – in the judgement of many – the best shot they had ever seen. Despite their very different temperaments and backgrounds it is clear that the two men had similar views about the inadequacies of current flight training. They also shared a common approach to how young and inexperienced fliers should be prepared for the most terrifying experience that they were ever likely to face. This is borne out by the similarities in their notes about gunnery techniques. It is Antony's writing on this subject, however, which is the most detailed and elaborate.

His personal experience had led him to conclude that while British warplanes were at least the equal of their German counterparts, and flight training of good quality, gunnery training was poor. This was a view that many RAF officers were to reach, but Antony seems to have grasped the problem and its implications more quickly and fully than most, and to have devoted himself to its analysis with unusual determination. His starting question was a simple one: why was it that a handful of pilots were successful, while the majority, no less brave and dedicated, were not. It was not the same question as 'Why Basil?', but it was so intimately related that it was one he pursued with particular tenacity.

His examination of film footage from British warplanes confirmed his suspicion that many pilots either ignored the basic principles of gunnery or simply did not know them. This was scarcely their fault during the first year of the war, when such gunnery training as was given consisted of teaching recruits to fire at a windsock or 'drogue' which was towed behind another plane. Like other critics, he recognised this provided a very poor guide to the actual conditions of air fighting.

Antony was no field-sports enthusiast, but having been brought up largely in the country, he knew that success with a gun depended on 'laying off' when firing, in order to allow for the movement of the target. What was required, he concluded, were radical changes in air-gunnery training which would enable pilots to understand that principle and – much more difficult – to follow it in conditions of aerial combat. His studies of the successes of First World War air aces such as Richthofen, Ball and McCudden convinced him that he had correctly identified the flaw in current training practices:

Each began his career as fighting pilots with a period of frustration, in which they were cramped by the difficulty of adjusting themselves to the conditions of their job. Once these first troubles were overcome, they felt their skills as pilots and their resource and resolution as fighters to be sufficient to give them success in combat with the enemy. Yet, there followed in each one a period of disappointment in which they had nothing to show for their best efforts but a series of dismal and at first inexplicable failures … It was at this point that each of them made the discovery on which his success in the future was to depend; that victory in combat is only possible to an expert shot using an efficient gun. Thereafter they all spent endless time, indeed every moment of their spare time, practising firing, lining up their sights and evolving various technical and mechanical aids to accurate gunnery. Success came to them when they thus appreciated where the gap in their efficiency lay.[3]

The result of his deliberations was the 'Fisher Trainer', a ground-based system which enabled recruits to fire at a simu-lated target that moved as it might in battle and to record their success. He constructed a prototype out of a range of materials (including pieces of a Meccano set) and subsequently demon-strated its worth to senior officers, including Air Chief Marshal Sir Hugh Trenchard. A young Polish RAF pilot drew a cartoon depicting Antony grappling with the components of the proto-type, spanner in hand, a look of deep concentration on his face, capturing the determination that he brought to his task. Today it hangs in the study of one of his sons.

Bearing in mind that Fisher was then a very junior officer and of a self-effacing disposition, his success in persuading senior officers to allow him to design and develop the Trainer was a considerable achievement. The grim resolve with which he went about it is also reflected in the earnest prose of a 32–page

handbook on the Trainer classified 'Secret' when it was printed
by the RAF in 1943:

> Unless a pupil can be taught to shoot accurately
> automatically, he will almost certainly forget everything
> but pressing the trigger when he goes in for the kill. If a
> pilot cannot shoot accurately for those few seconds in
> which he is in combat with the enemy, all his training is
> wasted from the day he was called up, so is all the time
> and materials that have been put into the aircraft and the
> training and equipping of the ground crews at the
> aerodrome at which he is based.[4]

Given the technical nature of much of its content, the handbook is a model of organisation and clear presentation – in contrast to his early attempts at political writing a few years later.
But just in case pilots forgot the fundamentals of accurate shooting, Antony helpfully composed the following verse:

> *Never forget in Air Fighting*
> *Close Range and accurate sighting,*
> *Range judging done on Spitters*
> *Makes a Heinkel give you jitters.*
> *Four hundred yards look right*
> *Because the span half fills the sight*
> *But this hun is so much bigger*
> *That you must not press the trigger*
> *Till you seem too ruddy close*
> *Then let go – he's had his dose !!*
>
> *Never forget in air fighting*
> *Close range and accurate sighting*
> *The Hun is protected behind*
> *Why!! That thought is most unkind*
> *Still you've got to shoot from the side*
> *And you may think you're taught to aim wide,*

But the bullet moves slower than light
And if you're shooting is right
You shoot where the Hun will be
That is, just prior to hitting the sea.

Never forget in Air Fighting
Close range and Accurate Sighting.

                    GOOD SHOOTING[5]

Given his determination and his non-conformist outlook
Antony would no doubt have been prepared to set his handbook to music if it would help him provide better training. Certainly a more conventionally minded man would not have
included, as Antony did, a glowing account of how the German
air ace Manfred von Richthofen – known as the Red Baron –
achieved fame by shooting British pilots out of the sky during
World War I.

Fisher's approach to training – for which he was to receive
the Air Force Cross – rested on the secure foundations of identifying the problems faced by inexperienced fliers and analysing
them correctly. His use of the Fisher Trainer represented a considerable advance on earlier programmes, but Antony appears to
have reached the conclusion that the same training objectives
could in fact be achieved even more simply and in conditions
which approximated still more closely those of air fighting. By
February 1943, when Antony was chief flying instructor at
Twinwoods Farm, Bedfordshire, he had abandoned the Trainer
in favour of the camera gun, which enabled pilots to aim at real
targets and subsequently to analyse the film footage with the
help of an instructor. His deputy, John Hall, then a flight lieutenant, recalls Fisher as a conscientious but reserved officer who
did not welcome intimacy. 'Antony ran things on the ground,
and I took charge of matters in the air. The curious thing is that
I do not recall his going near the cockpit of an aircraft. At the
time, I would not have had any inkling as to the reason for this
because I was not familiar with his earlier war experience.'[6]

Nevertheless, Hall believes that those who benefited from Antony's approach to gunnery training included not only those whom he instructed, but also those who were to serve under him as instructors – especially those who, like himself, were later returned to active service. Hall, who received the DFC for bringing down eight German planes when he returned to operational flying with 855 Mosquito Squadron, said later: 'I am quite sure that I was a better pilot as a result of serving under him, and without that experience I would not have presented much of a threat to the Luftwaffe. Indeed, I might not have survived.'[7] And in an obituary following Antony's death in 1988, Hall wrote:

> The present writer who served with Antony all those years ago, has every reason to be grateful for those qualities which served his country so well throughout his life – quiet analysis of a problem, readiness to reject current dogma in the search for an answer, originality and courage in devising and propounding an effective solution and practical ability of a high order in putting the solution into effect.[8]

A significant but unknown number of RAF pilots survived the war because of Antony Fisher and his commitment to raising the standards of gunnery training. Some may have realised as much, but none would have known the high price that Antony paid for the insights that made him such a dedicated instructor, or the part played by the late Pilot Officer Basil Fisher in their survival.

3

Freedom and the land

The last months of Antony Fisher's war were spent at the Air Ministry, an experience which did nothing to shake his growing scepticism about the competence of government. After several years of moving from base to base, however, his new Whitehall role at least enabled him to look for a permanent home and to renew his interest in public affairs.

In July 1945, Antony purchased Thurston Hall, in Framfield, Sussex, previously the home of the Labour minister and lawyer Sir Patrick Hastings. The house was just a dozen miles from his boyhood home at Ashdown Park and with it went 440 acres of Sussex farmland. Described by the auctioneer as 'one of the most beautiful and convenient situations in Sussex', the property included four cottages, chauffeur's quarters, ornamental gardens, a 3-acre lake, a waterfall, and grazing and arable grassland. According to the sale details the property constituted 'a model home-farm embodying the latest principles of cattle farming and cattle rearing'. At the auction, Antony also purchased a herd of 52 shorthorn cows.

Built in the 1920s in the style of an Elizabethan manor house, Antony soon reverted to its original and less grandiose name of 'Newplace'. It was typical of him that he should delight in the possession of a fine home, which he could share with family and friends without appearing too grand. It became his favourite subject for sketching, one which he drew and painted in every light and from every perspective. He and Eve were to raise four children at Newplace – Basil Mark, born in 1941 and named after his uncle (but always called Mark); Linda, born in 1942; Mike, born 1945; and Lucy, born in 1948.

Antony's interest in economic issues had already been sparked by his pre-war business activities. The economic difficulties which Britain faced as it emerged from the war – and the polit-ical failure to tackle them – now occupied his thoughts to an in-creasing extent. He had already made up his mind that the best means to eliminate poverty was by allowing business to perform its wealth-creating task subject only to the rule of law. Govern-ment's job was to ensure the citizen's safety and to provide a sympathetic framework of laws and institutions within which individuals could pursue their purposes. But partly through the legacy of war and partly because of the prevailing intellectual climate, a coalition government was seeking increasingly to cen-tralise economic decision-making, through planning, rationing and controls. If, as he feared, the Labour Party was elected at the General Election, the trend would not merely continue but ac-celerate. As a consequence the individual liberties for which his father and brother had fought would gradually be lost.

In reaching such views he was considerably ahead of those Conservatives who later came to share much of his outlook on economic issues, among them Enoch Powell and Keith Joseph. Indeed, when Fisher began to argue the case against big gov-ernment, neo-Keynesian economics and the plans for a (Euro-pean) Common Market, these two Tory intellectuals still believed in all of those things. His humility prompted some to suppose that his views were mere echoes of the intellectuals, mostly economists, with whom Fisher had begun to enjoy contact in the years following the war. In fact, on all large issues Fisher had already reached a settled opinion and was to hold to this with greater consistency than some of those whose larger personal ambition and intellectual sophistication enabled them to build public reputations. When a neighbour asked how his views on economics had been formed, he explained that he had worked them out 'when I ran a garage in the Hatfield Road', a reference to his pre-war car-rental company.

Issues which for many seemed complex and difficult seemed to Antony to flow simply and directly from moral principles derived from the scriptures and from a correct understanding of how a market economy functioned. These provided the stable foundation of his opinions on virtually all topics; later, others with deeper economic knowledge may have helped him express these more effectively, and awareness of Adam Smith's *The Wealth of Nations* and a modest number of economic and political texts may have confirmed his own beliefs and instincts and given him greater confidence in expressing them, but they did not fundamentally alter them.

Among Conservatives who later came to embrace similar views, some, like Keith Joseph, were motivated by a desire to help the poor – whose interests, they believed, had been damaged by the egalitarian measures introduced in their name. Others, like Margaret Thatcher, did so because they believed them to be key to national revival. Fisher appears to have shared some of Joseph's concern for the less well off, as well as his sense of public duty, but seems to have been motivated primarily by a desire to change policies and measures which struck him as quite obviously doomed to fail. As with the great Lord Anson, the desire to put right things which were obviously going wrong was extremely strong.

Antony's earnest demeanour and single-mindedness gave some impression of an ideologue, but I doubt whether he deserves the description. Political ideas did not constitute a secular religion as they did for many reformers – as a practising Christian Scientist he had no need for such a thing. He saw market ideas as the practical foundation on which action might be taken. In the opinion of Dorian, his second wife, 'Despite the firmness of his ideas I am quite sure that Antony would have changed them if someone had been able to demonstrate to his satisfaction that they didn't work in practice. But no one ever could!'

On his release from the RAF in December 1945, Antony had re-joined Close Brothers where, to his considerable delight, he found himself working with his old friend Terry Martens, just demobbed from the army. Again working in tandem, they were given joint responsibility for the company's 30 per cent holding in the Wolverhampton-based General Metal Utilisation Company, a task which they found far less stimulating than their former role. The two men felt that they had been consigned to a backwater and their enthusiasm for City life quite quickly waned. Martens began to think of escaping the English weather and Britain's equally drab economic climate by emigrating to Rhodesia, while Fisher started to reflect on wider political and economic developments, to read more widely, and to contem-plate a career in politics.

By the end of the war Antony had joined the Society of Indi-vidualists, probably the most appealing of the wartime organisa-tions which existed to preserve the ideas of classical liberalism against a background of growing state control. It was here that for the first time Antony met others of similar beliefs, including the society's founder, Ernest Benn. In the words of Richard Cockett, the author of *Thinking the Unthinkable*, a stimulating account of the counter-revolution in economic thought that took place in Britain between 1931 and 1983, Benn 'was as fervent a believer in economic individualism as his nephew Tony Benn was to be in arguing the case for economic collectivism'.[1] Fisher also met S. W. Alexander, a young and energetic Beaverbrook journalist whose pug-like features bore such an uncanny resemblance to Beaverbrook himself that he was rumoured to be his illegitimate son. Alexander specialised in economics and finance but his pas-sionate belief in free trade inevitably brought him into conflict with his proprietor's campaign for tariffs and Empire preference. Alexander consequently parted company from Beaverbrook soon after the end of the war to become editor of the *City Press*, where he campaigned earnestly for free trade, for an end to controls and for the private ownership of industry. In the 1945 General Election Antony campaigned on behalf of Alexander, who stood as the 'free trade candidate' for the two-member City of London constituency. But later that year he supported the Conservative candidate, Russ Assheton – later the party's chairman – at a by-election in the same constituency. This switch reflected a realisation that while the Conservative Party was very far from perfect, it was the only electable party that might be converted to free-market beliefs.

Another prominent member of the Society of Individualists was Oliver Smedley, a pugnacious ex-paratrooper of fiercely independent views who had won the Military Cross at Arnhem. Smedley ran the Cheap Food League, which denounced agricultural subsidies and campaigned for an end to the state marketing boards for agricultural produce, a cause to which Antony dedicated himself with equal passion and, ultimately, great success. Smedley also created the Farmers' and Smallholders' Association, which railed against the Attlee Agricultural Act of 1947 and of which Antony was for many years joint treasurer.

Today there is nothing remarkable about the opinions Antony began to advocate in a stream of articles and letters for the *City Press* and other publications in the late 1940s. These dealt with the fallacy of state planning, the perverse effects of government intervention in the economy, the harmful consequences of agricultural subsidies, the communist threat posed by the Soviet Union and the erosion of individual liberty arising from socialist measures at home. But at the time such views were held by a very small, often eccentric, minority. Although earnest and literal-minded, Antony was not eccentric, and those meeting the handsome, well-dressed and well-connected Old Etonian were struck both by his unconventional views and the depth of his conviction. For most people of Antony's background and class the conventional view was that the drift towards collectivism was probably inevitable, and that the best that could be hoped for was that the Conservative Party might somehow slow down the process. Moreover, many would have accepted that, while socialism had some unfortunate practical consequences, it was noble in theory. In contrast, Antony could detect no traces of nobility in socialist theory or practice. He consequently made no secret of his view that socialism was a great evil, a blight upon the land, and a violation of what he termed 'the moral code'. Nor did he have much respect for Conservative attempts to establish a *modus vivendi* with collectivism by means of 'Butskellite' notions[2] of a mixed economy and a political 'middle way'. 'Can there be any middle course between right and wrong?' he asked in an article in the *City Press* in April 1948. In the same article he declared: 'Those at one end [of the political debate] are right, and those at the other are wrong. Anything in between is still wrong, as any compromise with wrong cannot be right.' Repeating a favourite phrase, he concluded: 'Communism is the poison offered to the people; socialism is the cup in which it is given; and the welfare state is the tempting label on the bottle.'

Antony's fear that Britain was on the path to totalitarianism was to result in him appearing before Uckfield magistrates' court. On receiving his census form in July 1951, Antony decided that the information demanded could be used by an over-powerful state to destroy the liberty of the individual. He therefore tore it up. On receiving a second form he filled in only those parts of it which on reflection he thought dealt with matters that the government was entitled to know. Through his solicitor, Neil Buchanan, he offered profuse apologies to the census officials and to the court for any inconvenience caused, but added:

> In this country of ours the power of the state increases almost daily and legislation is no longer resisted … The best way undoubtedly of resisting is to get the legislation altered, but sometimes it is necessary to resist in the only way possible and to bear the penalty accordingly.

He was fined £5, with £3 costs.

Antony's hatred of communism and his growing unease about Britain's political direction was reflected in his choice of reading matter. High on the list was *Reader's Digest,* subscriptions to which Antony routinely gave as Christmas or birthday gifts – even to surprised university dons and others used to receiving more intellectually demanding texts. Fisher greatly admired the magazine's vigorous anti-communism, but no article was to produce such an effect as a condensed version of Hayek's *The Road to Serfdom* which appeared in the April 1945 edition. Although in most fundamental respects Antony's views were already formed, it is clear that Hayek's powerful polemic against socialism made a profound impression. Later he described how the book gave expression to many of his own fears and anxieties and how its combination of passion and rigour hardened his resolve to play an active role in reversing the political tide. Some of Fisher's collaborators believed that his knowledge of Hayek's book was strictly limited to the *Reader's Digest* version. In fact, Antony's own treasured edition of the full text, complete with copious underlinings, comments and smiling faces against paragraphs with which he particularly agreed, is now in his daughter's possession.

On reading the *Reader's Digest* article, Antony determined to meet its author – about whom he could have known little, despite the impact which Hayek's book had made on its publication. The meeting took place at the London School of Economics some time in 1945:

> It was for me a fateful meeting. My central question was what, if anything, could he advise me to do to help get discussion and policy on the right lines. I do not recall his exact words but have retained almost 30 years later a vivid impression of his message. Hayek first warned against wasting time – as I was then tempted – by taking up a political career. He explained that the decisive influence in the great battle of ideas and policy was wielded by the intellectuals whom he characterised as

'second-hand dealers in ideas'. It was the dominant intellectuals from the Fabians onward who had tilted the political debate in favour of growing government intervention with all that followed. If I shared the view that better ideas were not getting a fair hearing, his counsel was that I should join with others in forming a scholarly research organisation to supply intellectuals in universities, schools, journalism and broadcasting with authoritative studies of the economic theory of markets and its application to practical affairs.[3]

Fisher later liked to recall passing the office of Harold Laski, the most prominent socialist academic of his day and a leading Fabian, on his way to Hayek's door.

Antony left the meeting with serious doubts about the wisdom of pursuing a political career and with an inner resolve to give practical expression to Hayek's suggestion. Nevertheless, Terry Martens believed that despite Hayek's advice Antony applied for a Tory seat shortly before leaving Close Brother's and that his failure upset him considerably. Antony often felt set-backs deeply, but he was seldom deflected by them. If he did seek selection as a Conservative candidate, it is clear that he later had second thoughts and concluded the best course was to follow Hayek's advice and to try to improve the world by other means. For Antony, politics were merely the means by which the ideas and principles in which he believed might be put into effect. He had little interest in the political process itself, nor in the drama of parliamentary cut and thrust, and none at all in Westminster gossip. While it is possible to imagine him as a principled, con-scientious backbench MP, his palpable lack of guile and his un-willingness to compromise suggest that if he had achieved ministerial status his career would have been a brief one. No Sir Humphrey could have been found to protect a politician so de-termined to conform to principle whatever the political cost. This view is borne out by Ralph Harris, who was to become the first general director of the Institute of Economic Affairs:

He was constantly tempted to go into politics. He moved
in Tory circles … and in the early fifties there was a real
possibility of a safe seat and he asked me what I thought.
He felt that many Tories were deeply misguided and
direct entry into politics would be a short cut to getting
the message across instead of going along the long path
of convincing the intellectuals first. Had he gone in he
would have been like, say Lord Hinchingbroke, a non-
conformist champion of libertarian views without lasting
influence.[4]

Antony may have regarded his conversation with Hayek as a
turning point in his life, but Hayek could not subsequently remember it, probably because he gave similar advice to others
who said they wanted to help. But only Antony acted on that
advice and made it the central preoccupation of his life. As he
began to make headway in the achievement of that goal, he reported progress to Hayek, beginning a correspondence and
friendship that lasted until Antony's death. It is tempting to conclude that in Hayek Antony had at last found the father-figure
of which war had robbed him, one whom he could look up to
and whose counsel he could seek.

Shortly after meeting Hayek, Antony started work on *The
Case for Freedom*, an extended pamphlet of 86 pages in which he
sought to apply his thoughts to the problems of the day.[5] Unlike
Must History Repeat Itself? (published in 1974), it did not benefit
from the suggestions of friends. It therefore represents an accurate guide to Fisher's views and concerns as well his strengths
and weaknesses as 'a second-hand dealer in ideas'. In large part it
consists of an earnest if raw and simplistic exposition of the case
for free enterprise. 'The Community which comes nearest to
keeping its markets free', he writes, 'will be the most prosperous.'
Such societies, he argues, rest on a bedrock of principle and the
rule of law: 'Only by applying these can there be stability, happiness and prosperity in any community, and it is only in this way
that real freedom can ever be attained. Legislation based on

principle will tend to make a world composed of imperfect people run smoothly. Unprincipled legislation will force imperfect people to behave badly.'

Judged as polemic, the pamphlet is unimpressive: the prose lacklustre, the argument deficient and diffuse. It is difficult to believe that it would have greatly lifted the spirits of allies or converted the undecided. Indeed, readers may well have taken exception to his assumption that any principled approach based on the Christian ethic and the rule of law was bound to arrive at identical conclusions. In this spirit Fisher condemned the Attlee government for being 'unprincipled' when it is clear that what he disliked most about it was that its measures were firmly rooted in different principles from his own. Nevertheless, *The Case for Freedom* is remarkably perceptive in identifying a number of concerns and themes which were to dominate the political agenda over the next half century. These included economic issues such as inflation, currency-exchange problems, housing shortages (which Fisher correctly discerned were the consequence of rent controls), but also international problems such as communist expansion, the subversion of UN agencies such as UNESCO (from which Britain and America were to withdraw 40 years later) and the inadequacy of international arms-control measures as a means of controlling the proliferation of atomic weapons. He also rehearsed the advantage of professional over conscript armies at a time when national service was seen as part of the national order, criticised Marshall Aid on the grounds that it would hinder rather than help economic recovery, and registered strong opposition to a European super state. Finally he enjoined the reader to 'Insist on having government by principle: we cannot contract out of this world, so we may as well make a success of it!'

If we exclude his opposition to Marshall Aid, which is widely regarded as having been beneficial, the views he expressed half a century ago would now find support with many more than just those on the intellectual right in Britain and the US. Indeed, many of the goals which Fisher set out – privatisation, the abolition of exchange controls and the loosening of political control over markets – have been achieved. But probably only a very small number know that their realisation can be traced back to Fisher and a chance meeting which he was to have in 1949 with a young Conservative Party researcher called Ralph Harris.

Harris, who was Political Education Officer for the South-east home counties, had been invited to speak by the East Grinstead constituency agent on a subject of his choice. Since rationing of basic foods had still not ended, Harris chose to speak on the superiority of the price mechanism over rationing as a means of allocating scarce goods and enlarging freedom of choice.

> I felt this had really gone down quite well and after the meeting along came this earnest man to offer his compliments. He was tall, handsome, slim, elegant you might say, and he subjected me to a severe cross-examination about my views, where I had picked them up and what I had been reading. He was particularly anxious to know what I thought about communism, which he saw as the main threat to our future. I was somewhat surprised to learn he was a farmer, which is how he described himself, because he was so well dressed. I learned later that he was still dwelling on the war years, the loss of his brother in the Battle of Britain and the fight for freedom. But my first impressions were of a somewhat eccentric, extremely earnest man who responded to my inclination to make jokes with a somewhat puzzled look as he tried to work out my meaning.[6]

The conversation between the two continued as Fisher accompanied Harris on foot to East Grinstead station. On the way, Antony recalled his conversation with Hayek and outlined his plan to create an organisation which would seek to influence the climate of opinion to make it more receptive to free-market ideas. 'One day when my ship comes in I'd like to create something which will do for the non-Labour Parties what the Fabian Society did for Labour,' Antony explained. Before boarding his train back to London Harris – who doesn't seem to have taken more than a few seconds to decide that he would like to play a leading part in the enterprise – replied: 'If you get any further I'd like to be considered as the man to run it.'[7]

It was six years before Fisher was able to start laying the foundations of what became the Institute of Economic Affairs, but it seems that he never wavered in his choice of Harris as the best man to run it. For his part, Harris, who had gone on to become an economics lecturer and journalist, remained convinced that Antony's project represented the most promising means of pursuing goals which were already his own.

4

A chicken in every pot

In 1950, Antony left his job in the City to concentrate on his Sussex farm and to pursue a range of business and political interests. He liked country life and was seldom so content as when walking his Labradors in the grounds of his home. But he was not sentimental about the countryside: its principal purpose was to provide consumers with food, not to perpetuate a way of life. While his views on such matters were generally shared by political allies in the Society of Individualists and by fellow contributors to the *City Press* they found little support among farmers. Within the National Union of Farmers – which Antony criticised publicly for behaving as if it were a department of government – there was widespread backing for guaranteed prices and a complex array of subsidies, such as those for fertilisers, drainage and water schemes. Like fuel and food rationing, these had their origins in emergency laws enacted during wartime which had outlived their purpose. Worse still, in Antony's view, was wartime legislation that enabled the government to seize land which was not being farmed efficiently, much of those seizures made permanent by the Attlee government's Agricultural Act of 1947. In articles and letters to the press he railed against all such coercive powers, including those granted to the agricultural marketing boards to which producers were obliged to sell their output.

His most urgent task, however, was to place his own farm –
then losing £2,000 a year – on a more secure economic footing,
or face the possibility of selling up. Rabbits, which had overrun
huge areas of the English countryside, prevented him from
growing corn. There was also the problem that his farm manager
could not read a balance sheet or understand even the simplest
business figures. Antony steeled himself to dismiss him and find
a more numerate replacement. He also decided to become more
deeply involved in running the farm. Among his first decisions
were to expand his herd of shorthorns, to replace the farm's
work horses with the first tractors to be introduced to the area,
and to establish more clearly defined business criteria. His most
significant step, however, was the purchase of 200 day-old chicks
from a local hatchery with the aim of rearing them in a 12-foot-
square loose box with an electric fire on the wall to simulate the
heat of the hen.

Antony was already distinguished from his neighbouring
farmers by his smart appearance – more Savile Row than
Barbour – his unorthodox views about subsidies, and the slide
rule which he consulted before making decisions. His experiments in raising chickens, then very much a sideline that was
frequently left to the farmer's wife, were regarded as further
proof of his eccentricity. His elder son Mark later recalled:

> Everyone just laughed. The people on the farm just
> didn't believe that you could have 200 chickens in so
> small a space. Local opinion frankly doubted whether
> producing chickens on such a large scale could ever be
> economically viable.
>   When the time came to put the chicks on the market
> the man who looked after them approached the local
> chicken slaughterer, who said: 'I lost £1 on each of the
> 1,200 birds I sold last year, so why would I want your
> 200? Who is going to eat 200 chickens?'[1]

Even if few others shared his view, Antony was sure that

economies of scale could bring poultry within the budget of a huge market. Ironically, it was a state compensation scheme that provided him with the means not only to prove his point but also to challenge the conventional wisdom about much else. In August 1952, Antony's herd of 52 shorthorns contracted foot-and-mouth in the epidemic that swept through England, and the entire herd was destroyed. Anxious to continue with his experiments in poultry farming – then the least regulated sector of British agriculture – Antony used the compensation to fund a study trip to the United States.

While in the US, Antony visited the recently created Foundation for Economic Education (FEE), in Irvington-on-Hudson, just outside New York City, in the hope that this might provide the model for the institute which he and Harris had long been discussing. FEE specialised in the publication of simplified texts on how markets functioned. Fisher was much impressed by these and sent heavily underlined copies to Harris. Harris was less impressed, judging that a more scholarly approach would be required to influence economic opinion in Britain. But while FEE failed to provide the blueprint for which he was searching it did provide a valuable introduction to a former economics professor, Dr F. A. 'Baldy' Harper. In 1947, he had been a co-founder with Hayek of the international forum of classical-liberal economists, the Mont Pélerin Society. 'Baldy', who had left Cornell University after coming under pressure for using Hayek's *The Road to Serfdom* in his courses, in turn introduced Antony to his former colleagues at the Department of Agricultural Economics at Cornell. Antony visited the university's scientific broiler farm, where he was amazed to find 15,000 birds in a single building – and immediately grasped the full potential for large-volume production in Britain. Keen to demonstrate the role he had unknowingly played in British economic history, Baldy later declared, with evident pride, 'I introduced this man to his first chicken farmer!'

Antony also met Karl Brandt, a professor of agricultural economics at Stanford University. Brandt invited him to deliver a paper on British agriculture to a conference of the Mont Pélerin Society planned for Venice in September 1954. At that stage of the society's history it was unusual for businessmen to be invited to MPS conferences, let alone to be asked to speak. But his paper was sufficiently well received for him to be invited to become a member. It dealt with the powers taken by the outgoing Labour government, and concluded: 'I believe that agricultural legislation in England gives dangerous powers to the Minister of Agriculture. Under a Government or Ministers so minded, the agricultural legislation would fit easily into the pattern of complete dictatorship.'

At the time of Antony's US visit, the term 'broiler' – a mass-produced table chicken of either sex weighing 3–4½ pounds – was unknown in Britain, where poultry production was mainly carried on smallholdings. Although the techniques which Antony later employed to raise and process chickens were different from those that he observed in the US, the sight of thousands of birds being raised and prepared for the restaurants and dinner tables of New York amply confirmed his belief that chickens could be produced in much larger numbers in the UK, and at a fraction of the cost. According to Tony Pendry, who was later to become his business partner, 'Others went to the US to research broiler production and processing during the same period, and one or two grasped the potential for large scale production in Britain, but only Antony displayed the combination of qualities necessary for success, namely vision, ambition, and the readiness to take risks.'[2]

This insight was not the only valuable outcome from Antony's visit. Greater investment and research had produced a strain of chicken with a high conversion rate of feed into meat; compared to the scrawny but expensive farmyard fowls of home, the plump White Rock chicken matured quickly and produced meat of a consistent quality. Its development had been one of the key factors in the growth of American poultry farming into a multi-million-dollar industry. For large-scale production to take place in Britain it would be necessary to breed the chickens in the UK. Unfortunately, legislation outlawed the importation of both birds and eggs. Antony therefore disguised 24 fertilised White Rock eggs as Easter eggs by wrapping them in silver paper and bringing them back in his hand luggage. The eggs were then rushed to a hatchery near Framfield. When the 24 one-day-old chicks arrived at Newplace three weeks later, Antony's daughter Linda, then aged ten, was given the task of ensuring that they could reach food and drink. These chickens, to be used as breeders, were to be a key in the transformation of agriculture and of British eating habits.

Two important factors were to facilitate Antony's increasing success in the poultry industry: the first was development of drugs which controlled coccidiosis and fowl pest, and the other was the repeal of rationing on animal feed by the post-war Conservative government. At that time, farmyard fowls grew to market weight in 100–112 days. But Fisher's chickens were ready for market in 70 days, thus consuming less food, with the result that retail prices began to fall quite quickly. By May 1953, Fisher had 2,500 chickens and by August of that year that number had risen to 24,000. Initially, chicks were bedded on wood shavings under a hot-water brooder, but this was later replaced by Calorgas heating. Food was power-blown into silos and thereafter conveyed to the birds by an overhead rail system.

Such rapid expansion led to difficulties in finding sufficient market outlets. Antony therefore decided to prepare the birds for market himself rather than sell them to others. The result was a partnership with Tony Pendry, a young neighbouring farmer. Pendry had served as a lieutenant in the East Surrey Regiment in Northern Ireland, North Africa and Italy, where he was wounded and taken prisoner at Cassino in February 1944. On his return home from POW camp, Pendry had turned to farm labouring as a means of restoring his health. As his interest in farming deepened, he attended classes at the Surrey Farm Institute for ex-servicemen and in 1948 became a management trainee with Unilever, for whom he subsequently set up and managed small factories specialising in the packing and freezing of fruit and poultry under the Birds Eye and Macfisheries labels.

After returning to the family farm in 1953 and setting up his own table-poultry unit in 1954, Pendry was introduced to Fisher, who was looking for a business partner with just such a background. The two were not only complementary in temperament and skills; they were also linked by a common desire to forget harrowing wartime experiences and build new futures. But although they were to spend many hours together during a partnership that lasted eleven years, neither mentioned one word about their respective wartime ordeals.

Later the same year the two launched the Buxted Chicken Company, with Fisher as chairman and Pendry as managing director. It had a staff of 12, a cash investment of £1,000 and a bank loan of £5,000. A small concrete and asbestos processing factory in Gordon Road, Buxted, began operations in May 1954. Within a year staff numbers had increased to 40, and 20 local farmers were paying one shilling a pound to have their chickens processed, each becoming a shareholder and making a small contribution to advertising costs. Others acquired farms in order to participate in what was a unique free-enterprise co-operative based on Fisher's entrepreneurial vision and Pendry's managerial skills. Sainsbury's became by far their biggest and best customer.

By 1958, the Fisher family had 1,250,000 chickens between them. But in order to avoid a conflict which arose between Antony's interest as chairman of Buxted and their biggest supplier, Buxted acquired the family farms in the early 1960s.

Fisher's business style was open, direct and based on trust. According to Pendry:

> At first I was surprised by the unusual extent to which Antony was prepared to take people on trust. But I was also surprised by the relatively small number who took advantage – which did not prevent him from being hurt when they did. In the main, however, they treated him well because he had treated them well ... It was typical

that he should insist on selling discounted shares to the working directors of Buxted. This was long before the wider share ownership movement got going and there was no compelling reason for him to do so. I think he did it because he instinctively believed it was the right thing to do.[3]

Antony's initial experiments in factory farming had taken place in a disused cowshed. But this was to be replaced by four environmentally controlled chicken sheds for 100,000, each with a new cottage for a farm manager and assistant manager. On its launch, Buxted Chickens had confined its operations to rearing, plucking and chilling the birds, but by the end of 1957 the company, which was now handling 25,000 birds a week, also eviscerated, froze and packaged them. By the time the company was floated in 1962 with a capitalisation of £7 million it was running three processing plants – at Buxted, Aldershot and Boreham – to which a further three, at Dalton, Walesby and Sutton Benger, were to be added. The company also grew as the result of acquisitions, including that of Western Chickens of Chippenham in 1960. It also decided to buy its own hatcheries and to raise and process turkeys. By 1962, the original staff of 12 had grown to 2,000.

Newplace provided the ideal base from which to plan the expansion of this growing agribusiness as well as to raise an expanding family. As a parent Antony was as much a non-conformist as in other matters. Except to ensure that they were provided for in material terms, Antony took only a cursory interest in his children when they were small, and as they grew older he regarded the pranks and ragging of his boisterous and high-spirited family with amused tolerance, frequently joining in the fun. He seems to have taken for granted that they would share *his* interests at some later stage – in which expectation he was not disappointed – but he did not feign an interest in theirs. His elder daughter, Linda Whetstone, recalls:

As children we didn't see much of him. He spent much
of his time in his study at Newplace working on his
various schemes. When he was with us he was great fun,
often ragging and laughing and when we were old
enough to be interested in the things that interested him,
then we would join in his life … It might seem odd that
he didn't send any of us to university. This was not due to
his own experience of university life, which he enjoyed.
The fact is that he never really applied himself to our
upbringing – perhaps he expected the 'invisible hand' to
do it! He never disciplined us or made a conscious effort
to teach or train or guide us. If he did it was by example
because we all wanted to please him. Certainly, we were
not brought up in the generally accepted way. I only
went to school for four years in my entire life. The rest of
the time I was taught by governesses at home who came
and went for reasons I can't remember.[4]

Family discipline was left largely to Eve. Occasionally, at
Eve's insistence, Antony would try to impose a semblance of
authority on children who generally enjoyed the run of their
father's property, but afterwards he could sometimes be observed shaking with mirth. There was no rebuke when, as
teenagers, Mark and Mike drove their father's Land Rover on
to the frozen pond at Newplace to test the thickness of the ice;
when Mike pushed his father into the swimming pool in front
of guests; or when Mark threatened to pour a plate of soup
over his father's head if he did not stop lecturing the family
and their guests about the virtues of capitalism. An abiding
memory of Antony's youngest child, Lucy, is that of her father's
shoulders heaving with silent laughter as her mother tried un-
successfully to impose order at the dinner table. Most of
Antony's business and political acquaintances thought him so
earnest as to be totally lacking in a sense of humour, but Mark
recalls his father being prone to such acute attacks of giggling
that he could not speak, an aspect of his personality which

seems almost never to have been displayed outside the family circle.

Almost the only rules enforced by Antony were that his children must be polite and considerate to others, and must attend the parish church at Framfield with their mother and the Church of Christ Scientist at Haywards Heath with him on alternate Sundays. Had they been given a choice the children would have opted for the latter, not because of theology but because their father's unwillingness to exert control allowed them to hurl missiles from the rear windows of his Humber as it sped through the Sussex countryside.

Family holidays were equally carefree, especially when taken abroad. Antony strongly disliked the English weather and did not enjoy the holidays spent with relatives in Cornwall in the early years of his marriage. When business prospered, there were lavish holidays to foreign places, especially to Zermatt in Switzerland, where the family went six years in succession. Antony was generous both to his family and to friends, and exceptionally so when business ventures flourished. But an inner belief, not always justified, that these ventures were bound to succeed discouraged him from putting money aside for rainy days. As Buxted began to prosper the children were promised either a swimming pool or a tennis court; typically he provided both.

Antony's possession of the grandest house in the area and an attractive and energetic wife would have enabled him to play the role of squire had he so chosen, but he had no such ambitions. Eve, although far more gregarious, was also devoid of social pretensions. Although relative newcomers to Framfield, both were extremely popular, not only because of the prosperity that Buxted brought to the area, but also because of the Fishers' reputation as generous hosts and Eve's readiness to throw herself into the work of local charities. One former neighbour who called at Newplace one day to pick up her children remembers counting more than sixty adults and children at the house and, despite the fact that Antony was teetotal, noticed that nearly all the adults had a full glass. Antony, however, had no

small talk and unless a guest was interested in his views on political economy the conversation, although always cordial, could
be brief. In contrast, Eve greatly enjoyed company and clearly
made up for her husband's lack of interest in the small change of
social discourse. Both were members of the East Grinstead
Conservative Association, but Eve was clearly judged the greater
asset, for while Antony was largely concerned with discussing
the problems arising from socialist planning, Eve was an accomplished and energetic organiser and fundraiser, one whose help
could always be counted on. To Antony's increasing regret she
remained uninterested in the political issues which preoccupied
him and took no part in his schemes to improve the world. Her
interest in politics was genuine – sufficiently so for her to attend
seminars at Swinton Conservative College in Yorkshire during
the late 1960s – but it was of a very different kind. In the main
it was confined to the issues dictated by the party's electoral interest and centred on its leading personalities, to whom she displayed a natural deference. Antony, in contrast, had little respect
for most Conservative politicians of the day because of their reluctance to challenge the collectivist assumptions which shaped
the political agenda and informed policy in the post-war
period. He also held them responsible for failing to attack the
controls and regulations which he encountered in his working
life and which did nothing to remedy the country's relative economic decline.

By 1964, Buxted was producing 500,000 birds a week – compared to 10,000 during the whole of its first year of operation –
and Antony could claim to be Britain's, and probably Europe's,
biggest chicken farmer and a rich man. While most meat prices
soared, that of chicken fell – from 3s 8d a pound in the year in
which Buxted was launched to less than half that ten years later
– with the result that chicken was becoming the most frequently served meat. Success had not been smooth or painless,
either for Antony or the small chicken farmers. A combination
of rapid growth and price volatility meant that there were

several occasions when the venture might have failed. There had also been problems with planners and with the rating authorities, who refused to extend the agricultural exemption available to poultry houses. On occasions when the company's future seemed uncertain bridging loans, mortgages or generous overdraft facilities were needed to stave off disaster. Before Buxted was securely established a neighbour can recall Eve's mother, recently informed of the latest setback, declaring to her daughter: 'This time Antony is going to bankrupt himself, you, me – everybody!'

The smaller Buxted producers had sometimes responded to the bumpy ride by asking Antony to buy them out. On such occasions he would reply that he would prefer not to because he thought the shares would rapidly appreciate in value, but would be prepared to if they were adamant and first took independent advice. A few persisted, but those who followed Antony's guidance were well rewarded when the £1 shares eventually peaked at £600.

The actual running of the company was left entirely to Pendry, whose realism, management skills and sense of humour made him the perfect foil to the non-conformist Old Etonian whose greatest strengths as a businessman comprised an ability to think in broad conceptual terms, a readiness to take risks – if not always to evaluate them correctly – and the capacity to pick men and to inspire their loyalty. It is a testament to the effectiveness of their partnership that Buxted ceased its rapid expansion when the company came under new direction in 1965. The cause was a severe bout of depression, itself triggered by a nationwide fowl pest which led to the destruction of many hundreds of thousands of birds at Buxted. The outbreak alone would certainly not have proved fatal to the company's prospects, which despite increasing competition, remained excellent. Nevertheless, as Antony's depression deepened, he found it difficult to concentrate or make decisions. It was obvious to Pendry that important decisions requiring his chairman's involvement and consent could not be indefinitely postponed and after several months with no clear idea of when Fisher might return to full health, an offer to merge the company with Allied Foods seemed the best way forward.

On Pendry's testimony:

> Antony was not a hard man. Some can deal with the kinds of pressures and problems that arise in business, and cope. Antony could not. I sometimes felt that if he had been able to have a drink in the pub with a friend he could have forgotten his problems or put them in a better perspective, but he was not that kind of man. He seemed to have no really close friends and because of his religion he did not take a drink. Looking back at his life I can never decide whether the good fortune he experienced exceeded the bad, or whether the bad exceeded the good.[5]

Under the new arrangements, Eric Reed, the chairman of Allied Foods, became chairman of a merged company called Allied Farm Foods, while Tony Pendry shared the role of joint chief executive with Reed's brother. It was an arrangement which Pendry did not find congenial and he left shortly afterwards to become a consultant with British American Tobacco, later moving to Nabisco as a vice-president. Antony, who remained unwell for several more months, continued as a board member until August 1968, when Allied Farm Foods was sold for £21 million, of which Antony received around £2 million. Commenting on this chapter of his business career, Antony's second wife, Dorian, declared, 'Antony did more to put a chicken in every man's pot than any king or politician ever did.'

Later, when people expressed concern about factory-farming methods, Antony would point to the care his company had taken in keeping his chickens warm, fed, watered and submissive as a perfect example of the welfare state. Privately, he remained proud of his contribution towards turning a luxury item into a staple diet for millions.

Success in broiler production had also encouraged Antony to produce eggs. The Laughton Egg Company, based in Ross-on-Wye, in which he acquired a controlling interest, became one of the largest layers in Europe, but Antony quickly found his plans constrained by the Egg Marketing Board, to which all but the smallest producers were obliged to sell. Under the scheme, introduced in 1956, registered producers were required to grade their eggs and stamp them with a 'Little Lion'. The professed purpose of the Board was to stabilise prices for the benefit of the producer. But even before it came into existence Antony warned that its operations would destroy the incentive to produce fresh, quality eggs, and encourage over-production, while the cumbersome marketing arrangements envisaged would delay the arrival of produce to market. The result would be a thriving black market as consumers increasingly bought fresh, quality eggs at the farm gate, if necessary at a premium price. In an interview with his local newspaper, Antony also protested that the scheme 'intruded upon the inherent right of every citizen to carry on business without interference'. When officials became aware that the scheme was producing exactly the results forecast by Antony, prosecutions were brought against farmers who defied its provisions by selling unstamped eggs. Ministers reacted by ordering an advertising campaign featuring a farmer who urged television viewers and newspaper readers: 'Look for the Little Lion!' Increasingly, however, shoppers took against the Little Lion, and tried, if they could, to avoid him whenever eggs straight from the farm were available.

Antony's twelve-year campaign against the Board, involving letters and articles in national, local and trade newspapers, and protests to ministers and MPs, was conducted almost single-handed. But in 1964 he received welcome support from his elder daughter, Linda, then aged 22 and an external student at the LSE, who in a crisply written prize-winning essay predicted that efficient farmers would have nothing to fear from the Board's abolition, and that improved techniques would stimulate demand for eggs in the long term, while the taxpayer would be

saved an annual bill of more than £20 million.[6] In 1969, following a lengthy public hearing on the future of the Board as its
subsidy rose well beyond £20 million, its scope and powers
were drastically reduced, prior to its total abolition. According
to Sir Ronald Halstead, a senior businessman who sat on the
Egg Reorganisation Committee set up to advise the Labour
Minister of Agriculture, Fred Peart, and a major driving force
behind the reforms, 'Antony was an inspiration.'

5

Making the case for the market

By the autumn of 1954, Antony was sufficiently confident of business success to pursue his plans to transform the character of British political and economic debate through the creation of what was to become known as a 'think tank'. Although subsequently sometimes tempted to seek direct influence, Antony was adamant that the new organisation should follow the path of intellectual persuasion rather than political activism. In this he remained faithful to the advice given to him by Hayek nine years earlier.

It is often assumed that the purpose of think tanks is to develop new ideas. The reality is that many such bodies come into being in order to apply a body of existing ideas to current problems. In the process those involved hope to convert others to the philosophy which underlies their approach. This was the path taken by Antony when he began to lay the foundations of the Institute of Economic Affairs in 1954–5. As letters to friends and collaborators make clear, his actions were not intended as the first steps in a search for novel answers to Britain's worsening economic difficulties; he believed that the answers already existed, and the task was to explain them in a lucid and cogent manner in order to persuade others. It is also clear that from the outset he had a grasp of the means by which his goal was to be pursued. By targeting the opinion formers, or 'second-hand dealers in ideas' – university teachers, journalists and broadcasters – he hoped to reach those whom they in turn influenced. This approach reflected Hayek's view that yesterday's dissent becomes today's consensus, as described in his essay *The Intellectuals and Socialism*: 'Once the more active part of the intellectuals have been converted to a set of beliefs, the process by which these become generally accepted is almost automatic and irresistible.'[1] Given the limitations on resources, this approach made economic as well as strategic sense and although it was to be refined by those Antony brought in to run the IEA, its outlines were in his mind from the beginning. So too was the need to produce scholarly work of a high intellectual standard and to avoid being embroiled in party politics.

Antony's principal collaborator in the creation of the new organisation was his old ally Oliver Smedley, and it was at his suggestion that it was named the Institute of Economic Affairs. In a letter to Smedley of 1956, Antony wrote:

> Money spent on politics has very little effect on the actions of the average person. Most people are far too busy with their own affairs to get involved with the dreary subject of politics. It is of course necessary to have political machinery but if we are going to increase the number of people who are prepared to vote intelligently, we must start putting the right ideas in front of them at an early age. In my own case, it seems the best method is putting money into the Institute …
>
> My chicken business continues to grow rapidly. It has the advantage that it should increase my income considerably, but of course it is also taking up a lot of my time.
>
> The Socialists got round this idea by getting a rich man to support the London School of Economics and they put Lhaski [sic] and Dalton there. Lhaski [sic] and

Dalton between them must have done incalculable damage to sound thinking the world over. They teach young people at a time when they are actually exercising themselves in an effort to find out things. They are still at a formative age. Once young College and University students have got the right idea [economically] they will never lose it and will spread these ideas as they grow up. In particular, those carrying on intellectual work must have a considerable impact through newspapers, television and radio and so on, on the thinking of the average individual. Socialism was spread this way and it is time we started to reverse the process. It is probably impossible to do it in any other way.

He concluded:

Therefore the Institute of Economic Affairs has been formed to propagate sound economic thought in the universities and all other education establishments where we find it possible to do so. There are obviously many ways open to us, all depending on the amount of money available. The Institute is a charitable and educational organisation and therefore funds subscribed by businesses are not subject to tax. Where tax has been paid it can be recovered.

The latter point was also grasped by Smedley, who realised that the Institute's prospects of acquiring and keeping charitable status would be jeopardised if its activities were seen to be party political. In a letter to Antony in 1955 he wrote that it was 'imperative that we should give no indication in our literature that we are working to educate the public along certain lines which might be interpreted as having a political bias. In other words, if we said openly that we were re-teaching the economics of the free-market, it might enable our enemies to question the charitableness of our motives. That is why this first draft [of the Institute's aims] is written in very cagey terms.'[2] Once the Institute's publications began to appear, people could judge its educational and non-party political nature for themselves.

The IEA's first base was a cramped, £3-a-week room with one table and chair at Oliver Smedley's General Management Services, an umbrella organisation which housed a diverse range of free-trade organisations at 4 Austin Friars, a few dozen yards from the Stock Exchange in the heart of the City of London. Coincidence had already played a large part in the Institute's creation and its growth continued to proceed along largely spontaneous lines. As John Wood, who was to become a trustee in 1963 and the Institute's deputy director six years later, said in 1981, 'If, from the first the IEA had developed in a systematic manner, tidily implementing a detailed forward plan, it would have been out of character. There were no plans.'[3]

Typically, its first publication – *The Free Convertibility of Sterling* by Antony's friend and fellow *City Press* contributor George Winder – was brought out 'as a kind of experiment' before the Institute existed as a legal entity. The book, which advocated the abolition of exchange controls, was printed by Batchworth Press and appeared in June 1955. Antony, who signed the Introduction as 'Director of the IEA', invested £200 in the enterprise, which was lost when Batchworth went bankrupt. However, partly as a result of a review by the American economist Henry Hazlitt in his *Newsweek* column, the entire print run of 2,000 copies was sold within three months. Hazlitt, who was famed for the lucidity of his expositions on economic issues, was highly complimentary: 'For the last ten years many of us have been hoping for some clarity, courage and common sense on this subject in Great Britain, only to be repeatedly disheartened by the confusion or acquiescence on the subject. But at last the tide seems to have turned ...' Hazlitt went on to compliment Winder on 'a most lucid, thorough and uncompromising protest against continuation of British exchange control ...Winder has published something more effective than a mere polemic. He has written a sort of elementary textbook.'[4]

Heartened by the success of the publication, Fisher and Smedley gave formal expression to their plans for the new body on 9 November 1955 when they and a colleague of Smedley, J. S. Harding, met at Austin Friars to sign the trust deed. Its purpose was 'to establish a charitable body to be known as the Institute of Economic Affairs ... with the object of educating the British Public in knowledge of economic problems and their solution'. The trustees, who also approved 'The Rules', the IEA's constitution, each contributed £100 to the funds, while Smedley's company was given the task of looking after the Institute's secretarial needs at a sum to be decided. An advisory council was also set up, consisting of the Liberal peer Lord Grantchester, the economists Colin Clark (Oxford), Eric Nash (Aberystwyth) and George Schwartz, and the distinguished City Editor of the *News Chronicle*, Sir Oscar Hobson.

In June 1956, Antony wrote to a local Conservative MP, Major Frederick Gough (the only Conservative politician to take an interest in the birth of the IEA):

> After what I can honestly say is now many years of studying socialism, Communism, bad government, tyranny, whatever else you call it, I have come to the conclusion that possibly one of the only ways of defending the civilised community against completely false and wishful thinking is through such an organisation as this. Even if it isn't the only way, I do believe it is the cheapest. I therefore intend to give up all my other 'social' activities so that I can give as much constructive thought to the work of the institute as it is possible for me to do.

Gough subsequently helped organise a series of dinners at the Commons so that the founders of the new body could explain its aims and rationale to interested MPs.

The IEA's aims were set out in its first promotional brochure, which stated that its sole concern would be 'economic truth', unswayed by 'political considerations'. Its ultimate objective would be a society in which people would understand free-market economics, 'together with an understanding of the moral foundations which govern the acquisition and holding of property, the right of the individual to have access to free competitive markets and the necessity of a secure and honest monetary system'.[5] The new institute also promised 'to make available the works of the great economists so that they may the more easily be brought to the notice of the public', although it did not specify how this was to be achieved.

As with all of the enterprises with which he was to be involved, Antony believed that his most significant decision would be the appointment of 'the right man' to run it – or in this case, the right men. For the subsequent success of the IEA was to depend on two men: Ralph Harris and Arthur Seldon. Ever since their meeting in 1949 at East Grinstead, Antony had remained convinced that Harris was the ideal man to head the organisation about which they had talked and corresponded. There is no reason to think that he ever considered any other candidate. In a letter to Harris of June 1956 in which he formally offered him the job, Antony wrote: 'Our strength lies in the fact that we are not beholden to politics, that we are out to seek and spread the truth. We are not beholden therefore to any past political history or any particular business gimmick. Everything we do must be of the topmost quality and carry the stamp of complete sincerity and integrity.'

These sentiments were no doubt heartfelt. The emphasis which Antony placed on them, however, was possibly intended to make a favourable impact on Harris, who had always stressed that success would depend on high intellectual standards and an unwavering determination to steer clear of party politics. The son of a bus inspector, Harris had been born in Tottenham and had left school in 1943 to train as air crew before going up to Cambridge to read economics, where he took a first-class honours degree. But after two years with the newly formed Conservative Political Centre – then presided over by R. A. Butler – Harris left to teach economics at St Andrews in 1949, moving to the *Glasgow Herald* in 1956 to take over the leader-writer's position that was vacated when Alastair Burnet accepted a fellowship in the USA.

Although there was and is nothing remotely false about Harris, few would have guessed his North London origins. A slim, elegant, pipe-smoking figure with a Bertie Wooster haircut, usually sporting an embroidered waistcoat and possessor of a remarkable collection of hats, Harris could almost have passed as a member of the aristocracy. But the tenacity with which he was to assault the prevailing economic orthodoxy, and the obvious relish with which he did so, may have owed a great deal to his background. As he later acknowledged: 'I had a bit of a chip on my shoulder. If I met public-school boys I would mock their accents, because these were the people who would condescend to help workers along with little state hand-outs and subsidies and benefits.'[6] Antony was always indifferent to considerations of class. What recommended Harris to him was his energy, his ability to simplify complex arguments, and his bravura public speaking, which combined flair, brevity, humour and logic, a combination not exactly common among professional economists. Some years later a perceptive profile in the *Spectator* assessed Harris's strengths: 'He thinks fast on his feet and can reduce a complicated argument to its essence and make the essence seductive. He works at the anecdote, statistic, or joke which will encapsulate a difficult point.'[7]

Unlike some among what was later to be referred to as the 'New Right', he was not attracted to liberal economics because he equated them with permissiveness. For Harris liberty was not to be confused with licence. As the *Spectator* correctly observed: 'Lord Harris is no libertarian. A Christian with little theological but much moral interest, his morality is of a traditional English Protestant kind, more sin and sorrowful Cross than joy in Resurrection.' Along with Harris's acknowledgement of the significance of human fallibility, however, went a relish for public debate and an obvious delight in organising the intellectual resources necessary to win his case. Fisher had found the perfect intellectual salesman.

Harris was appointed General Director of the IEA at a meeting of the trustees at the National Farmers' Club in White-hall on 5 July 1956, on a part-time salary of £50 a month which he would be free to supplement from freelance journalism. This followed an interview with Smedley and assurances that Harris would abandon his parliamentary ambitions – he had twice stood in Scotland as a Liberal Unionist candidate. Given Harris's own views about the need to ensure that the IEA did not become embroiled in party politics – an imperative that he was to observe steadfastly – such assurances were superfluous.

Harris had always been intrigued by Fisher's plan to do for classical liberal economics what the Fabians had achieved for so-cialism. But his inclination to risk his career and prospects in order to run the new organisation had been strengthened by his dismay at the direction of politics since the two men had first talked. Whereas he had regarded Churchill as 'a liberal Tory of the better kind', he was soon to observe the Macmillan governments 'congealing into a Keynesian-collectivist mould'. According to Harris, in a lecture which he delivered in 1980, 'The last brave stand – until Mrs Thatcher came to power in 1979 – was in 1958, when Peter Thorneycroft and his two treasury colleagues tried to stop the remorseless subordination of taxpayer and private economy to the insatiable demands of State spending – and were driven by failure to resign from Mr Macmillan's government.' It was the departure of the Treasury team of Thorneycroft, Nigel Birch and Enoch Powell – the latter subsequently a friend of both Fisher and Harris as well as an IEA author – that strength-ened Harris's resolve to follow 'the path of radical reaction'.

As an article of faith, those involved in the creation and early growth of the IEA held that risk-taking was a vital dynamic in the functioning of a free society. To varying degrees all risked their own security or reputation, or both, by becoming involved in this wholly novel enterprise. But given that Harris had a young family to raise and that his new salary amounted to only half of what he had been earning as a journalist, the risk he took was the greatest. The collectivist bias in the economics departments of British universities at that time would have almost certainly made it harder for him to return to teaching if things went badly and might well have ruled it out completely. Although a capable journalist and pithy phrase-maker, his views might also have prevented him from rising to a senior editorial position on a major newspaper. He said later: 'I was mad! I didn't calculate the risk at all. Fisher's enthusiasm and my desire to return to London and do something were sufficient.'[8]

Although his appointment was soon put on a full-time basis, enabling Harris to move to London and begin work in Smedley's office in January 1957, doubts about the Institute's financial viability persisted for some months afterwards. An undated letter from Smedley to Fisher, evidently written soon after Harris's arrival at Austin Friars, expressed a pressing need:

> Ralph is installed and hard at work. To put things pretty bluntly, we simply must have some money in the Bank. I have been carrying the day-to-day expenses for so long – offices, staff, stationery. I think you said Harris was to get £10 a week and the secretaries £5. Where is it to come from at the moment? Can you relieve all our minds by putting the Institute in funds, on loans or otherwise? I can do no more.

Although there is no record of a reply, Antony evidently provided the necessary funds. In 1955 he contributed £250, and during the first years of the IEA's existence he provided £1,000 a year – approximately one-fifth of its total income – while also playing an active role in raising funds from other sources, starting with £500 from a prominent stockbroker, Sir Robert (later Lord) Renwick. His own contribution was to rise to £12,000 per annum, although later, when his fortunes declined, he expressed regret that he had not given still more when Buxted's success would have enabled him to do so. In order to protect the Institute against the risks arising from his death, and to assuage the anxieties of the Institute's permanent staff about the extent of their dependence on him, he thoughtfully took out a life policy for £10,000, subsequently increasing this to £50,000. In recognition of the risks taken by Harris in joining this hugely ambitious but uncertain venture, Antony later created covenants for each of Harris's three children and continued to fund these until he encountered serious financial difficulties some years later. Fisher's financial support was typically rendered with a minimum of bureaucratic fuss and paperwork. According to Harris, 'He was seldom very explicit about money. He would say, "I can cover that," and there would be no further complication whatever.'

The Institute's second appointment – that of Arthur Seldon as its editorial adviser and subsequently its editorial director – was no less inspired than its first, and of decisive significance. Seldon was then working as an economist for the brewers' trade association under Lord Tedder, the recently retired Marshal of the Royal Air Force. Seldon, of equally modest working-class origins, was an orphan whose parents had died during the Spanish flu epidemic of 1918 and whose adoptive father, an East End cobbler, had died when he was ten. Seldon had become a socialist as a schoolboy at Sir Henry Raine's grammar school in the East End of London. He later described how

> the working classes around me in the East End were
> taught that all the ills of the world, from sickness and
> unemployment through exploitation and imperialism to
> hunger and war were caused by capitalism. I later came
> to doubt and then resent, as an irresponsible assault on
> young minds, the heavily insinuated implication that the
> ills of capitalism would be ended by socialism. The most
> plausible excuse for the deception was that the ills of
> capitalism were all around them in their daily lives, but
> socialism was the new hope dawning in the new Russia,

cleansed of the Tsars, from which the parents of some
had fled.

Thus were the toiling masses misled for decades by the
most destructive *non sequitur* in British history, the
fabrication of only a handful of the leisured, mostly
affluent middle class men and women, from politicians to
scholars, who preferred to capture the machinery and
financial resources of government, first to do in the
welfare state what the best of them had been doing far
better voluntarily and, then, by nationalisation to create
the prosperity from which all would, they said, gain –
equally.[9]

After winning a place at the London School of Economics
in 1934, Seldon gradually absorbed the economic liberalism of
his tutors, including Hayek, Lionel Robbins and Arnold Plant,
whose research assistant he later became. As a result of this intellectual conversion Seldon joined the Liberal Party, where he
became an ally of those like Smedley and Lord Grantchester
who were struggling to preserve the party's increasingly tenuous
commitment to classical liberalism. It was Grantchester, recruited by Smedley and Fisher to assist in the creation of the
IEA, who commissioned Seldon to write what would be the
IEA's first paper on pensions, and it was he who subsequently
recommended Seldon as the man to take responsibility for the
Institute's editorial output. Conscious of the risks to career and
family prospects, Seldon continued working for the brewers
when he became Editorial Adviser in 1958, then part-time Editorial Director a year later, only giving up his work for the trade
association when he became full-time Editorial Director in
1961.

Seldon's strengths lay in the rigour of his thought, a profound grasp of the subtleties of market analysis, his meticulous
attention to detail and a rare ability to write lucid prose on
complex subjects in a way that was at once acceptable to scholar
and non-specialist alike. No less rare were his readiness to impart

the same skills to others and his patience in doing so. Seldon was
also among the first British economists to realise the significance
of the so-called 'Public Choice' school of economics, which
seeks to apply market principles to the analysis of political behaviour and was developed in the US by James Buchanan and
Gordon Tullock. It was Tullock who, in 1976, was to write an
IEA classic called *The Vote Motive*, which exposed how public
policy was distorted by party competition in the electoral
market.

It was while working for the brewing industry that Seldon
had first discovered his pleasure in using words well. Anxious to
develop his writing skills, he submitted samples of his work to a
correspondence school which offered courses in writing, only
to have them returned with a note saying that they were already
of sufficient quality to obviate the need for tuition. During the
next 30 years scores of economists, including two Nobel-prize
winners, acknowledged the improvements which Seldon had
made to their prose. Those who approached him in person with
manuscripts were often treated to a masterclass in fine writing,
delivered painstakingly but with much humour. To authors who
produced limp or leaden prose he would start by insisting:
'Listen to the sound of the words!' As the political philosopher
Shirley Robin Letwin observed: 'Arthur Seldon managed to
everyone's surprise to persuade economists to write in English
prose.'

To Harris and Seldon, Fisher extended the same trust and
friendship that he had displayed towards Tony Pendry. According
to Harris,

> When I started there was no job description. It was
> simply a matter of AGAF, which is how Antony was
> invariably referred to in the office, putting his trust in
> me, and soon, Arthur, and if there was any difficulty at
> any time, he would be completely supportive. Although
> hands-off, he wasn't above a bit of chastisement if we got

into difficulties through our own fault. But there was never any criticism of the publications ... As far as the policy on subjects was concerned it was really *laissez faire* because he trusted us.[10]

Fisher modestly acknowledged the limits of his own role at a party held to celebrate the IEA's thirtieth birthday in 1987:

It is exciting to see what they have all done which I had absolutely nothing to do with, having been a kind of catalyst. If it hadn't been for Tony Pendry there wouldn't have been any Buxted and if there hadn't been Ralph and Arthur there wouldn't have been any IEA. Ralph says I was very kind and didn't interfere, the reason being that I didn't know how to interfere, and I didn't know how to help, either ... It's entirely due to their efforts which have produced results. I don't claim any credit at all. I've always said that I'm a businessman and it is the thinkers who should be doing this.

Success seemed far from assured during the early years, however. Indeed, it was ten years before the IEA could truthfully claim to be exerting an appreciable influence on debate, and at least another five before its success looked beyond doubt. Seldon believes their slow start in shifting the predominantly statist climate of opinion was due to the fact that IEA studies of the welfare state could always be criticised as insensitive to the needs of the poor and lacking in compassion. It was also a reflection of just how few allies they possessed in this country. Indeed, the central beliefs held by Fisher, Harris and Seldon were shared by only a small number of academics prepared to speak out, no more than a handful of prominent journalists, and a few pro-free-enterprise bodies of marginal influence such as the Economic Research Council, Aims of Industry and the Society of Individualists all of which inevitably attracted more than a fair share of cranks. Among farming and business contemporaries Fisher's initiative in creating the IEA was regarded as further proof of his eccentricity. 'I remember in the 1960s at one of our poultry industry black-tie dinners, a speaker, a socialist farmer, made a joke at my expense,' Fisher later recalled. 'He said that Antony Fisher was employing the only two economists left in Britain who believed in free markets.'

The prevailing fashion in collectivist thought was especially strong among more vocal economists like Andrew Schonfield, Michael Shanks and those associated with the publicly-funded National Institute of Economic and Social Research. In Britain it had been reinforced by the perceived success of Keynesian demand management in controlling unemployment before the war and inflation after it. As Seldon observed: 'From these apparent successes the belief developed that government could deal with any and every economic problem, by regulation and direct management: not only in defence, law and order and the supply of money but also in fuel and transport, education and medicine, housing and pensions, local services and everywhere else.'

The IEA approach was very different. It began from the very opposite end of the economic spectrum: with the firm, where wealth is created, and with individuals organised in families, voluntary groups, co-operative organisations or partnerships. In Seldon's words:

> It recognised that some goods or services – the so-called 'public goods' – had to be supplied by government, national or local, and financed by taxes or rates ... But for the rest it opened up questions that had lain dormant for decades. Why should this or that service be supplied by government? Why could it not be supplied by people coming together in 'markets' where those who wanted things could choose between those who offered them? If markets were not feasible, was that because choice for buyers or competition among suppliers was impractical, or because government itself was putting legal or other

obstacles in the way of individuals with goods and
services …? In opening up the prospects, the IEA
released a shoal of questions that to many observers
seemed closed and settled.[11]

Moreover, it was in the interests of articulate and well-placed
lobbies, including the trade unions, that such issues should
remain closed. It was highly inconvenient that Fisher should
have identified and harnessed the intellectual and financial resources to prise them open. According to Harris, reminiscing in
one of the 'Intellectual Portraits' series of videos produced by
the Liberty Fund in 1999, 'We were like naughty schoolboys. We
had come from nowhere and didn't know where we were
going, and so liked the idea of throwing a little cracker down at
their feet [those of the economic establishment]. So, you see, a
lot of our thinking was deliberately intended to affront them
and wake them up. I think we enjoyed it and it was a necessary
part of this Hayekian challenge.'[12]

The IEA's iconoclasm meant that Harris and Seldon were
not invariably treated with the respect or courtesy which they
themselves extended to professional colleagues, but as a
'scorned, dismissed heretical minority'. In Harris's words, there
was 'a preordained path for the state to regulate, to plan and to
direct – as in war, so in peace. If you questioned it it was like
swearing in church. At times this overwhelming consensus in-
timidated us, and we sometimes held back. We often felt like
mischievous, naughty little boys.'[13]

Friends and allies, initially a very small club, did not discern
great reticence on their part. Even allies doubted whether the
IEA could achieve the counter-revolution in economic thought
at which it aimed. Norman Macrae of *The Economist* recalled: 'I
remember writing a polite review of *Hobart Paper Number 1* in
early 1960, but saying privately that I thought they would go
bust, and that only a fool would write *Hobart Paper Number 2*.
This last proved true prophecy because I proceeded to write
Hobart Paper Number 2 [on rent control] myself.' This admission

appeared in *Hobart Paper 100*, published in 1984, by which time it was easy to forget that the early activities of the IEA had been denigrated or simply dismissed as irrelevant by numerous Marxist, neo-Keynesian growth enthusiasts, and sundry other varieties of collectivist.

The Harris–Seldon partnership, which lasted for 30 years, worked because, in the words of Milton Friedman,

> they complemented one another – they fitted together like pieces in a jigsaw puzzle. Ralph, outgoing hail-fellow-well-met, an excellent public speaker, was an ideal choice for the 'outside'. Arthur was an exacting academic with a passion for precision, the ideal choice for the 'inside' role. Ralph was a brilliant voice for the Institute; Arthur an unrelenting enforcer of intellectual standards in the Institute's books and the celebrated Hobart papers he created. Ralph's interest in the politics of economics balanced Arthur's in the economics of politics.[14]

Harris's somewhat idiosyncratic management style, which involved keeping numerous balls in the air at the same time, combined spontaneity with exhortation and great energy as an organiser and networker. He maintained the fiction of keeping a diary but frequently gave the impression of not knowing what was in it and of being largely uninterested in matters of administration. Internal memos were a rarity, mostly scribbled on compliment slips. Staff were poorly paid but treated as friends and allies in a common cause who could count on support and kindness if they encountered ill-health or personal problems. Despite the meagre economic rewards, many of them remained with IEA for twenty years or more, including Harris's assistant, Joan Culverwell, Mike Solly, the publications manager, and Ken Smith, the librarian. A few occasionally muttered that Harris and Seldon were guilty of the very paternalism of which they accused successive governments and were better at advocating the market rate for the job than paying it – but then Harris and Seldon were not running a government-funded body or a profit-making business but a unique institution that developed spontaneously as a focal point, as a meeting place for a small but growing nucleus of market advocates, as a publisher, as a conference organiser and as, in Graham Hutton's phrase, 'a haven for non-conformists of all parties or none'. Had they attempted to run the IEA along more 'rational' business lines it would certainly have proved a less agreeable and rewarding place to visit. It might consequently have been less able to engage the sympathies of those journalists and scholars who were judged crucial to the success of their mission. Years later, a friend of Harris's attending a seminar on how to appoint think-tank directors caused raised eyebrows by pointing out that, because of his idiosyncrasies, Harris – a heroic figure in the eyes of many of those present – would never have been appointed if their criteria had been applied.

Although Fisher himself subsequently promoted the IEA as a possible model in the creation of other free market think tanks, he may have been slow to grasp the fact that success would not entail continuous expansion in the manner of a thriving business. According to Harris:

> He was by nature impatient for results and at times thought the IEA wasn't growing as fast as he would have wished. He would have liked it to burgeon like his chicken business where he started with 100 chicks and in no time had 50 or 100,000. We had to keep telling him this was not a war of big battalions, more like a platoon operation such as the SAS. Also it wasn't very like a business … It was all very compact and our impulse was to keep it that way. We knew personally everybody employed in it, their wives and families, and kept colleagues a long time.[15]

At first the work of the Institute was shared equally, but a division of labour, later formalised, gradually emerged. Harris, extrovert and seemingly unable to control a constant flow of ideas, acted as the IEA's principal spokesman and fundraiser; Seldon, more reflective and scholarly, ran the 'engine room' in which papers were commissioned and edited, promising writers given advice, and high editorial standards imposed. The division of functions was not rigid: manuscripts, proofs, titles, drafts, press releases, promotional literature, fund-raising letters and speaking notes were constantly passed for revision and improvement through the invariably open door between their adjoining offices. Those who visited from the economics departments of British universities were as impressed by the importance attached to lucid writing, something to which they were not necessarily accustomed, as they were by the sheer volume of work. Seldon once described his relationship with Harris as 'The Gilbert and Sullivan combination of producer and projector of the case for liberal capitalism.' It is an apt description, even if it overlooks the part played by Antony Fisher, the reserved and self-effacing impresario who had made the Harris–Seldon production possible and subsequently exported it to every continent.

From the beginning, the constraint on funds required the Institute's directors to think carefully about the kind of activities that would most effectively achieve their aims. An early brochure, published in 1957, referred to schemes to help public speakers, to supply lecturers and to distribute articles to newspapers. The IEA's founders also contemplated a journal, though this idea was not taken up until 1981. The early recognition, later strengthened by Seldon's 1975 *Pensions in a Free Society*, was that scholarly publications would provide the most effective means to pursue their objectives. Antony wanted to see an IEA publication 'on every topic that might be discussed'. But it was still not clear what *kind* of publications. It was clear they could not afford hardbacks, produce titles for Everyman or Penguin, build a sales team or expect to scale the list of bestsellers. Fisher's early correspondence with Smedley had shown a general awareness of the target audience, but Harris and Seldon refined this considerably. The ideal publication would be a lively monograph of around 10,000 words and, unlike publications from other economic research organisations, preferably possess an arresting title (IEA titles were to include *Down with the Poor*, *The Price of Blood*, *For Love or Money* and *Anything but Action*). It would be aimed at journalists on quality newspapers in the knowledge that if they were sufficiently impressed to review it or write about it in their columns, its effect would be multiplied. However, Seldon successfully argued that it should also have a reading list to stimulate the interests of students so that they could pursue the matters raised in further detail, and should be accessible to intelligent sixth formers or first-year undergraduates. According to Harris, it was partly to spare Fisher and other business supporters the labour of having to plough all the way through the *Papers* that they were accompanied by an executive summary which enabled the busy reader to grasp the essence of the argument, an innovation which was to prove highly popular with non-economist readers. Finally, there was a press release, the draft of which would pass between Harris and Seldon for improvement and amendment perhaps a dozen times until an agreed version emerged.

A further characteristic distinguished IEA papers from those of other economics institutes: their authors were instructed to take no account of the practicality of their ideas, to be daring and unconventional, and to persist, however inconvenient their conclusions. As Harris later commented: 'It was one of Arthur's most seminal principles that IEA authors must pursue their analyses fearlessly and indicate conclusions for policy without regard to what may be thought, in the short run, to be politically impossible.'[16] For that reason many politicians would put down IEA publications concluding that Harris and Seldon – and especially the latter – were incorrigibly naive, just as they were to leave IEA seminars or lunches saying much the same. Civil but combative in print as in person, the two men simply made no concession to the political preconceptions of their readers or their luncheon guests. It was for this reason that the Liberal MP

John Pardoe, one of the few in his party to be receptive to the IEA message, declared in 1971: 'You are a confounded nuisance to any politician who wishes to be left alone in his unresearched ambitions.' Yet only a few years on many of those visitors were to discover that the limits of the 'politically possible' had shifted, in large part because of the IEA's growing influence, reinforced by the formation of the Centre for Policy Studies and the Adam Smith Institute in the mid-1970s. What once had been condemned as politically impossible was now on the verge of becoming orthodoxy.

One other characteristic distinguished the IEA's publications and its work generally: a determination to remain independent of its financial contributors. This meant never seeking – or accepting – public funding, while resolutely resisting pressures that came from existing donors and not allowing new ones to attach strings. Seldon recalls telling potential benefactors: 'We shan't necessarily say what you want to hear.'

As the result of being copied by other British think tanks and many scores of similar bodies elsewhere, the form taken by IEA publications, with their emphasis on high academic standards and accessibility, is now familiar to all those who work in the area of public policy: ministers, special advisers, economists, civil servants, journalists and broadcasters. In its day it was an original conception. While generally sympathetic, a few Conservative intellectuals disliked the economic reductionism of IEA publications, the universal quality of their arguments and their unwillingness to consider non-economic ends and ways of thinking. But even such critics were inclined to accept that, had it shown any inclination to accommodate these wider criticisms, the IEA would not have done its work so well.

From the beginning there was never much disagreement about the strategy to be pursued. To use a favourite metaphor of Seldon's, the role of the IEA was that of high-level, long-range artillery. If correctly targeted, its 'shells' would make their largest impact on the intellectuals. But the Institute did not aim to engage the enemy in hand-to-hand fighting. Instead, its artillery barrage would enable others to move forward as infantry – those more directly involved in the political process such as the pressure groups Aims of Industry or the Freedom Association. That the fundamental aim was to shift intellectual opinion as it related to the role and scope of government was apparent to any but the most obtuse visitor to its offices. Indeed it was strongly implied by a quotation from Keynes which was given pride of place on the wall of its office at 2 Lord North Street (which they moved to in 1969) along with photographs of Hayek and Friedman:

> The ideas of economists and political philosophers, both when they are right and when they are wrong, are more powerful than is commonly understood. Indeed the world is ruled by little else. Practical men, who believe themselves to be quite exempt from any intellectual influences, are usually the slaves of some defunct economist.

An early problem faced by Harris and Seldon was to find authors of sufficient quality willing to write for an institute which paid little – a mere 50 or 100 guineas in the late 1950s – and, in the prevailing intellectual climate, promised even less in career advancement. Their solution was to write themselves. Seldon's book on pensions was followed by jointly written works on hire-purchase credit and advertising, both of which were then under criticism for being corrupting and encouraging improvidence. Although Harris and Seldon themselves made criticisms of the conduct of both spheres of business, credit companies such as United Dominions Trust and advertising companies such as J. Walter Thompson were relieved to find it on good authority that they were not guilty as charged – and promptly joined the Institute's small but growing band of financial supporters.

Among the first authors to be recruited from outside was

Professor Basil Yamey, a close friend of Seldon and the best man at his wedding. Yamey, a leading authority on competition theory, agreed to write on retail-price maintenance (RPM) after being subjected to a campaign of friendly persuasion. In *Resale Price Maintenance and Shoppers' Choice* of 1960 – the subject of Macrae's complimentary review in *The Economist* – he estimated that the cost of allowing manufacturers to determine retail prices was £180 million. He also calculated that repealing price maintenance would reduce prices of branded products by 5 per cent, thus saving the average shopper £3 10s a year. Fisher found the paper arid and excessively academic. 'I can remember saying to Ralph, who had sent me the draft, that it was so dull – couldn't I have more fun for my money?' When Harris explained that this 'was a marvellous piece of classical market analysis which identified a weakness in government policy by all parties', Antony readily deferred to the latter's judgement, as he was to do on all similar occasions. Indeed, helped by Yamey's very precise calculations about the cost of RPM to the consumer and its timing, the paper made a considerable impact on the media. Edward Heath, then President of the Board of Trade and a rising young politician, seized on the price-maintenance issue and forced its abolition through Parliament in the teeth of strong opposition from many in his own party, much of it stemming from understandable concern about the impact on small shops. When at the height of the controversy Heath lunched with Yamey, Fisher, Harris and Seldon, the future Tory Prime Minister pointed to Yamey and exclaimed: 'You are the cause of all my trouble!'[17]

To an extent, Yamey and the IEA were also the architects of Mr Heath's subsequent success. The repeal of RPM contributed very considerably to his reputation as a dynamic reformer. Antony commented: 'It may have been politically inexpedient [for the Conservatives] to take this action, but it certainly contributed to the reforming reputation of Mr Heath which propelled him into the leadership.' Given the later economic record of Mr Heath's government in abandoning its commitment to market principles following the Conservative Party's return to office in 1970, Antony had ample reason to reflect ruefully on the long-term and wholly unintended consequences of Yamey's paper. Nevertheless, the success of that publication confirmed both the soundness of the IEA strategy and the effectiveness with which it was being executed. Antony later commented:

> Here was a classic example of an intellectual working away in a backroom without any political power, ambition or intent, having a practical effect through attracting the attention of reviewers, civil servants and, finally, men of action. Subsequently, a mutual friend who knew Mr Heath well, told me how he tried to get Mr Heath … to tackle another pressing problem but Mr Heath explained that, having the choice between two reforms, he went for RPM because the case was fully documented. Here was tangible proof of Hayek's view that scholarly research should take pride of place over political campaigning.[18]

Despite the initial reluctance of the economics profession at large to take the IEA seriously, the clarity and rigour of its early publications began to encourage independent scholars to write for it. Among these were Alan Peacock, Jack Wiseman, Peter Bauer, W. H. Hutt and Alan Walters, all of whom had been at LSE or had taught there. Colin Clark, who had produced national income statistics for Keynes, and Graham Hutton, who became a member of the IEA's advisory council and an early trustee, were both ex-Fabians, and among the first in a distinguished list of leftist intellectuals who came to doubt their former beliefs and expressed those doubts positively through IEA monographs. Although criticised for 'naivety' by politicians, Seldon was quick to realise the strategic value of what he described as this 'infiltration in reverse'. Indeed, he went out of his way to encourage this process, as he made clear in a presentation to the 1959 Mont Pélerin Society meeting in Oxford: 'We are seeking authors with Fabian or similar origins but whose basic love of liberty enables them to come most of the way with us on particular subjects ... This infiltration in reverse can prove most profitable.' Harris and Seldon's widening Mont Pélerin Society contacts also enabled them to recruit economic liberals with international reputations, among them Harry Johnson, James Buchanan, Gottfried Harberler and Milton Friedman, who became a frequent visitor to the IEA's offices in the 1970s and 1980s. Among the IEA's many achievements was the introduction to a wide British audience of Friedman and Hayek, respectively leaders of the Chicago and Austrian schools of economics.

A stream of publications explained the moral and material foundations of market economies, the role of the entrepreneur – then far more than today a misunderstood and endangered species – the fallacy of state planning, the inflationary consequences of the Keynesians, the trade unions' role in unemployment, the unintended consequences of government economic intervention, and the corrupting and debilitating impact of the universal welfare state. During the first 20 years of its life – during which the staff increased from a single part-timer (Harris) to 12 – the Institute published some 3 million words in 250 *Papers* and *Monographs*, 62 of which ran to second or subsequent editions or reprints, while 70 were translated into one or more of 10 foreign languages. In all, a total of 1 million copies was sold, mostly to universities and schools, during the first two decades of the IEA's programme. Total income during this period amounted to £1.25 million, which Ralph Harris liked to compare with the annual budget of £1.8 million for the unlamented National Economic Development Council, and annual expenditure in 1981 was running at £200,000, which with equal pleasure Harris mischievously compared to the £480,000 budget of the Keynesian National Institute of Economic and Social Research, 70 per cent of which came from the taxpayer.

Expressed in general terms, the achievement of the IEA was to rehabilitate classical liberal economics and to demonstrate the enduring indispensability of market analysis as a foundation for public policy. In the intellectual war waged by the IEA against the advocates of state economic planning, these constituted huge victories with profound implications in the larger struggle between advocates of the free society and its enemies. The battles on which victory turned, however, were themselves of major significance, touching the lives of millions in ways that few may have appreciated. The most famous of these were fought over two issues that dominated British politics from the mid-1960s to the mid-1980s – namely, inflation and trade unions.

In 1960, the IEA struck a heavyweight blow against conventional opinion about the causes and cures of inflation by challenging the prestigious Radcliffe Commission report. Radcliffe, a lawyer rather than an economist, had been commissioned by Peter Thorneycroft, then Chancellor, to investigate the role of money in economic management, and took a largely dismissive view of its importance. The IEA asked three academic economists and two financial journalists of the old school to review the report with Thorneycroft, who had since resigned from the Macmillan government in protest over public-spending increases. Although there were minor differences between the authors they found that the official review had underestimated the importance of money in the control of inflation. In addition, their report, *Not Unanimous: A Rival Verdict to Radcliffe's on Money*, found that the way full employment had been pursued by successive governments was itself inflationary. Their findings were followed four years later by a full-frontal assault on full-employment targets written by Professor Frank Paish and Jossleyn Hennessy in *Policy for Incomes*.

'Monetarism' did not achieve international fame, nor enter the public vocabulary, however, until an address given by Milton Friedman to the American Economic Association in December 1967, when he famously argued that inflation was always and everywhere a monetary phenomenon and that its cure must necessarily involve strict control over the supply of money. Friedman later distilled the conclusions of many years of theoretical and empirical work in a lecture, 'The Counter-Revolution in Monetary Policy', organised by the Wincott Foundation in September 1970 against a background of steadily rising UK inflation. The essence of his lecture, which was to help him win the Nobel Prize in 1976, was expressed in the following words: 'Inflation is always and everywhere a monetary phenomenon in the sense that it can be produced only by a more rapid increase in the supply of money than in the quantity of output.' His lecture, which was published by the IEA, concluded: 'A steady rate of monetary growth at a moderate level can provide a framework under which a country can have little inflation and much growth. It will not produce perfect stability; it will not produce heaven on earth; but it can make an important contribution to a stable economic society.'[19]

The lecture was attended not only by Antony Fisher, who was to enjoy increasingly warm relations with Friedman and was later to be his close neighbour in San Francisco, but also by James Callaghan, the future Labour Prime Minister. Although in Britain 'monetarism' is invariably regarded as a Thatcherite phenomenon (and is sometimes used in such a way as to accommodate aspects of Mrs Thatcher's policies which have nothing remotely to do with Friedman's theories) it was during the Callaghan premiership, with Denis Healey as Chancellor of the Exchequer, that monetary aggregates were restored as key economic indicators by the Bank of England. Moreover, it was Callaghan, not Thatcher, who as Prime Minister sounded the death knell of Keynesian demand management when he told the Labour Party annual conference in 1976:

> We used to think that you could just spend your way out of a recession and increase employment by cutting taxes and boosting government spending. I tell you, in all candour, that this option no longer exists, and in as far as it ever did exist it only worked by injecting bigger doses of inflation into the economy followed by higher levels of unemployment as the next step.[20]

This speech, which signalled one of the most important turning points in British economic policy of the twentieth century, could have been written by a member of the IEA. Indeed, it may well have been inspired by the IEA's work over the previous decade since it was in fact drafted by Peter Jay, Callaghan's son-in-law. Jay had also been present at the Friedman lecture and counted himself an admirer of both Friedman and much of the work of the IEA, for which he had written on this subject earlier in 1976.[21]

If Friedman was the Institute's most celebrated advocate of monetary stability, Friedrich Hayek was its most famous and persuasive critic of trade-union power.

Hayek's view was that a return to market economics was possible only if the labour market was made more flexible by curbing the monopoly position of the uniquely privileged British trade unions. This view was supported by other liberal economists, most notably W. H. Hutt. In a seminal work entitled *The Theory of Collective Bargaining* published by the IEA in 1976, Hutt argued that the trade unions' claim that they could raise the living standards of their members through their monopoly position – what Hutt described as 'the strike threat' – was essentially false. Where demand for the product of their labour was flexible, a wage settlement above the market rate could be achieved only at the cost of higher unemployment; where it was inflexible a higher wage could be achieved only at the cost of destroying jobs or lowering wages elsewhere in the economy. Although Hutt did not say so, it followed that by abandoning their early role as workers' welfare organisations and registered friendly societies in favour of militant collective bargaining and coercion, the unions had proceeded down a historic blind alley – to the detriment of their members' interests no less than everyone else's. Hayek's analysis, which made a huge impact on Margaret Thatcher as Leader of the Conservative opposition from 1975–9, also indicated the harm done by the distortion of prices by trade-union activity. He wrote:

> If we want to preserve the market economy our aim
> must be to restore the effectiveness of the price
> mechanism. The chief obstacle to its functioning is trade
> union monopoly ... an exaggerated expectation of what
> can be achieved through monetary policy has diverted
> our attention from the chief causes. Though money may
> be one of them if it is mismanaged, monetary policy can
> do no more than prevent disturbances by monetary
> causes; it cannot remove those which come from other
> sources.[22]

Hayek's views were of course at variance with those of Friedman, for whom inflation was a purely monetary phenomenon;
the debate between them and their respective followers was to
preoccupy IEA authors and to constitute a fruitful source of
debate and inquiry for many years.

In the same year that Friedman delivered his landmark lecture,
Antony completed many years of work on what was to be his
most serious publication, *Must History Repeat Itself?*, eventually
published in 1974. The book, described by the *Sunday Telegraph*
as 'one of the most unfashionable books of the year', was sub-
titled: 'A study of the lessons taught by the (repeated) failure and
(occasional) success of Government Economic Policy through
the ages'. In the US – where it received respectful reviews – the
book was published under the title of *Fisher's Concise History of
Economic Bungling: A Guide for Today's Statesmen*.

A dedication to his brother was followed by the moving lines
of Laurence Binyon's poem 'For the Fallen':

> *They shall not grow old, as we that are left grow old.*
> *Age shall not weary them, nor the years condemn.*
> *At the going down of the sun and in the morning*
> *We will remember them.*

In his introduction, Fisher wrote, 'In the pages that follow I offer evidence which has convinced me that mankind is in much the same position as I was as an ignorant fighter pilot and in worse danger for being unaware of the need to correct that ignorance.'The text had been reduced by his friends Dr Rhodes Boyson, a Conservative MP, and John Wood, and 'rendered suitable for publication' by Ralph Harris. Although it displayed the same unwillingness to make concessions to contemporary fashion, the book was far better written and organised than *The Case for Freedom* and received greater attention. A leader in the *Daily Telegraph* applauded Fisher for his 'combination of the practical and speculative'. It accepted Fisher's thesis that the market economy was the best means of providing material welfare for rich and poor alike, but the *Telegraph* offered a rebuke: 'In a situation of vastly excessive public expenditure, a frightening momentum of monetary and wage inflation and almost irresistible trade union power, what needs to be documented now is how we find the road back to a market economy. It is not quite enough to say:"I would not have got here in the first place."'

A more apt criticism might have been that, if a government had attempted to introduce all of the proposals in Antony's book within the life of a single administration, the result would have been a legislative log-jam or revolution. For Antony had, in fact, signalled the route back to the market economy by means of a 10-point plan which could hardly have been more specific:

A new government must make its first priority maximising individual choice by removing the worst monopolies of all – those organised by the state – and withdrawing from the Common Market.

As a start the nationalised industries must be exposed to competition by removing barriers to entry. We must end state monopoly in coal-mining, gas, electricity, postal services, transport and nuclear power. At the same time radio and television and telephone services should be thrown open to competitive tender.

The buying and selling of all agricultural produce, currencies and metals should be freed. The National Economic Development Office and all other government 'economic planning departments' under whatever name, should be wound up. The power of the Bank of England must be ended, along with control over interest rates, the printing of money, and the fluctuating foreign exchange rates.

A number of government departments will become redundant and therefore a system of demobilising the civil service ... must be prepared ... Exchange controls must be wound up ... All forms of direct control over prices and incomes must be ended.

For good measure, Antony also advocated trade-union reform, tax credits for private healthcare and education vouchers, as well as the phasing out of tariffs and agricultural subsidies and reductions in every department of public spending except defence. He urged swingeing tax cuts with the ultimate goal of a uniform rate of income tax at 15 per cent, corporation tax at the same level, the abolition of capital gains tax, a flat rate of 20 per cent for inheritance tax, and the abolition of stamp duty.

Anyone reading Antony's book today would acknowledge that many of the suggested reforms have been achieved, although it was left to New Labour to remove from the Treasury the key power to determine interest rates. Moreover, the few parts of it which have not been achieved – for example, the abolition of capital gains tax, the phasing out of agricultural subsidies and the introduction of educational vouchers – remain favoured goals of economic liberals today. At the time, however, few outside Antony's immediate circle shared his view, and even some of them doubted whether the necessary political and moral will existed to reverse Britain's economic decline and possible descent into political chaos. Asked to review the book for the *Sunday Express* on 10 March 1974, Enoch Powell constructed an elegant essay on the book's theme without praising or criticising its author – perhaps because as a friend he felt it wrong to do either. To the question posed in the book's title, Powell believed that a pessimistic 'yes' was 'the natural reaction of anybody who lived through the last Parliament and watched Conservative members choke the lobby entrance to vote for legislation to fix prices and wages when they knew such legislation had invariably failed and had themselves personally said so to the electors and promised that there would be no repetition'. Powell argued that just as the remorseless increase in state spending and bureaucracy sapped the strength and initiative of the people of the ancient world, the same factors would destroy the political fabric of the new: 'The writing is on the wall for the Western democracies, and for Britain above all.'[23]

Although an admirer of Powell's intellect, Antony did not share his sense of doom. His own answer to the anguished question was that while British politicians displayed an innate tendency to repeat past errors, there was no necessary reason why they should not learn from their mistakes. Perhaps because he had observed at first hand the influence that the IEA was beginning to exert, Antony remained hopeful, as was apparent from an article about him in the *Christian Science Monitor* following the publication of his book:

> Antony Fisher, founder of Britain's authoritative Institute of Economic Affairs ... is a remarkable optimist. He thinks the situation in Britain today and in many other industrial countries is desperate. He thinks it will get worse. Yet, he says he is optimistic. He feels happier about things than he has for some time...The reason is that he feels sure that when present policies are shown to have failed and have failed for the umpteenth time because they cannot possibly succeed, people must try something else.

Events were to prove Antony right on both counts: economic conditions continued to worsen, but by 1979, the year in which Margaret Thatcher became Prime Minister, the British electorate was prepared to try something different. That there was a viable and coherent alternative available to them was in large part due to the IEA's growing influence and Antony's role as an intellectual entrepreneur during the two decades before Margaret Thatcher's arrival in Downing Street.

6

Educating Margaret

During the 1960s, two men, one a politician, the other a television writer and producer, formed long-lasting relations with the IEA that were to have far-reaching repercussions. The politician was Keith Joseph, the broadcaster Antony Jay. The separate but parallel stories of their relationships with the Institute demonstrate how at different levels the Hayek–Fisher strategy, executed by Harris and Seldon, was to succeed beyond all expectation.

In the early 1960s, Jay typified the attitudes and outlook of BBC journalists and broadcasters; attitudes which seemed to change more slowly than those of their colleagues in the print media. At that time, on his own admission, Jay was a walking anthology of neo-liberal platitudes: 'Like virtually all my colleagues I was anti-advertising, anti-capitalism, anti-industry, anti-monarchy, anti-selling, anti-profit; whatever made the world a freer and more prosperous place, you name it, I was anti-it.'[1] Jay began to question his beliefs only when he left the BBC to become a freelance writer and found himself working with businessmen. To his evident surprise he found that his new colleagues did not conform to his preconceived notion as greedy exploiters of consumers and workers, but were mostly decent people struggling to make a living. In a speech to the Headmasters' Conference in 1971, which was broadcast the following day on BBC Radio 4, he openly expressed doubts about his former

views. He also offered scathing criticisms of the prevailing anti-
enterprise bias of broadcasters and explained why such views
now struck him as hypocritical.

The broadcast had one consequence which, Jay says, was to
change his political philosophy more profoundly than anything
that had happened to him before or since. It was a telephone call
from Ralph Harris inviting him to lunch at the Institute of Economic Affairs:

> I found myself almost in a Samizdat world, a secret and
> subversive cell where heresies were propounded and
> revolutionary pamphlets were circulated. One that came
> into my hands quite early on was an extensive *Playboy*
> interview with Milton Friedman. I read it with
> tremendous intellectual excitement. All my adult life I
> had been irritated by economics and quite unable to
> understand it. Phrases like 'deficit budgeting' and
> 'aggregate demand' did not seem to relate to anything I
> understood. And then suddenly, reading the Friedman
> article, I discovered I could understand economics after
> all. It all fitted together. It made sense. Exposure to the
> IEA reading list showed me the futility of government
> planning, the role of competition, the operation of the
> price mechanism, the harnessing of self-interest to the
> public good, the functions of markets and their
> spontaneity (later demonstrated by car boot sales), the
> fallacy of government attempts to control prices and
> incomes, and the reason why the economic democracy
> of the supermarket is so much more sensitive and
> effective than the quinquennial referenda we call 'general
> elections': why Westminster's ballot boxes are so much
> less efficient than Tesco's checkouts, especially in serving
> the wishes of minorities.
>
> Unlike the economics I had been failing to understand
> all my life, the economics I learned at the IEA not only
> made complete sense of the economic world as I had

learned and experienced it; it also fitted together as a
complete system that was consistent, logical, and above
all, moral. It showed that capitalism was a better
guarantee of freedom, justice and equality than the
welfare state with its bureaucratised charity and
subcontracted compassion.[2]

Jay's tuition in market economics continued under Milton
Friedman, who later despairingly turned for advice to Harris
when unable to find an American programme-maker to
produce his television series, *Free to Choose*. Friedman wanted a
producer who could actually understand what he was talking
about, and without hesitation Harris recommended Jay. Their
collaboration led to the best televised exposition to date of how
a market economy functions, and a surprisingly popular television series.

Another consequence of Jay's intellectual conversion was the
television comedy *Yes, Minister*, and its sequel, *Yes, Prime Minister*,
which Jay wrote with Jonathan Lynn. At the time Jay was not yet
familiar with the Public Choice theory of economics pro-
pounded by Buchanan and Tullock but he had spent sufficient
time at the IEA to grasp the insights that lay behind it. The result
was the hilarious, fictional, but all too believable world in which
politicians and civil servants collide and collude, usually to the
detriment of the public whose interests are only served, if at all,
coincidentally. If the programmes had a message – and according to Jay it was never the makers' conscious decision to deliver
one – it was 'that those in political power are neither organised
or motivated to serve the public interest'. In Jay's words, its
corollary was 'that people are best left alone to pursue their own
interests in their own way with their own money'. Acknowledging his intellectual debt, he added: 'That is something I have
learnt through my connection with the IEA, and even if that
were all it would still be a cause for profound gratitude.'[3]

Jay's intellectual conversion may have been more rapid and
comprehensive than some others, but a continuous stream of

journalists were influenced through the 'lunches and launches' held by the IEA at its offices, first at Eaton Square, to which it moved from Hobart Place in 1961, and subsequently at 2 Lord North Street. As anyone who has lunched as the Institute's guest can bear witness, it can scarcely have been the quality of the food that drew them there. The appeal was to intellectual appetite, to the prospect of observing the post-war economic orthodoxy coming under devastating fire, and the expectation of hearing – and contributing to – a debate that was to suffuse a wider public and political stage. It is likely that many left such occasions feeling that they had witnessed a process that would change the agenda of British politics, and perhaps much else besides. Among senior journalists who acknowledged the IEA's role in influencing their views were William Rees-Mogg, Alastair Burnet, Paul Johnson, Andrew Alexander, John O'Sullivan, T. E. (Peter) Utley and Colin Welch. These, however, were merely the best known in a much longer list of journalists whose views underwent a change as a result of their contact with the Institute and who in turn influenced the way in which their readers thought about economic and political issues. Indeed, it is clear that the role of the Press was crucial in the transformation of the political and economic climate of the 1970s. As Richard Cockett has acknowledged, 'In the wider context there is nothing of equal importance in British newspaper history to the role played by the *Daily Telegraph, The Times* and the *Financial Times* in converting a wider public to monetarism.'[4]

Sir Alastair Burnet, a neo-Keynesian when he first came into contact with the IEA as editor of *The Economist*, later gave firsthand testimony of how intellectual opponents were 'turned':

> They came, it seemed, like spies in the night ... They
> were polite, even courteous, plainly intelligent fellows
> who enjoyed an argument. Only after a bit did it become
> apparent that they usually won their arguments. The
> well-drilled ranks of us Keynesians began to suffer
> uncomfortable casualties. The Butskellite regiments,

entrenched in the ministries and universities, had severe butchers' bills.

The intellectual concussion caused by the Institute of Economic Affairs conducted by Ralph Harris and Arthur Seldon ... upon the body politic and economic was cumulative and, eventually, decisive.[5]

A telling anecdote in an article written in 1978 by Jock Bruce Gardyne, one of the most intellectually able of his generation of Conservative politicians, provides an example of how the IEA's strategy of 'top down' intellectual conversion worked in practice:

> I cannot pretend that as a Tory back-bencher in the early 1970s, I regularly lectured my constituents about the vital importance of controlling the money supply. Yet at the last election I was confronted by a young working farmer who intervened in an argument over incomes policy to say that this was all nonsense: we were suffering from inflation because we had failed to control the money supply. He had seen Prof. Friedman on television, as had many millions of others, and had been deeply impressed.[6]

Professor Friedman's visits were, of course, regularly organised by the IEA.

Entertaining, almost always in the Institute's offices rather than in clubs or restaurants, proceeded at a prodigious rate and played an important role. On all such occasions there was strict adherence to the famous dictum of one of its most famous authors: 'There is no such thing as a free lunch.' Accordingly, all suitable occasions – from Christmas parties, to anniversaries, to the directors' birthdays – were used to promote the IEA's work and underlying message. Not all staff members felt able to match the directors' obvious relish for these occasions. Excusing himself from yet another Christmas lunch on the grounds of fading stamina, Martin Wassell, the publications manager (and for a time editorial director), explained that he had already attended many such events during the previous weeks. 'Do you know, Ralph, last year I attended twenty-nine IEA Christmas parties, lunches and dinners!' Evidently a little shocked that his colleague did not approach them with the same unqualified relish as himself, Harris replied: 'Do you know, Martin, *I* really rather enjoyed them!'

To such occasions MPs, researchers, academics, businessmen, donors and potential donors, as well as journalists and broadcasters, were invited. An established feature of the IEA calendar was the Hobart Lunch, held on the last Friday of each month, at which Harris presided in a manner not dissimilar to that of a genial master of ceremonies at an Edwardian music hall. As a result of these and other idiosyncrasies the occasion enjoyed a distinctive flavour of its own, which a growing band of regulars came to savour. Newcomers might initially be taken aback by the Editorial Director's somewhat direct greeting – 'I'm Seldon. Who are you?' – but most were also impressed by the affability and the evident sincerity of their hosts, and the scale of their ambitions. The popularity of the occasions also owed something to the fact that, thanks to Harris's breezy chairmanship, the speaker would not be allowed to exceed his allotted twelve minutes and so would finish on time. The ambience of the occasion was accurately conveyed by Shirley Robin Letwin:

> There was no resemblance either to a coterie like
> Bloomsbury or to a political pressure group like the
> Fabian Society ... It was more nearly like a common
> room with a highly unorthodox membership. Suits and
> ties, not sandals, were the norm. But Ralph Harris's
> ironic manner of presiding over the meetings, banished
> earnestness together with long-windedness, and made
> trade unionists, social democrats, and Labour Party
> members as welcome as businessmen, Hayekians, and
> assorted cranks.[7]

No politician, however important, could expect an easy ride

on such occasions. Praise, if due at all, had to be finely calibrated to match the achievement. At a private lunch for Mrs Thatcher shortly after she became Prime Minister, one of those present offered robust criticism of her government for not being bolder in introducing measures to reform state welfare and to reduce taxes. The Prime Minister visibly bridled. Harris, anxious to calm things down, proposed a toast 'to the best Prime Minister since Churchill'. At which point Seldon, risking the prospect of high honours for principles, raised his glass, saying in a clearly audible stage whisper, 'I'll take a *sip*.'[8]

If, to adapt Arthur Seldon's military metaphor, the journalists were the light artillery in the ongoing battle of ideas, the task of grappling directly with the enemy fell to politicians. In certain obvious respects Sir Keith Joseph Bt was ill-qualified in temperament or background for such bloody work. A man of nervous disposition with a known distaste for the more vulgar aspects of political life, Joseph had first entered public life out of a desire to raise the living standards of the poor. The failure of successive governments to achieve this aim, despite ever more ambitious plans for economic redistribution, encouraged a process of rethinking which was to lead him to the offices of the IEA and to a long-lasting personal friendship with Harris and Seldon. Although much more intellectually sophisticated than Antony Fisher, Joseph shared the latter's urgent and compelling desire to put matters right when they were manifestly going awry. His powers to recognise that things had gone wrong – and to discern the reasons – were at their greatest when he was freed from the cares and responsibilities of office. Indeed, he is probably the only significant Conservative politician to have made a substantial reputation chiefly while in Opposition. To those who teased that his sense of mission reflected a desire to undo the harm which he had done in office, he would ruefully concur. 'I did it! It was my fault!' or even, 'It's all my fault!' were frequent refrains. As Morrison Halcrow, the first of his biographers, has noted:

> Joseph's special kind of energy actually seemed to leave him with extra resources of energy when he moved from Ministerial office into opposition. His distaste for the conspiratorial side of politics saved him from some of the jealousies and point-making of opposition politics. A word constantly applied to Joseph was *anguish*; and, indeed, he devoted immense quantities of nervous energy to decision-making and squaring his conscience.[9]

Like Geoffrey Howe, Joseph visited the IEA soon after the Conservative defeat in 1964. According to Seldon, 'He said: "We are told we should know what you are up to and the ideas you have been working on." That was the first time any senior Conservative came to ask us what we were doing. He felt he should know.'

Joseph, a prodigious reader who sometimes required a suitcase to accommodate his weekend reading, asked many questions and took away a large number of IEA publications. According to Seldon, Joseph then remained silent for ten years until the Conservatives again lost office in 1974, when he returned for further guidance.[10] But Seldon's memory may be at fault. In fact Joseph, who had left his Fellowship at All Souls without any formal knowledge of economics, continued to read IEA publications and to consult the IEA directors on a range of economic issues during this period, even if personal relations cooled. According to Richard Cockett: 'Joseph was to become one of the most discerning and inquisitive consumers of the IEA's literature. He leaned heavily on it for intellectual support and developed his own philosophy of economic liberalism during the late 1960s ... Joseph used the IEA as an intellectual back-up system and as a sounding board.'[11]

The intellectual route which Joseph followed was not one of linear progression; it was full of detours and its most prominent feature – one which Joseph was to revisit on a regular basis – was the road to Damascus. Nevertheless, Joseph's influence, along with that of Geoffrey Howe and Nicholas Ridley, accounted for the fumbling and faltering progress of the Conservatives towards the free-market philosophy which was to be partially embraced at Selsdon Park, where the Shadow Cabinet met in January 1970. As events were to demonstrate following the party's return to power later that year, the commitment to the Selsdon approach was neither as comprehensive nor as deep as reports had suggested, and there is little reason to suppose that Edward Heath, the Conservative leader, ever subscribed to it as a matter of conviction. But in the wake of the Tory victory in 1970, hopes that the new administration would represent a radical break with the policies of the Butskellite middle way ran high at the IEA. Seldon wrote to Joseph shortly after the unexpected Tory victory:

> I must not burden you, but since I was turned away from
> the Conservatives by Lionel Robbins who taught me
> that they were doing more damage than Labour in the
> 1930s by socialising in the name of Capitalism, I have
> waited for the day when Conservatives like you would
> redeem their sins. I really do think that you could break
> Labour's hold on the working class and destroy socialism
> for all time.[12]

Seldon's analysis may not have been at fault but his prediction on timing was. He would have to wait almost ten years before a serious start was made in replacing the post-war consensus on the economy. Within eighteen months the Heath government had comprehensively rejected the free-market approach, awarding substantial handouts to 'lame duck' firms and industries and boosting consumer demand in response to rising unemployment in the traditional neo-Keynesian manner. When inflation consequently rose to unprecedented post-war levels, peaking at 29.6 per cent, the government reacted by introducing a prices and incomes policy to control the spiralling wage demands that resulted. Moreover, instead of privatising the nationalised industries in accordance with pre-election pledges it merely sold a handful of state-owned pubs in Carlisle and the travel agent Thomas Cook, while taking most of Rolls-Royce into public ownership.

But probably the biggest disappointment for Fisher, Harris and Seldon came with the performance of those politicians who had seemed most interested in their ideas when in opposition, especially Keith Joseph, Margaret Thatcher and Geoffrey Howe, respectively Secretary of State for Social Services, Secretary of State for Education and Solicitor General (and later Minister for Trade and Consumer Affairs) in Heath's government. Seldon, not a man to pull his punches, carried on a combative correspondence with Joseph for the first two years of the Heath government in which he pressed the case for private provision of social services, then gave up, more in sorrow than in anger. His last letter to Joseph (who spent more than any previous Secretary for Social Services) concluded: 'You have given nothing to those who expected something different from you.'[13] Others whom Joseph had met through the IEA complained that Joseph's radical impulses had been blunted by the civil service and that he no longer saw his old friends, perhaps because he was aware that their criticisms were justified.

The failures of the Heath government are beyond the scope of this brief biography, but it is clear that while Harris and Seldon were deeply dismayed by the conduct of the new government, Heath's intervention in the economy provided the IEA, on an almost weekly basis, with fresh proof to support its arguments. Indeed, it must sometimes have appeared that Heath was a helpful stooge in the IEA's efforts to re-educate the British – and the wider world – by demonstrating the disasters that flowed inexorably from intervention in the marketplace. 'It sometimes seemed that reality was on our side,' Harris said later. A succession of lucid and cogently argued publications criticised the government's industrial policy, its embrace of neo-Keynesian economics, its budgetary expansion, its doomed attempt to control the resultant inflation through prices and incomes controls, and its reluctance to use market mechanisms in the provision of welfare and education. Other publications assuaged the growing thirst for alternative approaches by arguing for strict monetary disciplines to counter the inflationary consequences of the 'Barber boom', for the privatisation of state industries, and the development of private alternatives to state provision of health, pensions and education.

Samuel Brittan of the *Financial Times* was among the first senior economic commentators to realise the full implications of the challenge posed to the prevailing orthodoxy during this period. He wrote in 1971:

> The unhappy state of relations between the Heath
> Government and the economic establishment has now
> reached the state where a little frank discussion could do
> no harm.
>
> The economic establishment, like the elephant, is
> easier to recognise than to describe. It comprises officials
> in the central policy-making department, Oxbridge
> economists interested in policy, and most of the
> economists likely to do time in bodies such as the
> Treasury, National Institute, NEDC, the late PIB ... An
> alternative focus is provided by the Institute of Economic
> Affairs, which has, with its propaganda for competitive
> markets, become a sort of anti-establishment.

It was to this 'anti-establishment' that Joseph and Howe, followed by Thatcher, were to turn after the Conservative defeat in February 1974. Some of his former friends among the economic liberals gave Joseph a cool reception, which given his propensity for self-criticism tended if anything to enhance his respect for their judgement. But he disarmed Harris and Seldon by saying, 'I'll understand if you think it's a waste of time. I came to see you ten years ago, and we've been discredited in between.' While Joseph displayed his customary level of intellectual curiosity, he appeared to have fewer reservations than formerly, and accepted virtually all of the criticisms made by Harris and Seldon of the government of which he had so recently been a leading member. Over a dinner which he gave for the two men at Lockett's (now Shepherd's) restaurant in Westminster, he explained his intention to create a new think tank which would take the arguments of IEA authors into the political arena. Unlike the IEA, the Centre for Policy Studies would fly a Tory flag, but there would be no formal links with the Conservative Party and it would be independent of it financially. To his considerable pleasure, Harris assured Joseph that he was not troubled by the fact that there would be two organisations promoting roughly the same message. In fact Harris and Seldon could not have been more helpful. They assured Joseph that competition was welcome wherever it occurred. The new body, while often drawing on the same authors, would be able to take its arguments to parts of the body politic which, owing to its non-partisan status, the IEA could not reach. Indeed, although a few of the Centre's publications might equally have been published by the IEA, it provided the logical next step for those who, having been persuaded by the Institute's analyses, wanted to give political expression to its views. Later Fisher visited Joseph to assure him of his personal support and to offer encouragement.

A speech which Joseph was to repeat before packed university audiences between 1975 and 1979 also underlines the significance of the IEA in influencing his views: 'It was *only in April 1974* [my italics] that I was converted to Conservatism. (I had thought I was a Conservative but now I see that I was not really one at all.)' On some occasions Joseph would say that until 1974 he had 'really been a kind of socialist'.[14] His change of view was in part due to the opportunity which opposition provided for reflection and partly to the influence of Alfred Sherman, an eccentric ex-communist who had fought the republican cause in Spain and had subsequently become a robust champion of capitalism. A trenchant critic of the Tory 'middle way' and of Heath's economic policies in particular, Sherman had given occasional speech-drafting help to Joseph and was later to draft most of his speeches. Nevertheless, if Joseph had been denied

the opportunity to reconnect with the intellectual allies he had
met at the IEA it is doubtful whether over the coming months
he would have had the confidence to break with the Heath
policies so emphatically. Moreover, without the IEA, there
would not have been a ready-made network of liberal economists and sympathetic journalists on which to draw for advice
and support. Nor does it seem likely that he would have contemplated the idea of creating the Centre for Policy Studies. According to Sherman, 'Had it not been for the Institute of
Economic Affairs, there would have been no Thatcher Revolution. They prepared the ground. They were the John the Baptist
of the 1950s and 1960s – *pace* Enoch Powell – the voice crying
in the wilderness.' In Sherman's description of the Centre's
original rationale can be heard echoes of Seldon's insistence that
his authors pay no regard for the politically possible:

> The Centre – it was agreed – was to act as 'outsider',
> 'skirmisher', trail blazer to moot new ideas and policies
> without committing the Party leadership; in the hope
> that sufficient headway had been made with public
> opinion and inside the Party, the leadership could move
> forward. Our job was to question the unquestioned,
> think the unthinkable, blaze new trails.[15]

Over the next five years Joseph was to consult Harris and
Seldon on all of the central economic issues of the day, and to
keep them regularly informed about his plans for the CPS. In
return, Harris and Seldon treated Joseph with the generosity
and hospitality that is traditionally extended to the prodigal son,
while providing an equally warm welcome to Joseph's new CPS
staff. Joseph acknowledged his debt to the Institute in July 1977
at the IEA's twentieth anniversary dinner when he declared that
the times were now propitious for the kinds of market-based solutions which the IEA had argued for: 'If the IEA did not exist,
how desperate would be the need to invent it.' In a tribute to the
Institute's founder he declared, 'All credit to that entrepreneur of

entrepreneurs, Antony Fisher, who perceived the need to mo-bilise Ralph Harris on one of the most successful entrepreneur-ial ventures of this half of the century.'

A still greater tribute to Fisher was delivered on the same oc-casion by Friedrich Hayek, his friend and mentor, in proposing a toast to the Institute. Referring to the ideas which they had discussed 30 years earlier during their first conversation at the LSE, he said:

> If these ideas influenced the aims of the Institute he created a few years later, I can now say honestly that it has achieved these aims far beyond what I then thought possible. At that time the creation of the desired intellectual climate was deliberately attempted only by the collectivists who, as Beatrice Webb told us in her memoirs, knew that if they converted the intellectuals to their philosophy its application would inevitably follow. I now believe that the change of opinion which has been brought about in the last 20 years is in large measure due to the efforts of this Institute, and is greater than anything the Fabians produced in a similar period of time.

In proposing his own toast to the Institute, Antony referred to the recent launch of similar bodies in Canada and Australia, and to the creation of a second UK think tank– the Adam Smith Institute:

> For those who ask for a concentrated effort I plead with all the power at my command for proliferation. We are getting near the truth, let it be propounded from as many sources as possible, and we must among many other tasks fill the aching void in bookshops of all kinds. Books which argue for big government abound, books which argue alternatively for the individual are dangerously rare. We have little time!

But while in 1977 the IEA could already point to considerable success in the moulding of opinion, Joseph's task, and that of the Centre for Policy Studies – to educate the Conservative Party – was only just beginning. Foremost among those to be educated was Margaret Thatcher, a political ally whose knowledge of economic issues was limited and whose approach to the subject largely instinctive. While an undergraduate she had read Hayek's *The Road to Serfdom* and remembered being impressed by it; Joseph advised her to read it again in light of their shared experience in government. She reported that it had helped make sense of many of the problems in government which they had encountered – and which they had arguably made worse. Thereafter Joseph proceeded to pass to her reading lists, articles and books, and in May 1974 asked her to become deputy chairman of the CPS. As she recalled in her memoirs:

> Whether Keith ever asked other members of the Shadow Cabinet to join him at the Centre I do not know: if he had they certainly did not accept. His was a risky, exposed position, and the fear of provoking the wrath of Ted and the derision of left-wing commentators was a powerful disincentive. But I jumped at the chance...
>
> From Keith and Alfred I learned a great deal. I renewed my reading of the seminal works of liberal economics and conservative thought. I also regularly attended lunches at the Institute of Economic Affairs where Ralph Harris, Arthur Seldon, Alan Walters and others – in other words all those who had been right when we in government had gone wrong – were busy marking out a new non-socialist economic and social path for Britain.[16]

This process continued after she was elected leader in 1975, but during the former period her Political Secretary, Richard Ryder, subsequently a junior minister in the 1983 Thatcher government and Chief Whip in the Major government, called at

the offices of the CPS in Wilfred Street on a regular basis for a
list of weekend reading. This was handed to him by the present
author – then a member of the CPS staff and on its board – who
in turn obtained much of what he passed on from the IEA. This
might typically include the latest IEA publication, articles by
Harris or Seldon, or pieces from journals and newspapers that
seemed to be of particular merit. Any suspicion that the Leader
of the Opposition was merely trying to seek the good opinion
of Joseph, her mentor, was dispelled when Ryder returned with
specific questions relating to last week's supply of reading materials. Joseph was also responsible for ensuring that Mrs Thatcher
struck up relations with the IEA directors, and through them,
Hayek and Friedman.

Shortly after she became Leader of the Opposition in 1975,
Harris arranged for Thatcher to see Hayek at Lord North Street.
Both parties were deeply impressed. According to Harris, 'although she is known as being a rather overpowering lady she sat
down like a meek schoolgirl and listened. And there was a
period of unaccustomed silence from Margaret Thatcher. She
said nothing for about ten minutes while he deployed his arguments.'[17] After Mrs Thatcher's departure, the IEA staff gathered
round the venerable philosopher-economist anxious to discover
what he thought of the first woman to lead the Conservative
Party. After an unusually long pause, he said with feeling: 'She's
so beautiful.' It was his only comment.[18]

A memorable exchange between Thatcher, Milton Friedman
and his wife, Rose, over dinner at a West London hotel in 1978
may have done as much as the IEA's published work to con-
vince her that the abolition of exchange controls could actually
strengthen sterling rather than weaken it. The meeting occurred
after Joseph rang at the last minute to apologise and to ask
whether Margaret Thatcher might attend in his place. According
to Harris, who was the only other guest, the meeting took the
form of a seminar, with Friedman answering her questions and
leading the discussion. The crucial first act in bringing the
British economy under the discipline of market forces, he

stressed, was to free the exchange rate and sweep away all controls. Although Geoffrey Howe, her future Chancellor, and Keith Joseph, her future Industry Secretary, had already been convinced of the case for abolition, Mrs Thatcher was evidently shocked by his advice. She replied: 'All the money will flow out of the country. What will happen – the bank rate will go through the roof!' Friedman replied: 'No, ma'am. No, ma'am.' And Friedman was off, explaining that by showing confidence in removing controls while sticking to monetary disciplines dealers might very well conclude that sterling was a currency to retain.[19] Friedman's advice proved sound. The abolition of exchange controls in October 1979 – powerfully advocated by John Wood and Robert Miller in *Exchange Controls for Ever?* published by the IEA in 1978 and echoing George Winder's first-ever publication 23 years earlier – was the first major step taken by the Chancellor after the General Election of May that year. Sterling, which had fallen as low as $1.20, rose to $2.00.

The Centre was also responsible for providing Mrs Thatcher with her first copy of Hayek's *The Constitution of Liberty*, although she seems subsequently to have acquired her own stock of the book so that she might use it to influence others. A copy was in her briefcase when she made her only visit to the Conservative Research Department – then regarded by Thatcher and Joseph as deeply 'unsound' – in the summer of 1975. Growing visibly impatient as one of the CRD desk officers extolled the virtues of pragmatism and the 'middle way' to a journalist, Thatcher reached inside her case and produced the book. 'This is what we believe,' she said. 'She banged it down,' reported one of those present, 'and then she delivered a monologue about the British economy.'[20]

Thatcher benefited from the existence of the CPS in a variety of other ways. By the time she challenged Heath for the leadership in February 1975, Joseph had mapped his own political philosophy with unusual clarity and rigour. After his own reluctant decision not to stand for the leadership there was no need for Thatcher to explain her own credo or even the policies which followed from its application and she made no attempt to do so. Instead, she made it known to parliamentary colleagues that she agreed with Joseph and would pick up the banner which he had raised.

Joseph's speeches, mostly drafted by Sherman, had the aim of moving the Conservative Party from the middle ground – 'a slippery slope to socialism and state control, whose results even socialists now disown' – to the 'common ground'. Of these speeches, perhaps the most significant was that delivered at Upminster in 1974 when, for the first time as a senior Conservative front-bencher, he accepted a long-standing IEA contention, namely that *both* parties were responsible for Britain's relative economic decline because of the collectivist nature of their measures. Further speeches – on the relationship between inflation, monetary growth and unemployment; on the importance of competition and choice; on the moral and political foundations of the market order; on the fallacies of centralised economic decision-making; on the significance of the entrepreneur; on the need to curb the monopoly powers of the trade unions – set out the foundations of what later came to be known as Thatcherism. In each case, Joseph rehearsed arguments made in more scholarly form by the IEA, arguments which were already familiar to the best informed members of the media as a result of the IEA's pioneering educational work.

According to Thatcher these speeches 'fundamentally affected a political generation's way of thinking'.[21] That change made possible reforms which had been almost universally regarded as politically impossible, thus arresting and reversing in turn 'the British disease', once judged by many to be terminal. By early 1994, two-thirds of Britain's state-owned industries had been sold off to the private sector, raising more than £50 billion for the Exchequer. Altogether, 47 major businesses with nearly 1 million employees had been privatised. The number of individuals owning shares tripled to 10 million and was to grow still further, as the number of those owning shares exceeded the number belonging to trade unions. Along with exchange controls, those on prices, incomes and dividends were abolished and more than 1 million council houses and flats sold off. Trade unions had been brought within the framework of the law and industrial relations transformed for the better. Moreover, the dragon of inflation had been effectively tamed, at least for the time being.

As Pulitzer Prize winner Daniel Yergin and Joseph Stanislaw have stressed in their book, *The Commanding Heights*,

> the most important consequence of privatisation was that, together with labour union reform, it changed the basic institutional arrangements that had defined Britain since 1945 – and that had brought Britain to a standstill by 1979. In that year 1274 working days were lost to strikes for every thousand people working. By 1990 that figure was down to 108 – less than one tenth. The political and economic culture in Britain had been permanently altered; Keith Joseph's intellectual revolution had, in good measure, and despite all the controversies, worked.[22]

Reflecting on the origins of the Thatcher revolution, Mrs Thatcher told an interviewer: 'It started with Sir Keith and me, with the Centre for Policy Studies, and Lord Harris, at the Institute of Economic Affairs. Yes, it started with ideas and beliefs. That's it. You must start with beliefs. Yes, always with beliefs.'[23]

Lady Thatcher has gone further than most prime ministers in acknowledging the role of ideas in history. But a more detailed account of the causal chain leading to Britain's transformation must necessarily include Antony's conversation with Friedrich Hayek at the London School of Economics in 1945, his chance meeting with Ralph Harris, and his success as a chicken farmer. Was Milton Friedman guilty of hyperbole when he wrote that 'the U-turn in British policy executed by Margaret Thatcher owes more to him than any single individual'? He was surely correct to judge that if Antony had not had the foresight and dedication to found the IEA – the most important source of Mrs Thatcher's ideas – her revolution would have been long delayed.

In describing his own role, Antony may have said that he didn't interfere 'because I didn't know how to interfere, and I didn't know how to help, either'. But such words underestimate the importance of his practical contribution. At the same time, the knowledge that his support could be counted on in foul weather as well as good lent a sense of security to the IEA's directors and staff during its early existence, when its budgeting was on a month-to-month basis. Antony's judgement about what needed to be done to improve Britain's economic performance was vastly superior to that of most businessmen. But he resisted any temptation to use his position as chairman of the IEA's board of trustees to hog the limelight or – to use an American expression – 'to grandstand'. He was content to have acted as the vital catalyst in the creation of the IEA, to have funded it generously when he was able to do so, and to have sung its praises on all occasions. These were rare qualities, as Harris was to discover when he tried to help create IEA clones in Europe:

> When the IEA became strong I travelled in Europe, sometimes with Antony, spending a lot of time in Italy, France, Belgium and Holland – curiously I was never invited to Germany – with the idea of establishing local versions of the IEA in those countries. I made contacts, and even planted seedlings and hoped to find equivalents of Antony to support and nurse them through their infancy and build up sponsorship. Yet in Italy we could get no industrial support, in France there was no notion of business contributions to anything other than trade associations.
>
> Antony provided the indispensable entrepreneurial element – the backing or financial guarantees or ready money when needed and help in finding fellow businessmen to join with him in pushing forward this enterprise in intellectual persuasion. In a word, he

provided the one thing that is still missing today from the
other countries of continental Europe, which made it
impossible to establish anything like the IEA there. There
are plenty of Arthurs and Ralphs in those countries, but
there aren't any Antonys, no venture capitalist in the
world of ideas ready to give it a try without seeking to
regulate or plan or control it ... Without Antony it is
hard to see how the very real – and we hope far from
finished – reversal of collectivism in Britain, and the
present ascendancy of free market ideas here, could have
ever come about.[24]

Antony's policy of benign non-interference helped ensure
that the Institute was not distracted by the kinds of splits and rows
which can occur between the strong-minded individuals which
think tanks tend to attract. Similar bodies, some based on the
IEA, have been rent by internal feuds or faction-fighting into
which outsiders have sometimes been drawn with attendant bad
publicity. But until Antony's death in 1988 and the retirement of
Harris and Seldon during the same year, relations between board
members and directors, and directors and staff, remained
remarkably good. Almost the only blip in this otherwise
harmonious state of affairs occurred over a matter of little real
significance. Examining the latest IEA publication to arrive
through the post in May 1984, Antony observed that it listed 1957
as the year in which the Institute had been founded, rather than
1955, when he and Smedley had laid its organisational
foundations. He recalled similar occasions when the same
mistake had been made. Feeling that this contradicted his own
oft-repeated emphasis on 1955, Antony wrote to Harris asking
him to put matters right: 'The constant repetition in IEA
documentation that it was created in 1957 takes away the value of
my effort, which quite apart from being incorrect is unfair to me.'
Antony also expressed the fear that the error would damage his
ability as a fundraiser if potential donors concluded that he had
exaggerated or misled them about his part in the Institute's birth:

> To maximise my opportunities for raising money for all
> institutes (including the IEA) it is necessary that I get a
> fair hearing for what I did achieve. All I am is a catalyst. I
> have not run any institute for any longer than I have had
> to. My abilities and inclination do not run in that
> direction … However, the starting-up process is as vital
> as it once was for the IEA … My request for due
> recognition in no way detracts from your wonderful
> efforts and tremendous success.

Harris's reaction was that the letter was out of character, and may
have been prompted by Dorian's understandable concern for her
husband's reputation. While he was sorry that his friend's feelings
should have been hurt it was palpably absurd to imagine that
anyone should think Antony capable of boasting or telling lies.

In his reply, Harris explained that he had always used the
later date of 1957 because it was the year in which Seldon's first
paper on pensions had appeared, and that he had tended to
think of the early publication by Winder on currency convertibility as being the publication of the Batchworth Press, 'and
frankly not being of the scholarly standard on which our success
has utterly depended'. However, he promised 'to think harder
about how we put the record straight'. Sensitive to the feelings
that might have been aroused by the peerage which he had received in Mrs Thatcher's first honours list, Harris added:

> The question of being 'unfair' runs wider than this
> historical detail. As I have told Arthur (and others) there
> is a gross disproportion in my getting a peerage and you
> (him and others) getting little or no public recognition.
> All I can say is that I shall not rest from trying to see
> more justice done, though I must report that my first
> priority for honours has recently been Fritz Hayek
> (whose prospects I'm told privately are made difficult by
> the fact of his living abroad, despite retaining British
> citizenship).

Repeated efforts by Harris to achieve recognition for his friend and patron did not, alas, bear fruit until the knighthood confirmed on Antony within a month of his death in 1988. Although no further action was taken in response to Antony's protest, his friend's letter assuaged any feelings of resentment which might have been harboured by a less self-effacing man, even though on the narrow issue of when the IEA had been founded Antony had clearly been in the right. A hand-written note by Harris to John Blundell, the present General Director of the IEA, attached to the file copy of the Fisher–Harris correspondence, reads, 'You might be interested in this scrap of history? It's the only example of a contretemps between AGAF and the Directors in 30-odd years of harmonious co-operation. May you be as blessed! My letter must have satisfied Antony, since I do not recall any further exchange on this question.'

7

A dream that failed

By the beginning of 1968, Antony had recovered sufficiently from the series of black depressions that had led to his resignation as chairman of Buxted. He now felt able to face up to problems in his personal life and to contemplate new business ventures. He and Eve had grown apart as the children had grown up, and in order to avoid the tension which now existed between them, he would spend as much time as possible in the couple's London flat or retreat to his study at Newplace whenever the opportunity arose. Earlier in his marriage he had been saddened by the fact that his proudest achievement – the creation of the IEA – was not something that he could share with his wife, but he now took this for granted. To a considerable extent the views with which the Institute was associated were, in fact, a source of friction between them, for they were at sharp variance with the policies of the Conservative Party, in which at a local level Eve was an important and popular figure. Unlike her husband, she was far from being an ideologue, but the political differences between them resembled those which were later to divide the so-called 'wets' and 'dries' in Mrs Thatcher's cabinets of the 1980s – except that the latter were not obliged to cohabit or face one another at the breakfast table.

As children, Mark, Linda, Mike and Lucy Fisher had been uninterested in their father's curious political activities. But the interest in politics of the older children grew as they progressed into adolescence. Their father's informal lessons in political economy now seemed to make sense, with the result that during the political arguments that took place between their parents they sided with their father. When as chairman of the East Grinstead Conservative Association Eve brought home party spokesmen for tea or dinner the consequences could be embarrassing, for she was frequently to find that the opinions of her guests were politely but very firmly opposed not only by her husband, but also by two or three increasingly self-confident children. Mark later recalled:

> We had all grown up with a great belief in free markets and the ability of politicians to produce exactly the opposite of what they said they intended, and to wreck everything in the process. We had begun to observe this with our own eyes. So there used to be a one-sided argument between the visiting dignitary and our mother on one side, and my father and the Fisher offspring on the other. I remember our local MP, Geoffrey Johnson-Smith, telling us how good the Common Market would be for us, and being rather startled to discover the strength of the opposition he encountered. I also recall meetings in the village hall when my mother would be on the platform with the dignitaries, with my father and the children sitting in the audience shouting, 'Boo'. It seems comic looking back, but also sad, and it must have been an embarrassing experience for my mother.[1]

Differences over politics were compounded by their religious differences and by the couple's sharply differing attitudes towards financial matters. Antony's business ventures were as ambitious as his plans to educate the British about economic reality, and generally entailed a high degree of risk. Eve, practical and methodical – qualities which made her a highly effective fundraiser for the Conservative Party as well as for local chari-

ties — feared that Antony's risk-tasking, combined with his reluctance to put money aside, would one day ruin them. Antony,
who had an instinctive belief that if only you worked and tried
hard enough you could make anything work — a belief that survived occasional evidence to the contrary — thought his wife's
fears to be excessive. Although a humble man, Antony's hugely
ambitious plans kept him on the move and ensured that nearly
all of his conversation was either about business or his increasingly strong desire to repeat the IEA success in other countries.
Eve, in contrast, preferred the simplicity and calm of village life
and the company of friends.

When the break came in 1968 Antony did nothing to dis-
abuse those who concluded that the decision had been Eve's. In
fact it was he who announced to Eve that he did not wish to
continue in the relationship any longer. Soon afterwards he
broke the news to his elder son in Eve's presence. Mark was
asked to go and purchase a house for his mother in the village,
which he succeeded in doing the same day. 'It was very civilised
if also very painful,' he recalled later. 'My mother took whatever
she wanted from the house, which she did without any argument ... So many people's parents were getting divorced it
seemed to be inevitable. Dad seemed happier and Mum seemed
happier ... it seemed to be an almost easier relationship once
they had parted. But at the time they were both devastated and
their sadness at their failure to make the marriage work never
left them.'[2] The Fishers' marriage had lasted 29 years; in the view
of family and friends they would probably have parted earlier,
but wanted to remain together until Lucy, their younger daughter, was sufficiently mature to understand, and it is likely that for
some time neither had wished to confront the problem. Following the divorce, both Eve and Antony were to enjoy extremely
happy second marriages with partners whose interests more
exactly matched their own. In the meantime, Mark, who was
running the family farm, moved his wife, Rosie, and their children into Newplace so that his father was not alone.

Even before the collapse of his marriage, Antony had begun

to consider a business activity that would take him outside Britain for part of the year. By that stage he knew that Buxted would be sold and his own role, already much reduced, would simply be that of shareholder. He told Mark: 'Look around for a project that we can do that is both business and fun, preferably in the sun.' No idea immediately presented itself. But some months later Mark read an article in the June 1967 issue of *National Geographic* entitled 'Imperilled Gift of the Sea', and written by Dr Archie Carr, an American zoologist. Carr described how the green sea turtle, one of the oldest surviving species, was threatened by uncontrolled hunting and by the loss of its nesting grounds. Dr Carr went on to argue that the creature might be brought back from the edge of extinction if it were domesticated in much the same way pigs or sheep had been many centuries earlier. Only one out of the 100 to 1,000 eggs laid by a turtle in the wild during a season actually survived to adulthood, he explained. But if successful, attempts to raise turtles for commercial purposes would strengthen the creature's chance of survival by reducing the incentives to hunt wild turtle. One or two per cent of hatchlings born in captivity could also be released into the wild – well above the survival rate in nature. Moreover, at a time when fears about the ability of the world to feed itself were growing, it seemed possible that the turtle could be the key in compensating for allegedly inadequate food supplies. Carr wrote: 'The green turtle is probably the most valuable reptile in the world, and it offers an expansible food resource for the future ... There is a ready market for turtle meat, a growing demand for clear green turtle soup, and a rising commerce in turtle hides for leather.' Carr went on to describe the plans of Robert Schroeder to breed the turtle on Grand Cayman, the largest of three Cayman Islands, where the seagrass on which the turtle feeds grows in great profusion.

Mark researched the subject further and discovered that there was almost no part of the green turtle which did not have a commercial use: virtually all of the meat was of high nutritional value, the shells could be used in furniture and jewellery, and there was considerable demand for turtle oil as well as for turtle soup. In addition, the Caymans had an extremely friendly tax regime, political stability, politicians who were anxious to encourage enterprise, unspoiled beaches, and limitless sunshine.

Mark showed the article to his father, whose reaction was as enthusiastic as his own. Following the *Reader's Digest* version of *The Road to Serfdom,* it was the second magazine article to change Antony's life. He wrote immediately to Schroeder expressing an interest in providing financial backing for his plans. Schroeder gave the letter to Irvin S. Naylor, an American entrepreneur and cigar-box manufacturer who had read the same article and been similarly excited by the commercial potential of breeding turtles. By coincidence, Antony's letter arrived on the day of Naylor's visit to Schroeder. Shortly afterwards, Antony left for the Caymans to investigate investment opportunities in person. While on Grand Cayman, Allied Foods was sold to Garfield Weston's company, British Associated Foods, which meant that Fisher had more disposable income than at any time in his life. Moreover, a meeting with Charles Hutchings, Director of Agriculture, convinced him that the Cayman Islands Authority would do everything in its power to support promising business ventures of almost any kind.

While on Grand Cayman, Antony had an investment idea of his own. Observing that the island's milk supplies were imported, and that milk was consequently sold at four times the price in England, he began to speculate as to whether a dairy herd could be maintained on the island. Antony consulted Hutchings, who assured him that provided the land was rock ploughed there would be no problem in raising grass with which to feed a herd. Antony later recounted to Mark that Hutchings showed him two fields where this had been done and also told him of a 100-acre tract on the south end of the island that he said could be reclaimed in a similar fashion. Mark recalled: 'The idea of an overseas business venture – whether in turtles or cows – in a warm and beautiful place which was also a tax haven, proved irresistible. Dad loved snorkelling, and I was a trained diver, which all added to the appeal of the place.'[3]

In October, Antony flew to New York to meet Irvin Naylor, the ebullient entrepreneur, to discuss a business plan that would enable Schroeder to give up his university job in order to create the world's first turtle farm. The two men established good relations and remained friends despite the numerous business problems that later befell them. Later that month Antony called his son from the US to say that the two men had launched a company in Grand Cayman under the name of Mariculture Ltd in which he had invested $20,000. The aim was to allow Schroeder to take the first steps in the creation of the farm while he and Naylor found financiers to back them. Naylor would be president, while he and Mark would join the board. He also suggested that Mark fly to Grand Cayman to set up home for his wife Rosie, then pregnant with their daughter Lucinda, and son, Giles, so that they could start the island's first dairy. Within weeks Mark had dutifully complied with his father's request and settled his young family on the island; their arrival was closely followed by that of 50 Brown Swiss cows.

But progress in both ventures was far from smooth.

> Setting up any kind of business there was, at best, difficult. In the case of the dairy, first we had to build sheds to get out of that blazing sun. Then we needed to build a desalinisation facility since cows, like humans and other animals, can't drink salt water. Once all that was done we bought and shipped 50 Brown Swiss cows – all were six weeks from calving – from the States to Cayman. Our goal was to have a dairy herd of 100–125 cows producing milk.[4]

Plans to grow grass for animal feed turned out not to be as simple as the Director of Agriculture had claimed. Torrential tropical rain turned the fields into a morass, then the sun baked them dry. Although deeply frustrating, the failure to produce animal feed would not be fatal to the success of the enterprise;

provided that freight rates remained at roughly constant levels it could be imported from the US and it would still just be possible to make a profit. Antony's younger son, Mike, however, who had inherited both his father's entrepreneurial instincts and his mother's practical nature, seems to have sensed that matters would not end well on Grand Cayman. Then in his early twenties, he asked his father: 'Why not invest in the Antarctic? There are no taxes, and the grass won't grow there, either!'

Despite a number of daunting difficulties – including the discovery of the near impossibility of harvesting the grass on which the turtles feed by means of an underwater harvester – the first steps in the creation of the turtle farm were encouraging and impressive. The first eggs, collected under licence from the coast of Costa Rica, were incubated on the porch of Robert Schroeder's house on Grand Cayman in 1969. Later, turtles captured in the wild were placed in large breeding pens where they mated and produced eggs. In order to facilitate the growth of the company, the Cayman Islands Authority granted an exclusive franchise to farm green sea turtles under the Cayman Protection Law of 1969. The company was also excused all import duties on equipment, feed, supplies, construction and other farm necessities.

Soon after his arrival on Grand Cayman, Mark attended a dinner of turtle, served in the local style, for those involved in the enterprise. Among those present was a young lawyer, John Maples, subsequently a Conservative MP and minister, whose firm had been asked to act on the company's behalf. Maples looked down with apprehension at 'a plate of rice in which there were bits of meat, huge gobs of fat and other gelatinous materials'. 'Now we know what's wrong with this business – the thing's inedible,' he declared.

Despite Maples's verdict, Fisher senior and Naylor made substantial progress in securing the company's financial base. In August 1969, 400,000 shares were offered and subscribed, thus generating US$960,000 for the company. The Fishers themselves took up $200,000 of the stock, while Naylor took up

$48,000. Many of those acquiring shares were Antony's friends or business acquaintances. Anxious that they should share the benefits of what he hoped would be a repetition of his success at Buxted, Antony had described the potential rewards that investment in Mariculture might bring, while also stressing the risks. Among those taking up the offer were Ralph Harris, Arthur Seldon and their respective wives:

> Antony offered to let Arthur and me have a small personal stake in it, which we accepted, Josie and myself, Marjorie and Arthur each taking £100 shares. For it looked as if he might enjoy the same sort of phenomenal success that he had enjoyed earlier. I recall him coming back from the Cayman Islands with colourful videos from the Caymans where he had been snorkelling and saying, 'You ought to see these: after all you are shareholders you know.' In the end, when the firm collapsed it tore him to pieces to think that he had persuaded people, including some big firms, like Unilever, to put substantial sums into it.[5]

Among other personal friends to invest was his former business partner Tony Pendry, who had put in £10,000. Pendry was used to assessing business risk on the basis of strict commercial criteria, but apparently did not do so on this occasion. 'I simply did it because it was Antony and I was fond of him.' There were evidently no hard feelings when the money was lost. Antony also introduced Mariculture to the Commonwealth Development Finance Company, which in 1970 took a 21 per cent stake worth £150,000 in the company and guaranteed a bank loan of £250,000. Antony was also instrumental in involving Dr Samuel Ayres, a California dermatologist who had pioneered hair transplants. Ayres invested $48,000 and subsequently joined the board. All of the stock was issued at the same value; none of the pioneers took shares at a lower price to reflect their still riskier initial investment at the start. Despite the fact that no profits were envisaged for several years, the growth of the company produced considerable excitement among investors. Shares rose from their issue price of $2 to peak at $14 before beginning their downward journey.

In his annual report to shareholders in 1970, Irvin Naylor declared:

> In our opinion these funds will now be sufficient to carry the Company to a point when it will make profits and have a positive cash flow in 1973. The prospects for your Company, assuming that we achieve our plans, indicate that sales in 1973 will be at a level producing substantial profits. World turtle supplies are being reduced rapidly. The human population explosion is resulting in the killing of the turtle population, and governments everywhere are passing laws aimed at protecting the survivors. Our success will mean the survival of the species so that we have the support of the conservationists...
>
> We cannot claim success until we have produced a steady supply of turtle and sold it at a profit. We are on our way to achieving the former and are beginning to deal with the latter. The continuing inquiries we make indicate an interest and demand for our products at satisfactory prices. Because of its unique character the venture is receiving publicity which in turn produces more such inquiries. Undoubtedly we have made mistakes but we have also learned much and your directors remain optimistic for the future.

The capture of male sea turtles is more difficult than that of females because they spend less time on land, but in April 1973, while collecting eggs in Surinam, an employee of the company captured two male turtles for the purposes of breeding and named them Hubert and Horatio. They went about the task for which they were intended with unexpected determination, and the good news was telephoned to Antony in London and to Irvin Naylor at his home in Pennsylvania.

Thanks to the enthusiasm of Hubert and Horatio, on 12 April 1973 the company scored the first-ever-documented breeding of green sea turtles – a landmark in turtle farming and conservation, although the resources required for the company to get to this level of development had greatly exceeded original projections. According to *Last Chance Lost?*, a sympathetic but detailed and authoritative history of Mariculture written by Peggy and Sam Fosdick and published by Naylor, 'The perseverance of a handful of gutsy, indefatigable businessmen and scientists had paid off. But the costs in time and money had been high. Perhaps, through the clear vision of hindsight, too high.'[6]

Nevertheless, in 1973 progress was there for all to see. The company's headquarters, spreading over ten acres, provided a home for 100,000 green sea turtles. It consisted of a complex of 140 concrete pens, a man-made breeding pond and nesting beach, nursery pens for newly hatched turtles, processing facilities, laboratories and offices. By 1973, turtle farming had become Grand Cayman's first – and only – export industry and its largest private employer, with a staff of 100. A promotional leaflet declared: 'There is something especially satisfying about it when one can contribute to scientific knowledge of an important species, add to the world's food supply, help strengthen Cayman's economy ... and at the same time engage in a successful commercial enterprise.' After overcoming a range of technical and feeding problems, the company's prospects looked brighter than at any time, not least because of the progress in marketing, and an increasing realisation that the commercial potential of turtle farming might exceed their already high expectations. Accordingly, despite tight financial constraints, the company planned a second farm and to double the size of the existing turtle stock to 200,000. 'We believe that the turtle food industry can become as big as the chicken industry in years to come,' Mike Goodier, the company's managing director, wrote in late 1973. 'Whether we build them ourselves or franchise the operation, we can see commercial turtle farms being established all around the world. Water temperature is a limiting factor, but the green turtle will flourish almost anywhere in the tropics, and it might even be that one could build a farm in a temperate zone, and use the warm water from an atomic power plant.'[7]

Nutritional analysis of the turtle showed that its flesh is homogenous – the meat and fat are not distinct as with beef. It is high in protein and low in calories and cholesterol. Ounce for ounce, turtle steak has more protein, less fat and fewer calories than either beef or chicken. Heartened by the news the company's marketing staff hired chefs to devise recipes for turtle steak, with such exotic names as Turtle Marengo, Turtle Gran Cayman and Turtle Scallopini. They also produced a turtle cook book and staged a turtle festival at the Sheraton Hotel in Jamaica, 'to celebrate the return of turtle to the menus of leading hotels and restaurants and its availability to consumer markets'. According to the Fosdicks: 'Mariculture investors appeared to have hit the jackpot. The executive chef of the hotel prepared turtle soup, keshi yena of turtle, patti shells, and turtle Wellington, pate, galantine, aspic, paprika, and Jamaican Way. Just to round out the appeal, the chef also made good old burgers and fritters.'[8]

A use could be found even for those that died in infancy. Anatomically correct hatchlings were freeze-dried and sold to companies in the US, including one Texas company that cased them in plastic and sold them as book-ends or paperweights. (The same company also used rattlesnake heads and other animal products until conservationists, claiming quite falsely that the animals had been deliberately killed, put the firm out of business – an augury of developments to come.) Leather exports went to Japan, where they were used in the manufacture of shoes, belts and watch straps, as did the freeze-dried turtles after the firm's Texas customer was driven out of business. The shell of wild turtles is a dull green, but as a result of being exposed to ultraviolet rays while being raised in shallow water, the shell of the domestic turtle was lighter and more attractively patterned. Because they were porous, light filtered through them, and they were sold as wall decorations and light shades in the US, Europe and Japan.

Analysis of the turtle's oil showed that, if suitably rendered, it had a potential use in cosmetics. Some researchers claimed that the oil – for which the actress Polly Bergen's company was to place orders worth $50,000 – removed wrinkles, while others believed that the oil held potential for steroid application. But pound for pound the most valuable part of the green sea turtle turned out to be its penis, whose alleged powers as an aphrodisiac were very highly rated among the Chinese. Accordingly, the 6-inch-long penis of the grown turtle was mounted on a card next to user-friendly instructions based on traditional Chinese practice: 'Hold the product in one hand and shave it with seven strokes up and then seven strokes down into a glass. Pour the residue through a strainer into another glass. Drink the contents of the glass.' Although Mariculture did not guarantee results, the company received one large order from China, and looked forward confidently to receiving more. According to the Fosdicks, 'From jewellery to watch fobs, gourmet soup to humble stew, potential wonder drugs to vast polyculture, Mariculture's future appeared bright. The World was Mariculture's market – a market in 1973, brimming with promise.'[9]

That promise was not served by the hike in oil prices which resulted from the Arab oil embargo of 1973, and the resultant world-wide recession which depressed demand for the company's products. But if the energy crisis was damaging to Mariculture, it was fatal to Caribbean Farms, the dairy which Antony and Mark had set up in 1968. Although unable to grow enough of the grass on which real profitability depended the dairy had at least met costs and sometimes made a small surplus. But the oil embargo was to lead to a trebling of animal-feed costs between 1971 and 1973, and to a decision by Antony and Mark to sell their herd at a fraction of its original price. In all, the Fisher family had lost well over £100,000.

The same period witnessed a much more insidious change which was ultimately to destroy Mariculture – a change in opinion of the kind whose nature and implications Antony was better equipped to understand than his business colleagues. The change was in attitudes towards the conservation of rare species, and the growth of a radical environmental movement in every Western country.

Until 1973, Antony and his fellow directors had assumed that conservationists would be on their side, and believed that they had done all they could to keep them informed of their progress and to retain their support. The company claimed as much in its literature. But in March 1972 they were provided with a token of changing attitudes of which they would have been advised to take greater account. Dr Archie Carr, the author of the *National Geographic* article which had first aroused the interest of Mark and Antony, argued in another article that, far from rendering poaching of turtles in the wild unprofitable, turtle farming could encourage it by creating additional demand. He raised the possibility of small non-profit pilot schemes that might lay the groundwork for a turtle-farm industry that 'would be able to spring into existence and from the beginning fill any new demand that it created'.

Carr's article concluded: 'For the time being, however, the only realistic course is a world-wide effort to discourage international traffic in sea turtle products of every kind. The demand can be built back quickly when the farms are prepared.'

Antony and his colleagues were puzzled by Carr's change of heart. Without his initial support the company might never have come into existence. They also had good reason to doubt his economics. According to an interview given by Naylor which bore all the hallmarks of Antony's influence, 'When demand rises, prices accelerate for a while, then drop drastically as they did in the chicken industry ... Today, in England salmon is cheaper than cod ... The availability of farmed turtle products would have made hunting and poaching of wild green turtles unprofitable, thus preserving the wild populations.'

Carr's article was followed by articles which were less measured and more hostile to Mariculture, some angry with claims that the company had increased the turtle population – which seemed probable, but could not be proved scientifically. Others claimed that the company's promotional literature had exaggerated the extent to which it enjoyed the support of conservationists. In a growing campaign against Mariculture it was evident that many were motivated by an innate hostility to the idea that an endangered species should be bred for profit.

Antony believed that Carr, by far the most influential and scholarly of their critics, might be won round. He therefore wrote to him setting out the arguments for allowing Mariculture the opportunity to prove its case. Copies of Antony's letter no longer exist, but Carr's reply showed little awareness of the company's progress, and was adamant that he would withhold his support:

> The salient point in our relationship to date is that I do not support Mariculture ... I see no reason why an individual whose main concern is with sea turtles and enhancing the chances of survival of the various wild species and sub-species should be expected to sing the praises of Mariculture, or to do anything other than deplore, and perhaps to stamp out, international traffic in sea turtle products.[10]

Written against a background of growing international concern about the fate of rare species, further letters from Antony and Irvin Naylor to Carr and other conservationists, some including impressive lists of contributions made by the company to conservation and scientific research, failed to stem the growing opposition to its operations.

Carr's critical article was followed by a still more hostile article by David Ehrenfeld, a student of Carr's, in the January/February 1974 issue of *American Scientist*, written after a discussion between himself and Antony before an audience in New York. Antony subsequently provided a powerful 12-page rebuttal which pointed to numerous errors and omissions in Ehrenfeld's case and in many ways appears to be better reasoned than the latter's expert testimony. Antony and Irvin Naylor also recruited distinguished scientists and more traditionally minded conservationists to support their case. To no avail; opinion had hardened against commercial organisations which sought to combine conservation with profit-making. The process by which public opinion and the views of legislators followed suit was, as Hayek warned in a different context, virtually unstoppable.

Attitudes towards conservation in Washington DC were already much influenced by the International Union for the Conservation of Nature (IUCN), a private organisation formed in 1948 to raise awareness of the need to protect natural resources. When Mariculture was launched in 1968, green turtles were not on its list of endangered or threatened species. But five years later, when representatives of eighty nations met in Washington to sign the Convention on International Trade in Endangered Species of Wild Fauna and Flora (CITES), the turtle was listed in an appendix of species that *could* be threatened if trade were not regulated. Antony and his fellow directors had no obvious reason to be concerned by this. If, as proposed, all trade in wild turtles was banned, Mariculture, which expected in time to produce all of its stock from eggs laid on the farm, would not be damaged.

Then, in December 1973, the Endangered Species Act was signed into US law replacing earlier and less stringent laws governing trade in rare species. Following the precedent established by CITES the green sea turtle was categorised as a threatened rather than an endangered species. This would have allowed Mariculture to continue its operations subject to regulations which the company's management regarded as fair and reasonable. As a result of mounting pressures from conservationists, however, the US Secretary of the Interior announced that the US Bureau of Sport, Fisheries and Wildlife – an agency of his department – was proposing to reclassify the turtle as 'endangered'. Such a step would have meant the banning of all imports of turtle products – thereby wiping out 40 per cent of Mariculture exports at a stroke, and threatening all exports if the legislation applied to products routed via the US to other countries. Attempts to reclassify the turtle in this way at first failed as a result of legal technicalities, but the threat of future reclassification hung over the company, preventing it from raising additional capital, distracting its directors from their task of running the business, and involving it in heavy legal costs.

Its problems would have been solved at a stroke if the US government had been prepared to regard the company's activities as farming: its operations would then have fallen outside the terms of the Act. The advice of the IUCN, however, was that its activities could not be classified as such because the company had not yet reproduced turtles from the hatched turtles – an impossibility given the creature's 30-year life span and the relatively short history of the company. Mark later recalled:

> Although we had made huge progress we had not yet completed the reproductive 'loop'. Despite intensive lobbying and support of distinguished scientists outside the scope of the legislation the conservationists would not accept that we were farmers. In effect they were condemning the company to failure and collapse. In the circumstances it was difficult to avoid the conclusion that they were jealous: the conservationists did not want businessmen to succeed in doing something that they could not hope to achieve themselves: the conservation of the green sea turtle. The fact that we hoped to make profits also seemed to enrage them.[11]

According to *Last Chance Lost?*: 'The directors were worn down. None had any more cash or credit to commit to Mariculture. They were weary of endless and fruitless fundraising attempts – disappointed, according to Naylor, "in some of our shareholders ... who could have put more resources into the company but chose not to".' The company went into receivership in August 1975. Later that month an advertisement placed by the receiver in the pages of the *Wall Street Journal* offered the company for sale for $2.5 million. The advertisement referred to the 'innovative technologies' developed by the company and the potentially 'lucrative' nature of the market for turtle products, but made no reference to the factors which had brought about its collapse.

Antony, who had already lost tens of thousands of dollars with the failure of Caribbean Dairies, felt obliged to meet bank guarantees amounting to a further $60,000, although in strict legal terms he could have left Naylor to pay this sum. His total losses amounted to more than $600,000. Like Mark and Naylor, he remained convinced that the company could have succeeded but for the change in the legislation threatened by the conservationists and the hike in oil prices. Although the company was always high risk, and mistakes were made, its subsequent history suggests that, but for these factors, it might have had a chance of success. Taken over by a German industrialist, Heinz Mittag, and renamed the Cayman Turtle Farm, the company's prospects seemed doomed the moment the US markets closed, despite the fact that by this stage the farm no longer required eggs taken from the wild. Subsequently taken over by the Cayman Islands government in 1988, the company made a small profit based on local consumption of its products and income from the tourists who visited the farm. Four years later at Kyoto, delegates to CITES agreed that despite their earlier misgivings commercial trade might after all be of benefit to rare species – provided that numerous criteria were met. They also promised to revisit the issue of turtle farming. Irvin Naylor, who had spent many months trying to change minds in Washington, said later:

> In my heart I then believed – and still do – that of the
> several companies which I started, Mariculture was by far
> the most important as it had a global perspective and
> growth potential which shadowed anything with which I
> had been involved. But no matter what we did we
> couldn't seem to win the conservationists' argument ...

one of our most bitter realisations was the fact that no
matter how successful our breeding programme, no matter
how many hatchlings we returned to the sea, no matter
how many yearling turtles we headcounted and returned
to their native beaches – those who were philosophically
opposed to the commercialisation of a purportedly
endangered species didn't want to have their thinking
clouded by the facts concerning our accomplishments –
accomplishments, which if allowed to progress, could have
guaranteed the survival of the green sea turtle.[12]

The collapse of Mariculture, the debts that Antony felt morally
obliged to meet as a consequence, combined with the losses
from the dairy herd, had wiped out virtually all of his cash re-
serves. As a 'gold bug' who understood the value of scarce metals
during an inflationary era, he had made successful gold investments during the same period, but had also lost more than
£250,000 as the result of investments in Flair Plastics, a
company based in Thetford, Norfolk, when it failed spectacu-
larly to live up to its name. Mark Fisher described the experience as 'a very expensive crash course in how not to run a
plastics company'. What had attracted Antony to the investment
was his belief that there was potential for using plastics in car
production. For whatever reason the orders did not materialise.
Instead the company attempted to meet what demand there
was, which was mainly for plastic inflatables such as lilos. Sadly,
a poor English summer depressed the demand even for these,
particularly ones that mostly refused to remain inflated, with the
result that the company incurred losses. Antony eventually with-
drew, having lost all of his original investment. In the long run
he was proved right – motor manufacturers were to rely increasingly on plastic, especially as door panels – but his investment and his choice of business associates, with whom he kept
faith long after it was prudent to do so, had been ill-judged, a
fact which Mike had been quick to recognise.

Now aged 60, Antony had little in the way of liquid assets.

He was depressed not only by this run of business failures, but by the thought that friends had suffered significant losses as the result of his actions. He had hoped that business success would enable him to pour funds into the creation of IEA-like bodies around the world, but if the Institute's success was to be exported he would need to find other ways of achieving his goal.

8

Exporting the revolution

Following the example of the Fabians, the first step in seizing
control of the political agenda had been an assault on the intellectual high ground. By 1975, substantial progress had been
achieved by the Harris and Seldon artillery in achieving their
objective, even if the practical men of affairs – the infantry, in
Seldon's formulation – were just beginning to grasp the nature
of the trench warfare that lay ahead. Antony, however, was less
sanguine than either Harris or Seldon about the outcome. In a
letter to a friend, he expressed doubts whether the change in intellectual opinion in Britain had come too late to effect a reversal. During the same year he told a journalist from the *Vancouver
Sun*: 'You might ask why I don't go and sit in a lovely house in
the south of France. But that to me would be sitting in a deck
chair on the *Titanic*.'

At a regional meeting of the Mont Pélerin Society at Hillsdale in September 1975, Antony gave one of a series of lectures
in memory of the Austrian economist Ludwig von Mises. It was
here that he met Dorian Crocker, whom he was later to marry.
But the doom-laden introduction to his remarks made an unlikely starting point for a romance:

> It is my purpose to provide convincing evidence ... that
> present world-wide developments are leading and will

lead to disasters of unimaginable proportions; that these
disasters will involve the death of countless millions from
starvation, disease, and human slaughter; that these
disasters, if they occur, will be the direct result of
unsound economic decisions and are therefore
inextricably inter-related.

Antony went on to offer a package of measures he considered
necessary to rescue the Western world 'from this extremely dangerous situation'. Despite the stark nature of his message Antony
seems to have made a favourable impression on Dorian, the rich
and attractive widow of George N. Crocker, a lawyer, political
scientist, author and columnist for the *San Francisco Examiner*.
Dorian had been expected to be escorted to the meeting by
Sam Husbands, a prominent San Francisco stockbroker and a
friend both of Antony and her late husband, but when Husbands had to withdraw, he asked Dorian, 'Please say hello to my
pal Tony Fisher.' The two talked at length, and exchanged ad-
dresses.

At this time Antony was at the nadir of his fortunes and at his
most gloomy about Britain's deepening economic malaise. In
such a mood he was inclined to doubt the wisdom of the IEA's
reluctance to become more directly embroiled in the current
debate about economic policy. A year later, on 4 August 1976, he
wrote to Ralph Harris:

> I find myself ever more bothered, bewildered and
> perhaps I could say frightened at the inability of the IEA
> to come up with economic solutions to the country's
> problems ... In the past I have been told that it would
> make the IEA 'political'.
>
> Since none of the political parties could possibly
> espouse the right policies as of now, one consequence
> might well be that 'general opinion' and even some of
> the 'converts' might once again brush the IEA aside for
> being too unrealistic ... at our last Trustees meeting this

issue was not raised. I was simply told by Arthur that any attempt at achieving definitive policies ... so splits up our academic writers as presumably to threaten the existence of the IEA.

Are we then down to the same 'consensus' problems as the political parties? If so, these are sad days indeed. We did not seem troubled about publishing Hayek and Friedman on money. This appears to have had its consequences. How about dealing with denationalisation on the same basis?

Despite such misgivings – which Harris was usually able to assuage – Antony was quite clear about one thing. The task now was to spread the IEA message further, and to accelerate the process as rapidly as possible. Here, too, in Antony's view, there was something to be learned from the Left. Instead of concentrating efforts through the activities of one or two organisations, the key to success lay in a proliferation of organisations and publications sharing a broadly common outlook and aims. In Antony's view there needed to be lots of IEAs, a growing international network of market-orientated individuals and organisations, and a much more extensive debate about the issues. Writing to an American banker to solicit funds, Antony wrote: 'I am only the catalyst. I look upon myself as the catalyst between the business world and the academic world, and am only too pleased to help such organisations. Proliferation is required because it is vitally necessary that common sense should be made available from as many directions as possible, particularly *not* just from one source in one place.' Evidently, neither advancing years nor declining personal fortunes had dimmed his missionary zeal. Over the next decade he was to urge his IEA colleagues to help him create similar bodies abroad, to contemplate the creation of specialist units within the Institute, and to consider establishing regional IEAs. With others, Antony even discussed the possibility of buying the *Spectator* as a vehicle for the cause of economic liberalism, and of creating a diverse range of autonomous institutions and publications that would supplement the work being done in Lord North Street. He also contemplated the possibility of setting up – 'in exile' – think tanks which would examine the problems of the Central and East European countries. In support of his proliferation strategy he declared: 'The echo is as important as the message.' In a letter to Ralph Harris in August 1975 he wrote that the need was for 'vehicles which would be able to follow the lead of the IEA without being the IEA'.

Given his frame of mind during this period, an offer to help build the newly established Fraser Institute in Vancouver proved difficult to resist. The offer came from Patrick Boyle, a Canadian industrialist who had been disturbed by the accelerating leftwards drift of both federal and provincial politics. At the national level, the Prime Minister Pierre Trudeau, reflecting the fashionable opinions of the day, had mused publicly about the imperfections of capitalism and wondered whether the market might not be extinct, so requiring a greatly expanded role for state welfare. At the provincial level, five members of the New Democratic Party government in British Columbia, including its leader, had signed a socialist manifesto. To those whose faith in the market order remained undimmed, the need to expose the collectivist tide of opinion to critical scrutiny seemed urgent and compelling. Boyle had enlisted a young economist, Dr Michael Walker, who had worked at the Bank of Canada and as an econometrician in the Federal Department of Finance, where firsthand experience had crystallised his growing doubts about the competence of big government. But Walker, though self-confident, obviously dynamic and forceful, was only 29, with no direct experience of fundraising or of how a think tank actually operated. On a visit to Europe, Boyle was told repeatedly of the increasing impact of the IEA, and subsequently invited Antony to serve as acting director.

Antony took up his new appointment on 23 May 1975 and although he was to remain little more than a year, the combination of a young and dynamic ex-civil servant and a mature, genteel, well-connected Englishman proved highly effective, even if the two did not always agree. In addition to spearheading the new institute's fundraising campaign, Antony also constructed a distinguished Editorial Advisory Board, and attracted speakers with an international reputation such as James Buchanan, Harry Johnson and Alan Walters. But according to Walker the most valuable service Antony performed was to provide a role model of how warriors in ideas should *behave*:

> He was the very model of a modest, reserved, self-effacing Christian gentleman. I was particularly impressed by his ability to remain calm, polite and unruffled when dealing with abrasive, impatient, opinionated young men – such as myself. Even in the most difficult of circumstance he was always kind and considerate. In particular, he treated most courteously those who did not share our views – which in those days was most of the population. In doing so he set an important example.[1]

Antony also impressed others with the courtesy with which he went about his task. Indeed, his Etonian background, RAF record and his gentlemanly demeanour appear to have proved greater assets in America than in Britain, especially when it came to addressing rich Canadians and Americans. According to the *Toronto Star* in January 1976, 'Antony Fisher is spreading a fundamentalist gospel of free markets – and doing it with the grace and charm that can only come from an English education.' Antony's arrival also meant that Fraser benefited from the experience of the IEA over two decades. 'We even cribbed a statement of what we did from an IEA publication,' said Michael Walker. 'Without the IEA's example it would have taken us much longer to achieve take-off. We, in turn, accelerated the development of other institutes.'

Antony took his fundraising task seriously. In private conversation, he seldom if ever made jokes or referred to his wartime experience, but realising their value in fundraising he did both when addressing audiences of potential supporters. A favourite story, designed to illustrate the disastrous consequence of government's good intentions, ran as follows:

> Two men were out for a ride on a motorcycle. Because it was a very windy and cold day they stopped and the driver suggested that his pillion rider should turn his overcoat round and wear it back to front to keep out the cold. The pillion rider did and they started off again. A few miles down the road the rider realised that his pillion rider had fallen off so he quickly turned round and rushed back down the road looking for his friend. Soon he found a group of people looking at the side of the road and two men bending over his friend who was lying prostate on his back. The motorcycle driver asked how his friend was, and one of the men said, 'Well, when we found him he was moving a bit, but since we tried to put his head back the right way round he seems to have stopped breathing.'

This anecdote was among a number of stories and exhibits which Antony kept in his wallet for use in speeches and to raise his spirits when despondent. His wallet also contained a typed version of Kipling's *If* – which comes close to expressing his own personal philosophy in dealing with the twin 'impostors' of Triumph and Disaster – and a quotation by Picasso confessing the bogus pretensions of modern art.

The Fraser Institute's first publication – *Rent Control: A Popular Paradox* – demonstrated Antony's strategy for a network of wholly independent institutes drawing strength from one another. Thus Walker republished this IEA study of the baneful effects of rent control in five countries (published in 1972 as *Verdict on Rent Control*), with the addition of a section on Canada which reinforced the same lessons of failure. Between October 1975 and April 1976 more than 6,000 copies were sold, making

Antony's mother, Janet Katherine
Mary Fisher *née* Anson, c.1914

Antony's father, George Kenneth
Thompson Fisher, as a captain in
the Norfolk Regiment during
World War I

Antony *(at left)* with his mother and younger brother Basil

Basil and Antony at
Eton College in 1931

RAF Central Gunnery School, December 1942. Antony is seated
at far left; 'Sailor' Malan is seated at centre

Antony *(at left)* with Tony Pendry, his partner in
Buxted Chicken and the company's managing director

Antony beside a broiler shed in Pump Lane, Framfield, Sussex in 1956,
part of the thriving Buxted Chicken Company

Aerial view of Newplace, Antony's home in Sussex from 1945 to 1978

Antony and his first
wife, Eve, in party
mood on a cruise in
the 1960s

Antony *(at right)* with his eldest son Mark in the Cayman Islands in 1972,
holding one of the turtles that were to prove so unprofitable

Left In Paris in October 1980, Antony *(at left)* with *(left to right)* Milton Friedman, Pascal Salin, Jean Pavlevski and Rose Friedman

Below A rare photograph, taken at the Institute of Economic Affairs in London in the early 1980s, of Antony *(at right)* with his mentor Friedrich Hayek and Arthur Seldon and Ralph Harris. *Left to right:* Harold Rose, Seldon, Harris, Hayek, John Wood and Antony

Antony and Margaret Thatcher at the Grosvenor House Hotel, London, celebrating the IEA's 30th anniversary on 7 April 1987

Antony celebrating his 70th birthday at a party held on a double-decker bus.
With Antony are *(from left)*: family friend Annie Stewart, granddaughter
Rachel Whetstone, daughter-in-law Rosie and eldest daughter Linda.
(The birthday cake was inscribed 'Must birthdays repeat themselves?', a
reference to Antony's 1974 book, *Must History Repeat Itself?*)

Antony on his last family holiday in Menton-St-Bernard at Lake Annecy in
France in August 1987. With Antony and his second wife Dorian *(at left, second
row from back)* are his four children, their husbands and wives,
and his grandchildren

Antony's widow Dorian being given the insignia of Sir Antony's knighthood by the British Consul General in San Francisco in September 1988. Antony died soon after the honour was announced and before he could be knighted

the institute's first publication a bestseller. Rent control was subsequently repealed in almost every part of Canada, and such controls as remained reflected the insights of the Fraser study. By the end of 1976 it had published eight books, three of which had similarly entered the bestseller list – a tribute to the drive and enthusiasm of Walker's colleagues John Raybould and Sally Pipes as well as to Walker's choice of authors and topics. By 1986, Antony was able to report to fellow members of the Mont Pélerin Society that the institute had sold 35,000 copies of its first publication in 44 countries.

Nevertheless, during the early years the institute's prospects remained uncertain. Walker was sometimes forced to forego his own salary in order to pay the secretaries. 'I recall driving Antony to the airport some time during 1976 at a time when it was not clear whether there were sufficient funds to continue. When I returned to the office I explained the situation to the staff and told them in their own interests they should take any opportunities that were open to them. The following day, as a result of an earlier approach from Antony, we received a cheque for $20,000 from Imperial Oil, the Canadian arm of Esso. So we lived to fight another day.'[2] Later, life at Fraser became hazardous in other ways. In 1983, when observers noticed similarities between the government of British Columbia's proposed economic reforms and advice tendered by Fraser, trade-union action erupted. Walker, described as the 'Robespierre of the Right' by the *Vancouver Sun*, was burned in effigy and received a sufficient number of death threats for police to mount a 24-hour surveillance of his home, while several bomb threats were received at the institute's offices.

Like the IEA, whose structures and methods it followed closely during its early life, the Fraser Institute has wisely kept clear of politics, refuses to take public funding and has maintained high editorial standards. But it gradually developed a distinctive approach and profile, partly as a result of Walker's television appearances and weekly newspaper columns, its measurement of a broad range of public-service performance, and a media archive intended to serve the interests of political balance.

With a staff of 50, it is now Canada's largest independent public-policy institute, with offices in Calgary, Toronto, Ottawa and Montreal, and has a better record of media exposure than any other public-policy organisation in Canada, including those supported by government. It has published more than 350 authors in 22 countries, and has sought innovative ways to promote its message, including the introduction of 'Tax Freedom Day' to bring home to the average taxpayer the portion of his working life devoted to supporting the government. Unlike the IEA and think tanks later established in the US, New Zealand and Australia, the teachings of the Fraser Institute have never been embraced comprehensively by a national government, but its influence has been pervasive and has spread beyond national boundaries.

By late 1976 Antony had helped broaden the base of Fraser's finances significantly, although many individual donations were modest and its future still uncertain. It was clear, however, that he had contributed all that he could to its success, and he therefore ceased to be a member of its permanent staff while remaining its international trustee until his death, doing whatever he could to promote its work.

Fraser received financial relief from an unexpected source in 1981 when a New Zealander called Bruce Hatherly, who had been working as a dishwasher, arrived at Fraser's offices seeking sponsorship for a board game called Poleconomy, a game that simulated the economic and political forces operating in a modern economy. Revenue accrued not only from the sale of the game but also from squares purchased by business advertisers. At a time when the Canadian economy was in recession and the institute's modest funding was actually shrinking, the decision to market the game with squares priced at $35,000 each turned out to have been inspired. Launched in Toronto, Vancouver and Montreal in September, in time for the Christmas buying season, sales reached 100,000 by the end of the year, producing income for Fraser of about $700,000. The institute's annual report for 1983 recorded: 'The Institute's proceeds from the sale of the squares provided a tremendous boost to the Institute's income and have for the first time given the Institute a cash buffer between revenue and expenses.' According to Walker: 'The game not only saved our bacon, but provided the first contribution to our endowment fund which was ultimately to provide a measure of lasting stability.'[3]

Poleconomy continued to bring in money for Fraser for a further two years. Learning of its success Antony introduced the game to Ralph Harris who, acting on behalf of the IEA, sold squares to British businessmen to the value of £100,000. Subsequent attempts to market the game in the US for the benefit of American think tanks were largely unsuccessful despite initial business interest.

Antony also had personal and professional matters on his mind that may have discouraged him from remaining longer at Fraser. In 1976, at the 29th anniversary meeting of the Mont Pélerin Society at St Andrews, held near Adam Smith's birthplace at Kirkaldy to mark the bicentenary of *The Wealth of Nations*, Antony renewed his relationship with Dorian Crocker. This was described as 'very cosy' by Antony's son-in-law Francis Whetstone. A few weeks later Antony visited Dorian in San Francisco and proposed. Dorian, although much taken with the idea, was initially uncertain, but in order to become better acquainted agreed to join him on a cruise down the west coast of South America. Dorian reported to Mike: 'Separate cabins, of course. We're conservatives!' During the voyage Antony repeated his proposal of marriage. 'I recall receiving a knock on my cabin door and finding Antony on one knee. He was so charming, so handsome ... any doubts I might have had disappeared. Anyone who thought him humourless or dull simply didn't know him.' Antony and Dorian were married at Pebble Beach Chapel, California, on 8 October 1977, with a reception following at a friend's home near Monterey, 120 miles south of San Francisco on the Pacific Coast. Afterwards, Antony moved into Dorian's apartment on Russian Hill in San Francisco, with its sweeping views of the bay. Their friends Milton and Rose Friedman were later to become neighbours and periodic dinner guests. (Friedman had won the Nobel Prize in 1976 and was in great demand by TV and film crews. Often he called Dorian and asked to borrow her huge lounge to conduct these interviews. She always agreed, and most such interviews from the late 1970s to the late 1980s took place in that apartment.)

Dorian was warm, rich, generous, attractive and vivacious, yet highly competent and with a strong character. To these formidable assets she added political views that Antony found highly congenial. She says: 'I had already learned a great deal about the market economics from my first husband, and so I didn't need to be converted. But after I married Antony I believed in them even more strongly! The whole purpose of Antony's life was to get others to believe in them too. I was extremely proud to help him in any way that I could.' Whereas Antony's sense of mission had been a source of tension and of intermittent conflict in his first marriage, it now ensured common interests, goals, friends. Dorian took copious notes of meetings which she then typed up herself, helped make travel arrangements, and organised dinner parties for Antony's associates and those who might provide financial support for any of the think tanks with which he was associated. In order that they did not live out of suitcases when Antony attended IEA board meetings, Dorian purchased a flat in Cadogan Square. Later, when it was necessary for Antony to attend meetings in New York, she bought a further apartment in Manhattan. Except on family occasions, entertaining was always related to work and arranged in considerable style. Russell Lewis, journalist and acting director of the IEA in 1992, recalls eating off gold plate when dining at the couple's London flat.

Although younger than Antony, Dorian made provision in her will that would have allowed Antony to carry on his work without financial worries in the event of her death. Fearing that Antony might be tempted to invest his legacy in an entrepreneurial activity that might not succeed, she stipulated that he was only to receive the income. 'Don't worry, the capital will be safe!' Dorian assured Antony's daughter Linda. Dorian also set out to establish good relations with Antony's family, organising and funding holidays with one or other of the Fisher children and their families – and on one occasion all of them – and conscientiously remaining in touch after Antony's death in 1988. While he was alive, Christmases were spent in Linda's Sussex manor house. 'Dorian enjoyed everything my father did and became an important part of it.You had only to be with them a short while to realise how pleased they were to be in one another's company,' Linda recalls.

The professional challenge which gave new purpose to Antony's life was a plan for a think tank which would explain the virtues of the free market to the mostly liberal (i.e. mildly socialist) NewYork City, the home of international capitalism.This was an idea Antony had discussed with Bill Casey, a NewYork lawyer with growing influence in the Republican Party and more widely in the American conservative movement.Again, the model was to be the Institute of Economic Affairs. Between them, Fisher and Casey – later to become Ronald Reagan's campaign manager and subsequently his Director of the CIA – identified potential donors, and were sufficiently confident of success to incorporate the new body under the name of International Center for Economic Policy Studies (ICEPS) in November 1977. According to Randy Richardson, a businessman and philanthropist, it was Antony who convinced Casey that such a body would be highly beneficial to New Yorkers. Antony's genteel demeanour combined with his missionary zeal distinguished him from others who were knocking on the doors of grant-making trusts at that time. According to Richardson, 'Antony was unlike most of the people who fund such institutions. He was not intensely interested in party politics, did not seem heavily influenced by liberal or conservative themes. And he had little interest in becoming involved in research. His seemingly sole interest was in convincing wealthy persons of the benefits of establishing units to study the operations of government. He was charming, and good at doing that.'[4]

As always, Antony believed that his most important task would be to find the right man to run the organisation. He was increasingly convinced that this would be Dr Edwin J. Feulner Jnr, who had established a reputation as a prodigious organiser and networker as the Executive Director of the Republican Study Group. He had met Feulner, who was now in his mid-thirties, when he had worked for £5 a day as an intern at the IEA while attending a course at the London School of Economics. Antony asked Feulner to go to see Casey at his office in the Pan Am building. 'Casey told me that he was fully supportive of Fisher's endeavours, he liked me, and he suggested that if I was interested the job was mine. I telephoned Fisher and told him of my conversation with Casey and he said, "Great, the job is yours." '[5]

Feulner located a suitable Washington branch office and with Fisher appointed director Harold Hochman from New York University as the institute's research director. But to Antony's dismay Feulner was to receive another offer – to become president of the recently created Heritage Foundation – that more accurately reflected his interests and personal circumstances.

> Quite suddenly, more funding was made available at Heritage. I had always had a clear idea about the kind of timely and focused policy papers that were needed to make an impact on the Hill, and now I was being given the opportunity to put my ideas into practice. By taking the position at Heritage instead of going to ICEPS, I was also spared the endurance test of having to commute from Washington to New York three days a week, a prospect which my wife didn't care for. Although Antony was dismayed, he was understanding, and we remained friends. I have another reason to be grateful: my days at the IEA as an intern impressed upon me the need for published work of accuracy and high intellectual standards.[6]

Feulner may have had yet another reason for being grateful to Antony. Without organisations such as the IEA which sought to influence the wider climate of opinion, the task of Heritage – whose primary goal was to provide the US legislature with up-to-date briefing from a conservative perspective – would have been more difficult.

A man of huge industry who might easily have become president of a major US corporation, Feulner went on to turn Heritage into the biggest and best-funded public-policy organisation in the world, with a budget of $30 million in 1999. The position at ICEPS then went to Jeff Bell, a former aide at the House of Representatives, who quit within weeks in order to run for the US Senate. Antony responded to these developments by taking up the reins of ICEPS himself as its executive director. While continuing to fundraise, however, he relinquished these to William Hammett, an abrasive libertarian who had previously run the Center for Libertarian Studies in New York. It was at Hammett's suggestion that the organisation later swapped its cumbersome title for that of the Manhattan Institute. Described by one colleague as possessing 'a whim of iron', Hammett displayed an instinctive grasp of the way in which intellectual debate on policy issues would develop, commissioned authors accordingly, and promoted their work aggressively and with flair. It was he who shaped the institute and is largely responsible for its pre-eminence, even if he frequently reduced his staff to tears and occasionally to rebellion.

Hammett's departures from the familiar IEA model caused Antony a certain amount of unease, while Hammett tended to regard Antony's suggestions, based on his London experience, as unwelcome interference. Disputes between them over whether or not the institute should follow the IEA in having an academic advisory council and whether its publications should carry an IEA-style disclaimer distancing it from the views of their authors took on an intensity which was not commensurate with their importance. Eventually, the two men fell out when Hammett reacted furiously to the discovery that Antony had approached a Manhattan donor on behalf of another think tank. For Antony the approach was simply part of his drive to spread the free-market gospel as broadly as possible in a world containing too few donors. But Hammett regarded Antony's behaviour as tantamount to treachery, and used the dispute effectively to bring his association with the institute to a close. Characteristically, Antony continued to praise the achievements of Hammett and the organisation which he had founded, but from which he was now excluded.

The institute's earliest preoccupation was with supply-side economics and its early reputation had much to do with George Gilder's powerful *Wealth and Poverty*, published in 1980, which celebrated the marvels of wealth creation and the moral dimension of the market, thereby challenging the economic pessimism of the day. During a series of forums held in 1980–81, Gilder, then a member of the institute's staff, described in cogent and accessible terms the role of incentives and other key aspects of supply-side economics. Following this success, Hammett offered $30,000 to a then-unknown and unemployed social scientist called Charles Murray, whose celebrated book, *Losing Ground*, sold 60,000 copies in five years and provided the basis of subsequent US welfare reforms.

In mission and operations, then, Manhattan did not follow the IEA model, but developed spontaneously on the basis of Hammett's instincts. Rather than waging an intellectual war against collectivism, Hammett took it for granted that the ideological battle had been won. The role of Manhattan was to show how its belief in economic choice and responsibility could be applied in a city such as New York, which, in the words of one of its publications, seemed 'stuck in a downward spiral of economic and social decline, ruled by a bloated government bereft of ideas'. The zero-tolerance approach to crime famously put into effect by Police Commissioner William Bratton and Mayor Giuliani owed its inspiration to an essay entitled 'Broken Windows', in the March 1982 issue of *The Atlantic Monthly*, by Harvard scholar James Q. Wilson and Manhattan senior fellow

EXPORTING THE REVOLUTION 149

George Kelling, whose subsequent book, *Fixing Broken Windows*, published by the Free Press in 1996, elaborated on its themes. The consequence was a series of police reforms that are credited with bringing about a two-thirds cut in the city's murder rate between 1993 and 2000, the reversal of the exodus of the population, and the transformation of New York City into the safest big city in America. Bemoaning the fact that similar reforms have not been put into effect in London, now experiencing the same problems as New York a decade ago, the *Daily Telegraph* declared in May 2000: 'The intellectual ammunition for that successful counter-revolution was supplied by the Manhattan Institute ... The disjunction between the priorities of the public and the new elite explains why we need a Manhattan Institute for Britain – and quickly.' Echoing words dear to Antony's heart, it concluded: 'Once the battle of ideas is won, politicians can be emboldened to speak "for the great silent majority".'

These reforms have not only been copied by most other US cities, but also by cities in Central and South America, where a new generation of politicians, avid readers of Manhattan's quarterly, *City Journal*, have shown themselves committed to dismantling the traditionally highly centralised power structures of their countries. In education this has meant growing interest in the institute's work on 'charter schools' – public schools that secede from local school districts to set their own curricula and standards – and the use of the IEA's long-favoured educational voucher. Manhattan also provides a rare example of a successful think tank that has been able to find a replacement to the man, or men, who brought it initial success, and to do so without controversy or decline. Thus, when after a long and acrimonious dispute with his board Hammett suddenly resigned in 1995 in order to go into business, the succession passed smoothly to Lawrence Mone, the institute's vice-president, who has since built on Manhattan's traditions and approach without any loss of vigour or sense of direction.

★

By the early 1980s, the proliferation of market-orientated think tanks which Antony so ardently sought was taking place in Britain as well as internationally. Harris and Seldon had expected competitors to appear much earlier, probably within a decade, but (although not a direct rival) the Centre for Policy Studies was not established until 20 years later. Likewise, the Adam Smith Institute was created in 1975 by Madsen Pirie, Eamonn Butler and his brother Stuart, all of whom had been at St Andrews University, where they had been active in university politics, before working in the United States on Ed Feulner's Republican Study Group and as professors at Hillsdale College, Michigan. The ASI did not achieve the influence of the IEA or enjoy the access to politicians of the CPS. However, in concentrating on the practical means by which market-based solutions might be introduced, it encouraged a rising generation of young Conservative politicians to think about specific political reforms. In monographs and books it set out how a policy might be introduced in practice. In doing so, it believed that it had identified a niche market in the world of ideas. Pirie saw the role of the IEA as that of the pure scientist, while the ASI was the 'policy engineer'.

In the final analysis, policy is shaped by politicians and those who directly advise them, and it is difficult to find an example of a Tory reform which directly followed from an ASI blueprint (although the institute once claimed paternity of the Poll Tax). Nevertheless, its creation added to a swelling chorus of free-market voices, and provided a valuable educational service to aspiring politicians who wished to ornament their CVs with details of ASI study groups or their authorship of ASI papers, for which Pirie's flare for publicity ensured wide media coverage.

From the ASI's early days Antony served conscientiously as a trustee. He was not in a position to contribute directly to its funds, or that of any other think tank at that time, but he and Dorian regularly hosted parties at their London flat to which potential donors were invited. Meetings of ASI trustees were arranged to coincide with those of the IEA so that Antony could attend both during a single visit. According to Eamonn Butler, 'Although he may not have realised it, Antony contributed greatly to our morale, especially during our early days. It was an enormous boost to have this distinguished, serious, well-connected English gentleman patting us on the back while telling his businessman friends that they really should listen to – and support – these brilliant young men at the Adam Smith Institute!'[7]

The ASI's field of specialisation increasingly lay in the mechanics of privatisation, and by the mid-1980s it had developed a considerable body of expertise on the means by which public assets could be returned to private ownership. It ran a successful annual privatisation conference which drew paying customers from businesses interested in acquiring the assets being sold off by the state, as well as civil servants from countries which were interested in emulating the Thatcher reforms. But the great benefit to flow from its work came with the collapse of communism in 1989. According to Richard Cockett:

> The ASI quickly extended its activities into the countries of the former 'Eastern bloc' advising the new Polish, Hungarian and Czech governments on the practical details of privatisation within a few months of the breaching of the Berlin Wall. The ASI's manual on privatisation was earnestly studied by a new generation of enthusiastic free-marketeers, born in previously Communist Eastern Europe, who now attempted to import Thatcherism – as purveyed by the ASI – to their own newly 'liberated' countries.[8]

Today, the ASI advises numerous governments, including those of India, Nepal and Guyana, on privatisation and related issues.

Meanwhile, the IEA gave its blessing to a Dr Digby Anderson, a young sociologist from Nottingham University who sought guidance about how to set up an independent unit to examine social issues. They also gave him useful advice, house room, and £10,000 as seed money. In explaining the sudden presence in their midst of this non-economist, Harris and Seldon were apt to say that his goal was to do for sociology what the institute was doing for economics. A more precise statement of Anderson's plans was that he intended to expose the prevailing liberal ortho-doxy on social theory and practice to critical scrutiny. The Social Affairs Unit, as it was to be called, opened for business at 2 Lord North Street in December 1980, subsequently moving to its own offices when it was prosperous enough to do so. In its early years it concentrated on critical evaluations of the welfare state, and, in particular, its tendency to produce vested interests which worked at variance with its purported aim. Early publications included *Breaking the Spell of the Welfare State* (1980), *The Pied Pipers of Education* (1981) and *Who Teaches the Teachers?* (1986).

Anderson, an ordained priest who also writes entertainingly about food and what its preparation reveals about changing values and mores, went on to examine the role of morals and manners in maintaining a free and orderly society, and the regulation of hazard and risk in commercial society. If the welfare state withstood his attack – just as it has resisted Arthur Seldon's devastating economic critique – the SAU can at least justifiably claim that its arguments have entered the mainstream of debate. Moreover, it can also show that its work on ethical and cultural issues has contributed to an understanding of why the welfare state – and the culture of sentimentality which sustains it – has remained intact; why the Thatcher administration shrank from reforming it; and why, having been told to 'think the unthinkable', Frank Field, Tony Blair's first Minister of State for Social Services, was sacked before any such thoughts could be clothed in deeds.

The influence of the SAU cannot be measured as easily as those bodies, such as the ASI, which were intended to have a direct impact on policy. But it has an undoubted impact on opinion, not least because of the *brio* with which Anderson has pricked and provoked liberal sensibilities and the huge amount of publicity its publications have attracted in relation to its modest size and budget. In a single year during the late nineties, for instance, the SAU received major coverage in more than 60 articles in every national quality paper, with a combined readership of 28 million, while radio and television programmes featuring the SAU's work reached still larger audiences.

In Anderson's judgement, the SAU's debt to Antony and the IEA is organisational, the Unit having based its fundraising and publishing techniques on those of the Institute. 'In this sense, it is a Fisher think tank,' he says. Moreover, whereas Arthur Seldon broke with the previous practice of economic research institutes by producing well-written and accessible monographs with arresting titles, Anderson has gone one step further by producing publications which are not only well written but which the general reader might actually wish to buy. One example was *Faking It: The Sentimentalisation of Modern Society,* which included a highly controversial chapter by the philosopher Antony O'Hear on the mob grief and hysteria following the death of Princess Diana. Among those who joined the massed attacks on O'Hear's startled head as the book rocketed into the bestseller list was Prime Minister Blair. To his surprise O'Hear found himself defended not only by John Humphrys of the *Today* programme but also by the *Guardian*: 'The pillorying of O'Hear is like the rage of Caliban having seen his own face in the glass; it suggests he has come dangerously close to the truth.' The Atlas Economic Research Foundation (created by Fisher in 1981) and the two Fisher Memorial Prizes won by the SAU have helped the Unit spread its message beyond British shores, especially to the USA, where some of its ideas have been developed by others.

The achievement of Anderson in his own writing as a journalist and in that of the best of his two hundred or more authors, has been to reveal the inherent defects and contradictions of contemporary liberal society. In the words of an editorial in *The Times*: 'The Social Affairs Unit is famous for driving its coach and horses through the liberal consensus scattering intellectual picket lines as it goes [and] for raising questions which strike most people as too dangerous or difficult to think about.'

In 1980, encouraged by the success of the Fraser and Manhattan institutes in America, and by the recent emergence of the Social Affairs Unit and the Adam Smith Institute in Britain, Antony began to think about how this relatively new phenomenon might be truly internationalised. Some of those he consulted expressed the view that the IEA model would not suit countries which, unlike Britain and America, lacked a tradition of political pluralism. In such societies, think tanks of the IEA variety would tend to fall under the control of a rich individual, family or political faction, or so he was advised. Undeterred, Antony conceived plans for an organisation which would assist in the creation of free-market think tanks world-wide and guide them through their infancy. Although now of pensionable age, he displayed remarkable vigour in creating the Atlas Economic Research Foundation, the name of which was suggested by a favourite classical quotation: 'Give me a lever and I will move the world.' The lever, he said, was the IEA and the fulcrum nothing less than market forces.

Antony found offices for the new organisation, incorporated it as a non-profit public-policy institute, established a board, raised start-up funds, and employed a part-time secretary and part-time fundraiser to assist him. Based in Montgomery Street, San Franciso, the Atlas mission was to discover, encourage, and support 'intellectual entrepreneurs' with the potential to create independent public-policy institutes, and to continue backing them during the early years as their programmes matured. In launching the new body, Antony quoted Lincoln: 'With public sentiment, nothing can fail; without it nothing can succeed. Consequently, he who moulds public opinion goes deeper than he who enacts statutes or pronounces decisions.' An appeal for funds concluded: 'If either the people or their representatives in government choose the wrong course, there will not be another opportunity. Democratic capitalism will have ended for decades, perhaps for generations.'

Among those Antony had consulted about the creation of Atlas was his mentor and friend Friedrich Hayek. In a letter which he allowed his friend to use for fundraising, Hayek wrote:

> I entirely agree with you that the time has come when it
> has become desirable and almost a duty to extend the
> network of institutes of the kind of the London Institute
> of Economic Affairs.
>
> The future of civilisation may really depend on
> whether we can catch the ear of a large enough part of
> the upcoming generation of intellectuals all over the
> world fast enough. And I am more convinced than ever
> that the *method* practised by the IEA is the only one
> which promises real results   I have sometimes despaired
> that this can be done at all. But the last thirty years of the
> Institute's work has made me more optimistic ... you
> have developed a technique by which more has been
> achieved in the right direction than in any other manner.
> It would be money well spent if large sums could be
> made available for such a concerted effort.[9]

Antony continued to report to Hayek on his progress, each
letter setting out details of think tanks planned or created, funds
raised, books published, and press coverage achieved, as well as
generous praise for the individuals responsible. Each prompted a
gracious reply from the Nobel Laureate offering congratulations
and further encouragement, a pattern which continued until
Antony's death eight years later.

Guidance to those interested in duplicating the IEA success
story included detailed advice about legal structures, fundraising, budgets, staffing, publications, finding and commissioning
authors, editing manuscripts, marketing, media relations, and
how to keep politicians at arm's length. In addition to a 35-page
document entitled 'Guidelines for Establishing a Public Policy
Research Institute' there were seminars, workshops and conferences for the staff of newly created institutes, and for those planning to start them. Antony's emphatic views about how these
institutes should be run – based entirely on the IEA model –

were firmly espoused. They should of course be completely independent of party politics and government funding; but in
order to preserve intellectual and editorial independence,
funding should come from a multiplicity of sources. Publications should be of a high intellectual standard while remaining
accessible to the intelligent layman, and their aim should be to
measure the relative costs of public and private provision of
goods and services.

Marriage to Dorian provided the means by which Antony
could advise and encourage in person the directors of the infant
think tanks that were springing up around the world. It also provided him with a proud and energetic assistant who shared his
missionary zeal. At the end of their working day, Dorian would
pour a whisky for herself and a Coke for Antony before reading
out items which she had clipped from newspapers and magazines for his interest.

Following the first Atlas seminar in Vancouver in September
1983, Dorian edited a 50-page manual on do's and don'ts for
public-policy institutes. It concluded with a quotation from *The
Diary of Beatrice Webb*: 'The ball has been set rolling down the hill
at a fair pace. It looks as if the bulk of the working men will be
collectivists before the end of the century. But reform will not
be brought about by shouting. What is needed is hard thinking.'
By 1983, as a result of hard thinking and some hard practical
lessons, the ball had been set rolling in the opposite direction,
and at a rapidly increasing pace. The first successes of the
Thatcher administration, combined with the growing reputation of the IEA, meant that Antony now received an increasing
stream of inquiries about the means by which the intellectual
tide had been turned. The buzz of excitement, first experienced
in London, as collectivist panaceas were criticised and then rejected in favour of individualism and free markets, was now
being sensed much more widely, for example in North and
South America, Australia and New Zealand. The last eight years
of Antony's life were consequently his happiest and most fulfilled. He believed that the think tanks he had created or helped

had demonstrated a proven means by which nations might escape from poverty through the adoption of limited government, free markets and the rule of law.

Some of those who contacted his San Francisco office had already made tentative steps to start think tanks and wanted to become part of a wider network of sympathetic organisations. Others wanted practical advice about how to do so, funds, or both. Some would have prospered without Antony, but membership of the Atlas network meant they could attract speakers with international reputations, which in turn enhanced their credibility and fundraising potential. And according to Linda Whetstone, who became director of the UK arm of Atlas in 1984, 'Each could learn from the others about those techniques which were likely to be most effective in raising funds or in marketing, but most importantly, organisations could pass the best research and policy ideas from one to the other, and so avoid the need to reinvent the wheel. The process and network began to achieve a momentum of its own.' When, for the last time, Antony spoke at a meeting of the Mont Pélerin Society at St Vincent in Italy in 1986, he was able to report that the Atlas network included 30 such bodies in 20 countries, with more starting up every year. Today, Atlas supports and works with around 150 market-orientated think tanks. It played a pivotal role in many of their start-ups, and provided funding or other support to most of them at some point in their development. To date, it has raised $22 million, more than 90 per cent of which has been devoted to grants and programme expenses.

Atlas has been particularly keen to assist institutes based in countries where the struggle for economic liberalism is at a relatively early stage of development, most notably in Latin America and the Eastern Bloc countries of Europe. In both regions the growth of such bodies has been remarkable. When the Berlin Wall came down in 1989 there was a significant number of economic liberals within the crumbling Soviet Union who had benefited from contact with free market institutes in the West. These joined an army of committed international economic liberals in the West who were waiting to move into eastern Europe and the disintegrating Soviet Union to convert their ailing economies to the virtues of capitalism. Virtually all of the Eastern and Central European countries have availed themselves of the help on offer from the Atlas Foundation since the collapse of the Wall.

The advice given in 1980 by Antony to Hernando de Soto, an evangelical Peruvian of free-market beliefs, was as consequential as it was opportune. It was offered at a moment in the history of Peru when there were real fears that the Marxist guerrillas of Shining Path might achieve their revolutionary goals. De Soto, whose writing had made him a prime target of the guerrillas, argued that it was not capitalism that accounted for the wretched poverty of so many of his fellow countrymen, but the fact that they were denied a full role in the capitalist process. By granting legal titles to the homes and land of the poor it would be possible for them to move from the black economy, where only subsistence livings were possible, to the mainstream economy. Such a transfer would enable the poor to use their assets more productively – as collateral to expand their businesses, for example. The assets of individual Peruvian farmers and traders might be meagre. Collectively, however, they amounted to many millions of dollars, and the consequences of bringing them into more productive use would be considerable. De Soto was confident of his analysis, but unsure about how to gain a hearing in the public arena.

Following a lecture given by Friedrich Hayek in Lima in 1979, de Soto asked the distinguished visitor for advice about how best to promote free market solutions; Hayek strongly advised him to speak to Antony Fisher, and gave de Soto Fisher's telephone number. Later de Soto and Fisher met in Washington and San Francisco, and again during Antony's visits to South America.

On the foundations of Antony's careful and painstaking advice, de Soto created the Instituto Libertad Democracia (ILD) in Lima in 1984.

'Antony gave us enormous amounts of information and advice on how to get organised,' he says. 'It was on the basis of his vision that we designed the structure of the ILD. He then came to Lima and told us how to structure the statutes, how to plan our goals, how to build the foundation, what to expect in the short and long term ... He was very generous with his time, his ideas and contacts. What I remember best of Antony, aside that he was a consummate gentleman, is that he had the uncanny ability to get to the heart of any issue. He was able to transmit in clear and precise terms how one should get organised in intellectual terms to deal with a problem ... I remember him with affection and gratitude.'

Later, the Atlas Foundation provided the ILD with a range of practical assistance, contacts and publications.

De Soto's offices were bombed and his car was machine-gunned by Marxist guerrillas, but he survived and his ideas were embraced after Alberto Fujimori was elected president in 1990 on a platform of economic efficiency and anti-terrorism. Fujimori appointed the controversial think-tank director his most senior economic adviser. De Soto's formalisation programme extended legal titles to 1.6 million of the country's 2.3 extra-legal buildings and brought 280,000 illegal small businesses into the mainstream economy.

De Soto subsequently broke with Fujimori over the latter's refusal to initiate democratic reform, and returned to run the ILD. At first the organisation possessed a broad economic agenda. But it now focuses exclusively on programmes to create the legal underpinnings of market economies in Third World and former communist countries.

Since 1994 de Soto and the ILD have given advice to more than a dozen heads of state from Asia, the Middle East and Latin America. De Soto is sustained in his work by his original insight into the cause of poverty in his own country: 'The poor live outside the law because corrupt legal systems and warped rules force them to. It's this "legal apartheid" that explains why some peoples thrive and others don't.'

In some cases, the support of Antony and Atlas was marginal to the success of the recipient, in others crucial. Among those in the West which owe their existence to Atlas is the Dallas-based National Center for Policy Analysis (NCPA), which has exerted a considerable influence on the conservative tax and welfare agenda since the early 1990s. The Center was established after Antony heard its president, John Goodman, then economics professor at the University of Dallas, speak at a conference on nationalised health care at Stanford in 1980.

> Afterwards Antony approached me, and said that the most effective means of promoting my views on the subject would be to set up an independent public policy institute. He offered practical advice about how this might be done. He convinced me that I should become what he described as an 'intellectual entrepreneur'. I am absolutely convinced that I would not have founded the Center if we had not met. Through Atlas, Antony provided $25,000 in start-up funding, as well as further funding through the early years, introductions to potential donors, and good advice.[10]

The Center achieved national prominence when a package of 'pro-growth' tax cuts designed by the Center and the US Chamber of Commerce formed the core of Newt Gingrich's 'Contract with America' in 1994. It did so again when its proposals for investing social-security funds in the US stock market – first explained to George W. Bush by Goodman when he was managing partner of the Texas Rangers baseball team – were taken up by the Republican candidate during the US presidential campaign. In order to achieve wider understanding of the proposals, the Center has funded the development of a computer model by economists at Texas A&M University which allows visitors to compare the expected return on their social-security tax dollars with what they would have obtained on the stock market.

Goodman attributes the Center's ability to provide a stream of innovative ideas about tax and welfare reform to an early decision not to allow its programme and priorities to be distracted by the shifting vagaries of Washington opinion. 'Like the IEA, we didn't wish to be restrained by current views about what was judged politically possible.' Accordingly, it decided against opening an office in the US capital, a decision which was reversed only when the organisation was judged sufficiently mature not to be damaged by establishing a small permanent staff there. 'We also decided to stay out of the mainstream economic debates, which were being dealt with by others, and to concentrate on the far more difficult issues of health and welfare.'[11] Among other successes, the Center is widely credited with playing a major intellectual role in defeating the health-care proposals of Hillary Clinton. Goodman, who has opposed state health-care schemes the more he has understood Britain's National Health Service, has pioneered the idea of 'medical savings accounts' as a means of maximising competition and choice within health-care provision.

Without mentioning Atlas by name, Antony referred to the work of a 'family of 40 institutes in 20 countries' when he attended a dinner to celebrate the 30th anniversary of the IEA at Grosvenor House in April 1987. Antony, who was accompanied by Dorian and Mike, told those present, including the Prime Minister, Mrs Margaret Thatcher: 'The example of the IEA has surely demonstrated that this type of independent educational activity is as vital to the well being of the community as the great teaching establishments, libraries, museums, galleries, and other charitably-financed activities.'

For Antony and his family the evening was a proud and joyous occasion. Tributes to the Institute poured in from distinguished academic and public figures, confirming beyond any conceivable doubt that the age of unlimited government was drawing to a close, and that the central role of markets was finally being acknowledged. Lord Cromer, a former governor of the Bank of England, declared: 'I cannot fail to look back over 30 years with wonder and respect at what the IEA's inspiration and effort have achieved. What a bleak world it would have been had the institute not come into being and been so ably piloted.' Lord Blake, the Oxford historian, said, 'No single body has contributed more than the IEA to the long overdue destruction of *étatisme* and to the recovery of Britain.' Mrs Thatcher was equally fulsome in her praise. Paying tribute to Antony and to the Institute's founding directors, she declared: 'They were the few. They were right. And they saved Britain.' Referring to the record of her government, she added: 'What we have achieved could never have been done without the leadership of the IEA.' Despite the sincerity of her tribute the Prime Minister was in fact irritated by having had to sit through ten other speeches, and consequently having to speak so late in the evening. She therefore concluded with a final, unscripted flourish: 'Speaking as the eleventh speaker and the only woman, I hope you will recall that it may be the cock that crows, but it is the hen who lays the egg!'

The remaining period of Antony's life was spent, as had been most of his days following the collapse of Mariculture and his effective retirement as a businessman, in supporting the think tanks whose promotion had become his life's work. But fading health increasingly sapped his strength, forcing him to cut down on his commitments and travel. In the spring of 1987, with the help of the British-born head of the Institute for Humane Studies, John Blundell, Antony, now in his 72nd year, began the search for someone to replace him as president of the Atlas Economic Research Foundation. Blundell suggested a retired businessman, who had strong free-enterprise views, might be suitable, but on learning that the man spent several days a week on the golf course, Antony typically ruled him out of contention. Later he realised that Blundell, a highly effective manager and fundraiser, met the criteria more exactly than any of the other contenders. Blundell moved the organisation from

San Franciso to Fairfax, Virginia, after Antony's death, and under him Atlas continued to expand rapidly and to greatly increase its income. When he was appointed general director of the Institute of Economic Affairs in 1993, the position was taken by Alejandro Chafuen, an Argentine professor of economics who had previously worked with Antony at Atlas and who had already played a remarkable role in helping to foster the growth of classical liberal ideas in Latin America. Chafuen's appreciation of the cultural and ethical – as well as the economic – foundations of free societies made him the ideal choice.

By the spring of 1988 it was clear to the family that Antony's illnesses were terminal, even though he continued to work whenever able. In a letter to his elder daughter dated 24 April, he wrote:

> As you will know from Dorian's letters the doctors, with their modern diagnostic equipment, have written me off on two counts – a weak heart and bone cancer. Our general doctor, Morris Noble, is a wonderful man and I like both the other specialists. However, they offer no hope of a cure, just the best they can do in whatever time remains. Several of their pills have side effects, some of them quite unpleasant.
>
> I do have an alternative. I can give Christian Science a chance. This I have virtually never done with my health. I seem to have been off to the doctors at the first sign of trouble. It is and always has been difficult to *prove* any cure ...
>
> This being the case, I, with Dorian's full approval and telling none but you and the doctors, would like to give CS a chance.

His letter concluded: 'Times might be difficult, but I am convinced that a complete cure is possible if I have the confidence and understanding.'

Six weeks later, on 11 June, following strong representations by friends and admirers, Antony was knighted for 'public and political services' in the Queen's Birthday Honours list. Telephoning to congratulate his friend, Harris joked that the citation should have been for 'private and anti-political services'. Harris reported: 'Antony chuckled in agreement, but said he would keep the knighthood anyway!'

The award lifted Antony's spirits. Three days later he was back at his desk dealing with correspondence. In his last letter to Harris he wrote:

> I am delighted to be getting better and just hope it speeds up. I cannot let this moment pass without expressing my profound gratitude to you for the many ways in which you have brought about my knighthood. My own part is so much like planting a mustard seed, or perhaps even an acorn. It was you and Arthur and now a growing team … who have done all the work – without which my little effort would never have been noticed.
>
> But we all have to realise that 'neither is he that planteth anything neither he that watereth; but God giveth the increase' (First Corinthians: Chapter 3, verse 7). I think it was my Linda who referred to the knighthood as a 'crowning glory'. I like to think of it more as a good starting point for a major effort that will prove, conclusively, that there is a method by which the world can be saved from its perpetual economic tribulations.

Despite his faith in the possibility of a recovery, Antony steadily weakened throughout the remainder of the month. On 8 July, exhausted by looking after him, Dorian finally allowed him to be admitted to St Francis Memorial Hospital, where he died from a chronic heart condition the following day. Ten days later, in accordance with his wishes, members of his family scattered his ashes from the yacht *Naiad* as it sailed into the Pacific, while a Christian Science practitioner knelt in prayer.

On 28 September in a moving and eloquent speech at a thanksgiving service held at St Lawrence Jewry in the City, Lord Harris paid tribute to his friend's unique combination of qualities:

> As an Old Etonian, he had substance, style, self-confidence. But there was no conceit, no sense of superiority, nor the least remoteness from ordinary people. Antony was the most uncomplicated, honest, and upright man I have ever known. But perhaps his most endearing quality was modesty ... It owed everything to his private devotion to Christian Science, his awe for God's creation, and his simple instinctive belief in freedom for people to work out their own destiny ...
>
> Antony was a non-conformist. He was touched by the goad of divine discontent. If things were out of order, he could not turn his back, but must do whatever he could to set them right.

By the standards of his early and middle years, Antony was a poor man at the time of his death. His total estate amounted to around £20,000 which was apportioned between his two daughters, the Church of Christ Scientist, and the Institute of Economic Affairs. His greatest legacy, however, was a rapidly growing world-wide network of organisations which were increasingly to help shape the political agenda of an expanding portion of the world during the decades to come.

9

Antony's legacy

As a member of Margaret Thatcher's Shadow Cabinet in 1975, Keith Joseph hesitated to use the phrase 'market economy' for fear of the reaction. He briefly entertained the idea of referring to 'a social market economy' until being persuaded that the word 'social' was a weasel word that drained the subsequent words of meaning; instead, he tried for a time to do without labels. It is a measure of how much opinion has changed that during the campaign for the Labour leadership in 1994, Tony Blair waxed enthusiastically about 'a dynamic market economy'. Indeed, today, except in conditions of protracted warfare, it is difficult even to imagine, either in Britain or more generally, a reversal of the process by which state ownership and centralised economic planning have given way to market forces. Even the present economic down-turn seems most unlikely to halt or reverse it.

From the outset of this continuing transformation, the Institute of Economic Affairs has played a pre-eminent role in contemporary British economic and political history. The scale of its achievement has been deservedly acknowledged by Richard Cockett:

> By the mid-1970s ... the IEA had, over the course of twenty years, developed a coherent set of free-market

ideas, applicable to all areas of the economy. They had
articulated a coherent set of principles, the principles of
economic liberalism, applicable to a modern economy,
thus fulfilling Hayek's 1947 hope that the economic
liberals would refine and develop liberalism into a
modern vibrant philosophy ... Suffice it to say ... that
the IEA's greatest achievement was to develop and
publicise – 250,000 Hobart Papers had been sold in
several countries by 1970 – a modern programme of
economic liberalism, unrivalled in its intellectual
eminence by any other comparable institute in the
world.[1]

Although often dismissed as politically 'naive', those who ran
the IEA during its formative years were shrewder than their
critics. Seldon in particular had no doubt about the results of
success in the battle of ideas. In a letter to *The Times* in August
1980 – before any of the Thatcher reforms were complete, and
at a time when the Cold War was still being contested – he
boldly expressed absolute confidence that the result would be
the triumph of capitalism over socialism: 'China will go capitalist. Soviet Russia will not survive the century. Labour as we
know it will never rule again. Socialism is an irrelevance.'[2]
Where Seldon and Harris were guided primarily by intellect
and analysis, Antony was guided by instinct and moral precept.
As Lord Harris said in his final tribute to his friend: 'In setting
up the IEA, Antony was guided by the simple – sophisticates
might say naive – moral precept that right would eventually
triumph over misguided might.'

It is, of course, very likely that a renaissance of economic
liberal thought would have occurred even if Hayek had not put
the idea of the IEA into Antony's head in 1946, although it
might not have begun in Britain. It is also possible that Mrs
Thatcher might still have become Tory leader in 1975 and Prime
Minister in 1979. But it is worth remembering that the sense of
purpose which so impressed many of her parliamentary col-

leagues (and appalled others) derived from her commitment to a coherent set of economic principles. So, too, to a large extent, did her self-confidence. That commitment owed much to the pioneering work of the IEA over the previous quarter of a century. Without a strong attachment to those principles she might not have become leader. And even if she had become leader, the Tory reforms of the 1980s might not have been carried through. Antony's role as catalyst in the process of change was a pivotal one. The linkages were cleverly traced by Oliver Letwin in *The Times* in May 1994, in the words already quoted in the Introduction: 'Without Fisher, no IEA; without the IEA and its clones, no Thatcher and quite possibly no Reagan; without Reagan, no Star Wars; without Star Wars, no economic collapse of the Soviet Union. Quite a chain of consequences for a chicken farmer.'

Socialists customarily argue that history is moved by large impersonal forces in which the individual counts for little, even if the comrades are surprisingly quick to detect the influence of 'right-wing' conspirators when their aims are frustrated or their heroes toppled. It was a view which Antony found repugnant. Moreover, his personal qualities and those of the individuals he recruited were crucial to the success of their endeavours. His strategy of facilitating the activities of others rather than trying to direct affairs himself means that any attempt to describe his achievements must shift the focus of attention away from Antony himself. Self-effacing and reserved, Antony remains in the shadows while the spotlight moves centre stage to those he recruited, funded or simply encouraged. But his qualities of humility and modesty, combined with his remarkable persistence and loyalty, contributed to the stability and harmony of the institutes with which he was associated. Such qualities inspired trust in those he appealed to for money, and not unimportantly they contributed to the avoidance of damaging clashes of ego and ambition. Antony's practice of treating ideological opponents with courtesy and respect also seems to have rubbed off on those less naturally polite than himself.

With some exceptions – most notably Ralph Harris, John Blundell and Alejandro Chafuen – Antony was not always well or generously treated by those who ran the think tanks that he started or helped. Although he seems hardly ever to have complained about this, he was too sensitive a man not to have been hurt by their behaviour. Yet there are several instances of his continuing to praise – and support – individuals whom he knew to be actively engaged in diminishing his role in their success. His forbearance in this regard was a reflection of his character and of deeply held religious beliefs. Similarly, the courage and obvious incorruptibility of Harris and Seldon were important factors in building the IEA's reputation and in winning the grudging respect of opponents, thus making it easier for them to admit the possibility of error, if they so chose.

Coincidence also played a major role in the story. If Antony had *not* read the April 1945 issue of the *Reader's Digest*, if he had *not* chanced to meet Ralph Harris three years later, if Buxted Chickens had *not* prospered, and if the somewhat reclusive Lord Grantchester had *not* recommended a young economist called Arthur Seldon to write the IEA's first paper on pensions, then Britain's post-war economic and political history would have been different. On the occasion of the Institute's 25th anniversary, John Wood reflected in a similar vein. He concluded his somewhat whimsical observations about the role of coincidence in the Institute's history by asking: 'Is it too much to discern here, not for the last time in the Institute's history, the faint silhouette of an invisible hand?'[3]

Not all of the institutes which Antony founded or encouraged were a success; some never got off the ground, some collapsed for lack of money, some were led by prima donnas who lacked the requisite skills or style. At the time of Antony's death, the Atlas network comprised around 35 bodies operating at either local, state, national or international level in the disciplines of economics, law, social and political theory, urban studies, environmental studies and education. This number has multiplied since then and continues to grow. In that it provides a degree of institutional coherence and communication, Richard Cockett has compared the role of Atlas to that of the Comintern, except that, as he pointed out, economic liberals would never accept state funding. The comparison is also unfair in another respect: Atlas does not seek to impose conformity or control; nor would the institutes accept such subordination.

The cumulative impact of the Atlas institutes is impossible to assess, and difficult to keep up with. However, the practical consequences of their programmes can be seen not only in successful reforms undertaken in Britain, Canada and the US, but also in Italy, Spain, Central and Eastern Europe (where the influence of IEA-type institutes is admittedly difficult to separate from other influences), India, Argentina, Brazil, Chile, Mexico, Australia, New Zealand and parts of Africa. Combined with the revolution in information technology and the retreat of state controls, the wider acceptance of market economics has created the possibility of the first truly global economy, integrated and interconnected, in which work and output are networked around the world. This process of globalisation arouses considerable apprehension, but it also offers the prospect of rising standards of living, expanding human liberty and a diminishing risk of war as growing international trade encourages interdependence.

Antony would have enthusiastically welcomed these developments and focused his energies on identifying obstacles and proposing remedies. He would have rejoiced that think tanks in remote places, inspired either by the success of the IEA, Manhattan or Fraser, and some supported by Atlas, are doing just this, some with distinction. But he would have been perturbed that new developments threaten to restrict economic freedom – most notably hyper-regulation (much of it coming from Brussels) and radical environmentalism. He would also be dismayed that despite his heroic attempts to undermine the welfare state, its fractured and decaying edifice remains intact, and that consequently, in Britain and elsewhere, the proportion of national wealth consumed by the state shows no early sign of declining. There would nevertheless be encouragement for think tanks who have explored the (non-economic) factors that account for the longevity of the welfare state, and plaudits for those who have found innovative ways to advance the argument for private provision of health care, education and welfare.

There is little doubt about what Antony's response would have been to familiar and unfamiliar problems. Having found the fulcrum that he believed would enable him, with others, to change the world – the independent, non-party-political think tank – he would have wanted more of them.

Judged by the usual standards, Antony was not perhaps a great man (an over-used epithet anyway which seems to be reserved largely for scholars, soldiers and statesmen), but then he was not a conventional man, and so does not match conventional criteria. Those who knew him well are unlikely to quarrel with the judgement that he was an unusually good, even fine, man. In following a unique vocation to identify the way to prosperity and freedom, he helped reshape the political agenda of our world.

Notes

1   A defining moment

1 Richard Hough and Denis Richards, *Battle of Britain: The Jubilee History* (Hodder and Stoughton, 1989), p.177
2 ibid. p.178
3 ibid. p.180
4 Antony Fisher, *Must History Repeat Itself?* (Churchill Press, 1974), p.xv
5 Linda Whetstone, "Sir Antony Fisher", *Tanker Talk*, 1989
6 *Dictionary of National Biography*, vol 1. (O.U.P. 1921 edn)
7 *Letters from G.K.T.F.* (published by his widow, undated)
8 ibid.
9 ibid.
10 ibid.
11 ibid.
12 ibid.
13 Tim Card, *Eton Renewed* (John Murray, 1994), p.46
14 Interview with Russell Lewis, 1988
15 Bernard Fergusson, *Eton Portrait* (John Miles, 1937), p.33

2   Marriage and war

1 Richard Hough and Denis Richards, *Battle of Britain: The Jubilee History* (Hodder and Stoughton, 1989), p.156
2 *The Times,* 20 August 1940
3 Antony Fisher, *Notes on Instruction and Maintenance of the*

Fisher Front Gun Trainer (original typescript, 1940)

4 ibid.

5 ibid.

6 Interview with the author, May 2001

7 ibid.

8 *Tanker Talk,* 1989

3   Freedom and the land

1 Richard Cockett, *Thinking the Unthinkable* (HarperCollins, 1994), p.69

2 i.e., those of R. A. Butler and Hugh Gaitskell

3 Antony Fisher, *Must History Repeat Itself?* (Churchill Press, 1974)

4 Interview with Russell Lewis, 1999

5 Antony Fisher, *The Case for Freedom* (Runnymede Press, 1947)

6 Interview with Russell Lewis

7 Quoted in John Blundell, 'How to Move a Nation', *Reason* magazine, February 1987, reprinted in John Blundell, *Waging the War of Ideas* (IEA, 2001)

4   A chicken in every pot

For coverage of some of the material in Chapter 4, see also John Blundell, *Waging the War of Ideas*, (IEA, 2001).

1 Interviewed by Russell Lewis, 1999; and by the author, February 2001

2 Interviewed by the author, September 2000

3 ibid.

4 Interviewed by Russell Lewis, 1999

5 Interviewed by the author, 1967

6 Linda Whetstone, 'A Free Market for Eggs', *Essays in the Theory of Pricing*, (IEA, 1967)

5   Making the case for the market

For coverage of some of the material in Chapter 5, see also John Blundell, *Waging the War of Ideas*, (IEA, 2001).

1 From 'The Intellectuals and Socialism', reprinted in *Studies in Philosophy, Politics and Economics* (Routledge Kegan Paul, 1967), p.182

2 Richard Cockett, *Thinking the Unthinkable* (Harper Collins, 1994), p.130

3 John B. Wood, 'How it All Began', *The Emerging Consensus* (IEA, 1981), p.249

4 *Newsweek*, 25 July 1955

5 Quoted in John Blundell, 'How to Move a Nation', *Reason* magazine, February 1987, reprinted in John Blundell, *Waging the War of Ideas* (IEA, 2001)

6 Ralph Harris and Arthur Seldon, *A Conversation with Harris and Seldon* (IEA, 2001), p.35

7 *Spectator*, 4 May 1985

8 Blundell, 'How to Move a Nation'

9 Arthur Seldon, *Capitalism* (Blackwell, 1990), p.26

10 Interview with Russell Lewis, February 1999

11 Arthur Seldon, 'The Essence of the IEA', *The Emerging Consensus?*, p.xviii

12 *A Conversation with Harris and Seldon*, p.40

13 Blundell, 'How to Move a Nation'

14 *A Conversation with Harris and Seldon*, p.70

15 Interview with Lewis

16 Speech given on the occasion of the IEA's 30th anniversary, April 1987

17 Fisher, *Must History Repeat Itself?*, p.110

18 ibid.

19 Quoted in Harris and Seldon, *Not from benevolence...* (IEA, 1977), p.29

20 Speech to Labour Party Conference, October 1976

21 Peter Jay's paper, *Employent, Inflation and Politics*, was published by the IEA in January 1976

22 Suda Shenoy, *A Tiger by the Tail* (IEA, 1972), p.119

23 *Sunday Express,* 10 March 1974

6 Educating Margaret

1 Ralph Harris and Arthur Seldon, *A Conversation with Harris and Seldon* (IEA, 2001), p.77

2 ibid., pp.78–9

3 ibid., p.80

4 Richard Cockett, *Thinking the Unthinkable* (Harper Collins, 1994), p.188

5 *A Conversation with Harris and Seldon,* p.67

6 Quoted in 'How to Move a Nation' by John Blundell, *Reason* magazine, February 1987, reprinted in John Blundell, *Waging the War of Ideas* (IEA, 2001)

7 Shirley Robin Letwin, *Anatomy of Thatcherism* (Fontana, 1992), p.80

8 Marjorie Seldon (ed.), *Letters on a Birthday: The Unfinished Agenda of Arthur Seldon* (printed for private circulation, 1996)

9 Morris Halcrow, *Keith Joseph – A Single Mind* (Macmillan, 1989), p.37

10 *A Conversation with Harris and Seldon,* p.50

11 *Thinking the Unthinkable,* p.197

12 ibid., p.205

13 ibid., p.207

14 See Andrew Denham and Mark Garnett, *Keith Joseph* (Acumen, 2001), Ch.10

15 *Thinking the Unthinkable,* p.38

16 Margaret Thatcher, *Margaret Thatcher: The Path to Power* (HarperCollins, 1995), p.250

17 *A Conversation with Harris and Seldon,* p.53

18 *Thinking the Unthinkable,* p.176

19 *A Conversation with Harris and Seldon,* p.56

20 John Ranalagh, *Thatcher's People* (HarperCollins, 1991), p.ix

21 *Margaret Thatcher: The Path to Power,* p.53

22 Daniel Yergin and Joseph Stanislaw, *The Commanding Heights* (Simon and Schuster, 2000), p.123
23 ibid., p.124
24 Interview with Russell Lewis, February 1999

7   A dream that failed

1 Interview with the author in March 2001, based on earlier comments to Russell Lewis
2 ibid.
3 ibid.
4 ibid.
5 ibid.
6 Peggy and Sam Fosdick, *Last Chance Lost?* (Irwin Naylor, 1994), p.98
7 ibid., p.166
8 ibid., p.113
9 ibid., p.119
10 ibid., p.41
11 Interview with the author in March 2001, based on earlier comments to Russell Lewis
12 *Last Chance Lost?*, p.186

8   Exporting the revolution

1 Interview with the author, May 2001
2 ibid.
3 ibid.
4 Letter to the author, December 2000
5 Interview with the author, September 2000
6 ibid.
7 Interview with the author, August 2000
8 Richard Cockett, *Thinking the Unthinkable* (HarperCollins, 1994), p.306

9 Letter from Friedrich Hayek to Antony Fisher, 1 January 1980
10 Interview with the author, March 2001
11 ibid.

9   Antony's legacy

1 Richard Cockett, *Thinking the Unthinkable* (HarperCollins, 1994), p.157
2 *The Times*, 6 August 1980
3 John B. Wood, 'How It All Began', *The Emerging Consensus?* (IEA, 1981), pp.248–9

Appendix

Free-market think tanks around the world
compiled by Linda Whetstone

This appendix contains details of organisations in whose start-up or development Antony Fisher played either a direct role or an indirect one via Atlas. The basic information provided in each entry has been supplied by the institutes themselves: further details can be found on the relevant websites.

Atlas is associated with many more organisations than are included here and their names and contact details can be found on the Atlas website, www.atlas.atlasUSA.org.

The Acton Institute for the Study of Religion and Liberty
161 Ottawa Avenue NW
Suite 301
Grand Rapids, MI 49548
USA
Tel: +1 616 454 3080
Fax: +1 616 454 9454
Email: info@acton.org
Web: www.acton.org
President: Rev. Robert A. Sirico
The Acton Institute was founded in 1990 with Atlas playing a

key role in its early stages of development and growth through essential leadership and support.

It exists to promote understanding of sound economic and moral principles and their role in promoting a free and virtuous society. The institute maintains programmes designed for a variety of specific audiences, including future religious leaders, scholars, clergy, business people and civic leaders, as well as broad-based outreach activities, including regular publications and community events. Each of our programmes, both domestic and international, is designed with one purpose in mind – to demonstrate the role of morality as a sustainer of freedom and an educator of individual responsibility.

Adam Smith Institute

23 Great Smith Street
London SW1P 3BL
UK
Tel: +44 (0)20 7222 4995
Fax: +44 (0)20 7222 7544
Email: info@adamsmith.org.uk
Web: www.adamsmith.org.uk
President: Dr Madsen Pirie
Director: Dr Eamonn Butler
The Adam Smith Institute was founded in 1977. Antony Fisher took a close interest in our work and encouraged us to set up sound structures. He joined the board in the early 80s and was an enthusiastic, optimistic and creative member, always urging us to strive to achieve more ... and it worked! Atlas has been hugely helpful as a source of assistance, ideas and contacts with like-minded groups.

The Adam Smith Institute thinks of itself as a 'do tank', rather than a think tank. Its key strength is in designing practical policy initiatives that are both politically and commercially deliverable. It has been at the leading edge of policy innovation for more than two decades; an intellectual pioneer of policies such as privatisation, contracting-out government services and internal markets. Building on this expertise, the institute now advises governments around the world on public-service reform.

The institute makes a strong intellectual case that a lower tax burden leads to a more dynamic economy. Its scholars have argued that regulation of economic life is a legacy of the desire to control and confine, and that less regulation not only lowers costs, but opens opportunities for the development of innovative ideas.

The Albanian Centre for Economic Research (ACER)
1 Qemali Street
Bldg No. 34/1, 5th Floor, Apt 4
P.O. Box 2934
Tirana
Albania
Tel/Fax: +3554 229 069/225 021/259 637
Email: zpreci@interalb.net
Web: www.acer.org.al

ACER was one of the first non-governmental organisations founded in Albania, legally recognised in 1993. Antony Fisher's most important legacy to ACER has been its mission and objectives, the importance of independent opinions (non-partisanship) and above all the need to offer well-researched ideas, with measurable impact, in the public-policy environment. He was responsible for shifting our focus from a strong state mentality towards the analysis of Albania's present transition to a free-market economy.

Atlas broadened our contacts and introduced us to scholars and others of liberal thought by financing us to attend their international activities. Presentation of ACER on its web page has helped its international credibility at a time when Albania has a philosophical and conceptual vacuum. Atlas's assistance has been significant in the formation of an independent voice supporting the market economy and free society and with an increasing impact on the regional and local environment.

Allegheny Institute for Public Policy

835 Western Avenue
Pittsburgh, PA 15233
USA
Tel: +1 412 231 6020
Fax: +1 412 231 6037
Email: Aipp@alleghenyinstitute.org
Web: www.alleghenyinstitute.org
President: Jake Haulk, Ph.D.

The Allegheny Institute was founded in 1995 with both financial and moral support from Atlas. It is a non-partisan research
and education institution whose mission is to formulate and
promote conservative public policies at the local government
level based on the principles of free enterprise, limited and accountable government, individual freedom and responsibility
and a reverence for traditional values. We believe these principles
are the foundation of human dignity, happiness and prosperity
for all Americans.

The Allegheny Institute has worked successfully to defeat the
stadium-tax referendum in 11 western Pennsylvania counties
and promoted Pennsylvania's electric choice program and its
successful implementation amongst other things. It has produced over 80 reports on subjects ranging from airline mergers
to economic freedom in Pennsylvania and welfare-to-work
programmes, as well as sponsoring conferences and hosting
events featuring nationally known speakers.

Association for Liberal Thinking

GMK Bulvari No: 108/17

Maltepe

Ankara 06570

Turkey

Tel: +90 312 230 8703

Fax: + 90 312 230 8003

Email: liberal@ada.net.tr

Web: www.liberal-dt.org.tr

President: Atilla Yayla

The ALT was founded informally in 1992 and formally in 1994. Atlas funded Atilla Yayla's participation in their international events and held its 28th workshop in Ankara. It also funded publications in Turkish, including Hayek's *Road to Serfdom*, and the network of Atlas institutes has enabled young and talented members of ALT to increase their contacts, improve their academic work and the work of ALT.

ALT introduces to the Turkish public the richness of the intellectual tradition of liberal democratic civilisation; to promote values like liberty, justice, peace, human rights, the rule of law, tolerance; to encourage development of academic researches; to contribute to finding effective solutions to Turkey's problems within a liberal perspective. It has no direct links with any political party or movement.

ALT regularly holds national and international symposiums and panels in various cities of Turkey. It publishes a quarterly academic journal, *Liberal Thought*, and *Free Line*, a free youth journal which prepares young talents for future intellectual engagements, and both Turkish authors and translations of foreign authors.

Asociación Nacional de Fomento Económico (ANFE)

Avenida 8 y calle 27

San José

P.O. Box # 3577–1000

Costa Rica

Tel: +506 253 4460

Fax: +506 253 4497

Email: anfe@anfe.or.cr

Web: www.anfe.or.cr

President: Enrique J. Soler

The Asociación was founded in 1958 and collaborates with Atlas on different projects. Anfe's purpose is to defend private enterprise in Costa Rica. We believe that the state should be the servant of the citizens and not the citizens the servants of the state. We promote the reduction in the size of the state in our country, which is involved in many commercial activities (monopolies) and which should be opened to competition in the private sector so that the consumer can benefit from cheaper and better services.

We carry out research, run seminars and academic and cultural courses and have published almost 100 titles, such as *The Convenience of Privatisation*.

Association pour la Liberté Economique et le Progrès Social (ALEPS)

35 avenue Mac Mahon

Paris 75017

France

Tel: +33 143 80 55 18

Fax: +33 148 88 97 57

Web: www.libres.org

Le Journal des Economistes et des Etudes Humaines and

L'Université d'Eté de la Nouvelle Economie

Centre d'Analyse Economique

3 avenue Robert Schuman

13628 Aix en Provence

France

Tel: +33 442 96 54 20 (*Journal*); +33 442 64 21 65 (Université)

Fax: +33 442 96 96 30 (*Journal*); +33 442 59 38 87 (Université)

Web: www.ieeh.asso.fr

President: Professor Jacques Garello

ALEPS was founded in 1969 by a group of scholars and businessmen, most of them members of the Mont Pélerin Society. They knew of the work of the Institute of Economic Affairs, and Antony Fisher visited Aleps many times. In 1978 began the great adventure of the Université d'Eté de la Nouvelle Economie in Aix en Provence and ALEPS was introduced to Atlas by Leonard Liggio. In 1979 the Institute for Humane Studies Europe was founded by ALEPS, later to become the Institute for Economic Studies. This new institute developed programmes of economic education for students. Seminars were organized in different European countries, with a special interest in Eastern and Central Europe, in Romania, Bulgaria, Russia, Czechoslovakia, Hungary and the Baltic countries.

Aleps organises a yearly award for classical liberal intellectuals and many conferences and meetings to provide free-market arguments to French politicians and decision-makers (a huge challenge!). They publish two quarterly reviews (*Liberté economique* and *Libéral et croyant*), a weekly economic letter (*La*

Nouvelle Lettre), and *Le Journal des Economistes et des Etudes Humaines*, edited by Prof. Jean Pierre Centi and the Institut Européen des Etudes Humaines, a common subsidiary of both IES Europe and ALEPS.

In 2000, ALEPS created a website, www.libres.org, with a daily comment on economic, political and social events, an economic dictionary (1000 words), book reviews, a bibliographic guide, and a lot of other materials (audiovisuals).

A large part of ALEPS's developing activity is due to the intellectual and financial support of Atlas.

Atlantic Institute for Market Studies

Suite 521
1657 Barrington Street
Halifax NS
B3T 1G9
Canada
Tel: +1 902 429 1143
Fax: +1 902 425 1393
Email: aims@aims.ca
Web: www.aims.ca
President: Brian Lee Crowley

Atlas was directly responsible for the opening of AIMS's doors in 1994 by providing the first donation and invaluable guidance. It has linked AIMS with the knowledge and resources of the global network of think tanks, resulting in an almost continuous state of innovation and improvement in our day-to-day operations.

AIMS is an independent and non-partisan economic and social-policy think tank working to broaden the policy debate by making Canadians more aware of the range of options for resolving our economic and social problems. Of particular concern to us is the role that markets can and should play in our region's efforts to escape underdevelopment.

Institute projects have dealt with topics as diverse as the impact of transfer payments, health-care reform, property rights in the fisheries, deregulation and restructuring of the electricity industry, school choice, aquaculture, fiscal policy and management of natural resources.

AIMS has been three times a finalist for the Sir Antony Fisher Award. The institute won the award for its first book, on federal transfer payments and their impact on Atlantic Canada, as well as for a paper several years later on the gathering crisis in Canada's public health-care system.

The institute enjoys considerable success in communicating its work to a regional and national audience of policy makers, opinion leaders and the general public. Not only is AIMS frequently mentioned in the national media, but it has also been cited in international publications such as *Time* magazine and the *Wall Street Journal*. The institute's website gets over 20,000 requests a month, and its monthly e-mail newsletter goes to nearly 10,000 people.

The Atlas Economic Research Foundation

4084 University Drive, Suite 103
Fairfax
Virginia 22030-6812
USA
Tel: +1 703 934 6969
Fax: +1 703 352 7530
Email: atlas@atlasUSA.org
Web: www.atlas.atlasUSA.org

The Atlas Economic Research Foundation works with think tanks and individuals around the world to advance a vision of a society of free and responsible individuals, based upon private property rights, limited government under the rule of law and the market order. The organization is dedicated to discovering, developing and supporting intellectual entrepreneurs worldwide who have the potential to create independent public-policy institutes and related programs which advance our vision; and to provide ongoing support as such institutes and programs mature. Atlas is a nonprofit 501(c)(3) organisation that is supported solely by donations from individuals, foundations and corporations.

The Barry Goldwater Institute for Public Policy Research

500 East Coronado Road
Phoenix
Arizona 85004
USA
Tel: +1 602 462 5000
Fax: +1 602 256 7045
Email: info@goldwaterinstitute.org
Web: www.goldwaterinstitute.org
President: Michael K. Block, Ph.D.

The Goldwater Institute's original executive director, Michael Sanera, consulted at length with then President of the Atlas Foundation, John Blundell, before establishing the Institute in 1988. Atlas's advice and support was integral to the institute's effectiveness.

The institute is an independent, non-partisan research and educational organization dedicated to the study of public policy. Its mission is to advance the principles of limited government, economic freedom and individual responsibility – the principles championed by the late Senator Barry Goldwater. To promote these principles, change public opinion, and assist Arizona leaders in developing public policy, the Goldwater Institute conducts research on timely issues through the use of research papers, workshops, commentaries and policy briefings. The institute has been particularly effective in encouraging innovative public policy in Arizona, including school choice.

Beacon Hill Institute
Suffolk University
8 Ashburton Place
Boston 02108
USA
Tel: +1 617 573 8750
Fax: +1 617 720 4272
Email: dtuerck@beaconhill.org
Web: www.beaconhill.org
President: David G. Tuerck

David Tuerck founded the Beacon Hill Institute in 1991 following his attendance at an Atlas meeting in 1987 to hear Peruvian thinker Hernando de Soto, at which he resolved to establish an economic think tank in Boston. With the support of Massachusetts businessman Ray Shamie, the institute was set up at Suffolk University.

The BHI believes in the superiority of free and open markets and the primacy of the individual and of private initiatives in improving the lives of all individuals. It is an independent, non-partisan economic research organisation that applies a market-clearing approach to the analysis of tax, fiscal and regulatory issues. BHI combines innovative solutions and state-of-the-art econometric methods in the analysis of public-policy issues.

BHI analyses range from exhaustive policy studies to brief background articles. It promotes discussion of the issues through forums and lectures, through *NewsLink*, its quarterly newsletter, and through its website.

The Buckeye Institute for Public Policy Solutions

4100 North High Street

Suite 200

Columbus

Ohio 43214

USA

Tel: +1 614 262 1593

Fax: +1 614 262 1927

Email: buckeye@buckeyeinstitute.org

Web: www.buckeyeinstitute.org

President: David J. Owsian

The Buckeye Institute was legally established in 1989 by Sam Staley as the Urban Policy Research Institute. Atlas provided the seed money and its mission and function is modelled after the Institute of Economic Affairs. It publishes rigorous peer-reviewed policy studies while engaging in the broader public debate.

It is Ohio's leading public-policy research organisation whose mission is to educate Ohio's policy makers, citizens and media on market-oriented public-policy solutions. It offers policy alternatives consistent with a respect for individual liberty, private property and limited government.

The Buckeye Institute proactively develops its ideas with the assistance of 50 scholars from 23 universities and colleges throughout Ohio. Through publications, lectures and special events, the institute distributes these ideas to policy-makers and key opinion-leaders to make meaningful change.

Capital Research Center

1513 16th Street, NW

Washington DC 20036

USA

Tel: +1 202 483 6900

Email: RHUBERTY@capitalresearch.org

Web: www.capitalresearch.org

President: Terrence Scanlon

The Capital Research Center (CRC) was founded in 1984 by Willa Ann Johnson who had worked at the Heritage Foundation. She sent an associate to meet Antony Fisher and Alex Chafuen in the early 80s. They, along with John Blundell, were interested in how think tanks can move ideas into public policy, and in creating more market-oriented think tanks serving different geographical areas, professional disciplines and policy-making functions, and in finding people of diverse talents to staff them.

CRC studies critical issues in philanthropy, with a special focus on non-profit 'public interest' and advocacy groups, their funding sources and policy agendas (open and hidden), and their impact on public policy and society. CRC supports individual liberty, a free-market economy, and limited and constitutional government. These are the wellsprings of the economic growth and wealth creation that make philanthropy possible.

CRC sponsors a website monitoring the environmental movement, www.green-watch.com.

Cascade Policy Institute

813 SW Alder
Suite 450
Portland OR 97205
USA
Tel: +1 503 242 0900
Fax: +1 503 242 3822
Email: info@cascadepolicy.org
Web: www.cascadepolicy.org
President: Steve Buckstein

Cascade was founded in January 1991, with Atlas providing guidance, financial resources and encouragement. Its mission is to explore public-policy alternatives that foster individual liberty, personal responsibility and economic opportunity in Oregon. It publishes policy studies and quarterly newsletters, organises community forums, sponsors educational programmes and provides public speakers.

It runs the Oregon Better Government Competition, opening the public-policy process to all Oregon's citizens. Several winning proposals have been passed into legislation, and reports have been requested from around the US and from countries as far away as New Zealand.

The Children's Scholarship Fund, Portland, is facilitated locally by Cascade and improves educational opportunity by providing several hundred four-year scholarships for Portland low-income families so they can send their children to the schools of their choice.

The Center for Free Market Environmentalism Political Economy Research Center (PERC)

502 S 19th Ave Ste 211

Bozeman

MT 59718-6827

USA

Tel: +1 406 587 9591

Fax: +1 406 586 7555

Email: perc@perc.org

Web: www.perc.org

Executive Director: Terry L. Anderson

PERC was founded in 1980, and interaction with Atlas-associated organisations has helped get its message out in countries as far apart as New Zealand, Guatemala and Turkey. In 1992, in conjunction with the Pacific Research Institute, it won Atlas's annual Sir Antony Fisher Award with the book *Free Market Environmentalism*, which was one of the first descriptions of free-market approaches to environmental protection. Our mission is to provide market solutions to environmental problems and the award focused attention on the book, which is now used by many colleges as an essential resource in understanding these solutions. PERC works with Atlas in many other ways.

We accomplish our mission through research and policy analysis, outreach and education programmes.

PERC has taken free-market environmentalism from the intellectual fringe to policy-makers at the state and national level, who now use innovative FME ideas to shape sophisticated new environmental policies, details of which can be seen on our website.

The Centre for Civil Society

B-12 Kailash Colony
New Delhi 110048
India
Tel: +91 11 646 8282
Fax: +91 11 646 2453
Mobile: +91 98111 45667
Email: parth@ccsindia.org
Web: www.ccsindia.org
President: Dr Parth J. Shah

The Centre for Civil Society was founded on 15 August 1997, the 50th anniversary of Indian independence, inspired by the story of Fisher, Hayek and the IEA. Atlas strengthened the desire of the founder president, Parth J. Shah, to return to India to start a think tank while he was a professor in the US. In addition to funding, Atlas workshops provided training in the mechanics of running the centre and Atlas's international conferences have helped us become an active member of the global community of think tanks.

Our work has changed the debate on education policy in favour of markets, and created an understanding of self- or market-regulation in India. Our programmes include the following: Liberty and Society Seminar, a 4-day residential training for college students in libertarianism, 5–6 seminars across India every year; a summer research internship programme of 2–3 months for college students from India and abroad, average 7 students per year; the annual B. R. Shenoy Memorial Essay Competition for school and college students and the general public; and a 5-day programme that imparts a liberal viewpoint to business journalists, especially those working with the non-English language press. We run dialogues and lectures on policy issues and we offer the facilities of our extensive library in Delhi to students and researchers. We have built an extensive student network – young fighters for the cause.

The Centre for Independent Studies

38 Oxley Street
St Leonards
NSW 2065
Australia
Tel: +61 (0)2 943 84377
Fax: +61 (0)2 943 97310
Mobile: 041 1114653
Email: glindsay@cis.org.au
Web: www.cis.org.au
Executive Director: Greg Lindsay

Greg Lindsay founded the CIS in 1976, the same year that he first spoke to Antony Fisher and before he learned about the IEA. Much of what he learned subsequently came from observing and interacting with organisations like the IEA and the Fraser Institute, and the IEA model was adopted as a guide.

Since its establishment, the CIS has become the largest independent policy-studies organisation in Australia. It has pioneered studies in economics, political theory, law and social policy. Its output includes books, monographs, occasional papers and other publications as well as its quarterly journal, *Policy*. Activities include a comprehensive lecture and seminar programme and the annual John Bonython and Acton Lectures. Its annual public-policy conference, *Consilium*, is considered to be an event of the highest prestige and features speakers from Australia, New Zealand and the Pacific as well as from Europe and North America. Other activities include its student seminar programme, Liberty & Society, established in 1996.

Centre for Research into Post-Communist Economies
57 Tufton Street
London SW1P 3QL
UK
Tel: +44 (0)20 7233 1050
Email: crce@crce.freewire.co.uk
Web: www.crce.org.uk
Director: Ljubo Sirc, CBE
Administrative Director: Lisl Biggs-Davison

The CRCE was founded in 1983 to influence developments in Eastern Europe in the same way as the IEA influenced Great Britain. Antony Fisher was chairman of the trustees, Atlas provided support, and a home was provided at the IEA until 1999.

The CRCE researches the problems of countries in transition from communism to democracy and market economies. A forum is provided for academics, specialists and journalists to discuss individual countries and their progress, and to meet reformist economists and politicians involved in transition.

CRCE recognised and supported young economists behind the Iron Curtain in the mid-1980s, published their work and invited them to meetings. After 1989, many of the economists emerged as prime ministers, finance ministers and national bank chairmen – key figures in the post-communist world. All remain in close contact.

The demand for research into the transitional economies of Central and Eastern Europe continues. Research must suggest the alternative systems and policies to replace the disintegrating communist ideology, in Eastern Europe and throughout the world.

In 2001 the CRCE's work was recognised by HM the Queen, who invested Ljubo Sirc with the CBE for services to the promotion of democracy in Central and Eastern Europe.

Centre for the New Europe

23 Rue du Luxembourg
1000 Brussels
Belgium
Tel: +32 2 506 4000
Fax: +32 2 506 4009
Web: www.cne-network.org
Email: info@cne-network.org
President: Hardy Bouillon

The CNE was founded in 1994 and is a pan-European policy-research institute based in Brussels, Belgium, maintaining a German office in Trier. It reflects and stimulates debate on economic, political and social issues and receives financial and network support from Atlas.

Through its analysis and the solutions it proposes, CNE argues for a free-market economy in a society based on individual liberty and responsibility. CNE firmly believes that economic liberty goes hand in hand with prosperity for all.

CNE publications offer market solutions to policy problems. These include papers and studies on full employment, the reform of the welfare state, health-care policy, and other timely economic, social and environmental topics.

The research undertaken and published by CNE aims to promote all initiatives which further these objectives and nourish public debate.

Centro de Divulgación del Conocimiento Economico (CEDICE)

Avda Andrés Eloy Blanco (Este 2)

Edif Camara de Comercio de Caracas

Los Caobos

Caracas 1060

Venezuela

Tel: +58 212 577 9674/571 1719

Fax: +58 212 576 0512

Email: cedice@cedice.org.ve

Web: www.cedice.org.ve

President: Aurelio F. Concheso

CEDICE was founded in 1984 after a meeting with Sir Antony, who explained how Hayek had told him of the importance of liberty and how ideas can influence the course of political events. CEDICE's founders identified and contacted others in Caracas and the response was overwhelming. Atlas's support enabled the running of workshops in Venezuela on education and freedom that have had an important impact.

CEDICE's mission is to promote freedom, the market economy and individual liberty in Venezuela and South America. Our organisation teaches economic courses and conducts seminars. It also publishes, prints and distributes books and other materials espousing individual liberty, and teaches a basic economics course for university journalism students and courses for journalists about the free market. The impact of this course has been remarkable in the resulting column inches about economic freedom and free enterprise.

CEDICE established a bookstore as a bridge between the general public and other classical liberal Latin-American institutions. With the support of 40 bookstores, we have sold more than 90,000 books and donated more than 50 collections containing libertarian ideas to universities.

Centro de Estudios en Educación y Economía, AC

15 de Mayo

1531 Pte. Col. Ma. Luisa

Monterrey

CP 64040

Mexico

Tel: +52 83 44 48 24

Fax: +52 83 42 74 33

Email: ceeejrer@prodigy.net.mx

President: Alejandro Garza Laguera

The centre was founded in 1982 after Rolando Espinosa attended the Fraser Institute's annual meeting in Vancouver, by invitation of Antony Fisher, so that he could see how it operated and share ideas with them. He had been impressed with the methodology of the IEA when he first met Antony Fisher there in 1981 and wanted to learn more about it. This was his introduction to the international movement of free-market intellectuals and the international network of market-oriented institutes.

Centro de Estudios en Educación y Economía, AC, is a research and educational institute whose mission is to promote the principles of a free-market economy in Mexico. It was the first to publish books in Spanish of the main free-market intellectuals, including Mises, Hayek, Michael Novak, etc. They are sent to the centre's primary audience: Mexican universities. It also researches key policy issues and sends the results to members of the Congress, policy-makers in the executive branch and the nation's news media.

Centro de Investigaciones Económicas Nacionales (CIEN), Guatemala (National Economics Research Center)

12 calle 1-25 zona 10

Edif. Géminis 10

Torre Norte of. 1702

Guatemala City

Guatemala

Tel/Fax: +502 2 335 3415

Email: macena@cien.org.gt

Web: www.cien.org.gt

Executive President: Ing. María del Carmen Aceña de Fuentes

CIEN was established at the end of 1982 after Juan Bendfeldt met Antony Fisher. His ideas and the circumstances in Guatemala led to the establishment of CIEN as a public-policy institute. Its mission is to promote economic development in Guatemala through the adoption of sound public policies based upon the technical study of economic and social problems.

CIEN publishes monthly reports, a quarterly review of the economy and forecasts, an annual review and perspectives, and occasional papers, and it monitors and analyses legislative proposals in Congress. The institute offers public lectures, conferences and an annual summer course in economics for journalists. Major reports are published in book form. Over the years, the institute has become increasingly recognised for its free-market position and it has spearheaded policy and legal changes that produced the privatisation of state-owned enterprises. This included the creation of an open market for radio-communications in parallel with the sale of the national telephone company, a legal framework which has been hailed by some as the most advanced in the world. CIEN participates in the International Economic Freedom Index.

Centro de Investigaciones y Estudios Legales

Libertadores 350

San Isidoro

Lima 27

Peru

Tel: +51 1 441 3424

Fax: +51 1 442 6161

Email: eghersi@tsi.com.pe

Director: Enrique Ghersi

CITEL was founded in 1988 following encouragement from Antony Fisher and with great support from Atlas when no one else would help. CITEL makes proposals for legal changes including new laws on arbitration, public registry and the proposal of a new constitution.

Civitas: The Institute for the Study of Civil Society

The Mezzanine

Elizabeth House

39 York Road

London SE1 7NQ

UK

Tel: +44 (0)20 7401 5470

Fax: +44 (0)20 7401 5471

Email: info@civitas.org.uk

Web: www.civitas.org.uk

Director: Dr David G. Green

Deputy Director: Robert Whelan

Civitas was founded in January 2000 but it grew out of the Health and Welfare Unit of the Institute of Economic Affairs, which was founded by Antony Fisher. The unit, set up in 1986, developed to the point at which the trustees felt it would prosper as an independent body. Consequently it became independent and moved out of the IEA office in 2000.

Civitas has benefited from the efforts of the Atlas Foundation to bring together those who, in their different countries, are working towards the ideal of restoring those institutions which we describe as constituting civil society, being distinct from both the market and the state.

Civitas publishes on a variety of social policy issues, including health, welfare, crime, the family, education and, more generally, the institutions necessary for a free society to flourish. In parallel with the publishing programme, a regular series of lunches, seminars and conferences bring together people who are interested in particular topics from different viewpoints, in an attempt to improve the quality of public debate.

The David Hume Institute

25 Buccleuch Place
Edinburgh EH8 9LN
UK
Tel/Fax: +44 (0)131 667 9609
Email: Hume.Institute@ed.ac.uk
Web: www.ed.ac.uk/~hume/
Director: Professor Brian Main, FRSE

The David Hume Institute was founded in 1985 and is partly modelled on the IEA, though it is more specialised in its interests. Co-founder Sir Alan Peacock has been connected to the IEA for nearly 40 years as trustee, author and mentor.

The DHI is named after the famous Scots philosopher and economist. It is inspired by Hume's *Political Discourses* (1751), which laid the foundations of the economics of law and its application to such important policy issues as the scope of government, the international economy and the efficiency of the legal system. It seeks to appeal to an international audience and from the outset it received support from eminent economists, including the Nobel Prize winners George Stigler and James Buchanan and other contributors from the UK, Europe and the United States. It is gradually receiving more coverage in the national press and its conferences and seminars are well attended.

The Dumont Institute for Public Policy Research

71 South Orange Avenue
PMB 260
South Orange
NJ 07079
USA
Tel: +1 201 530 0877
Email: bob@dumontinst.com
Web: www.dumontinst.com

The institute was founded in 1990. It has benefited from the research of other think tanks, and the Institute for Humane Studies, Atlas and the Heartland Institute, among others, have helped the Dumont Institute develop. Atlas provided guidance and encouragement and helped fund attendance at several conferences.

The Dumont Institute publishes policy analyses, policy briefs and occasional papers. It also publishes the following journals: *Journal of Accounting, Ethics & Public Policy, Commentaries on the Law of Accounting & Finance, Commentaries on Law & Economics, Commentaries on Law & Public Policy.*

ESEADE Graduate School

Uriarte 2472
(1425) Buenos Aires
Argentina
Tel: +54 11 4747 0018
Fax: +54 11 4772 7243
Email: postmaster@eseade.edu.ar
Web: www.eseade.edu.ar
President: Armando Braun

ESEADE was founded in 1978 following the same advice that Hayek (the first chairman of our Advisory Board) gave to Antony Fisher, which is not to commit any effort to politics but instead to concentrate on the education of young people and their understanding of freedom. The Atlas Foundation has been supportive of several activities at our schools, giving us scholarships for students to be able to attend our courses or helping the financing of our academic journal, *Libertas*.

ESEADE is a graduate school teaching economics, political science, management, finance and corporate law. It aims not only to give students the basic tools in their professional work but also a clear understanding of the importance of a free society and its values.

The Ethan Allen Institute

4836 Kirby Mountain Road
Concord
VT 05824
USA
Tel: +1 802 695 1448
Fax: +1 802 695 1436
Email: eai@ethanallen.org
Web: www.ethanallen.org
President: John McClaughry

The Ethan Allen Institute was founded in 1993 and Atlas contributed directly or indirectly some $25,000 from 1993–95. It also sponsored attendance at a valuable management workshop.

Our mission is to influence public policy in Vermont by helping its people to better understand and put into practice the fundamentals of a free society, individual liberty, private property, competitive free enterprise, limited and frugal government, strong local communities, personal responsibility and expanded opportunity for human endeavour. The institute's report *Reviving Health Insurance in Vermont* (2000) has had a significant impact on the state's health-care reform debate otherwise dominated by socialist health-care advocates. Its forthcoming report *School Children First* is expected to have an even greater impact in the coming school-financing debate.

Our monthly Statehouse Roundtables bring to a legislative audience the knowledge of free-market oriented (and other) experts on education, health care, electricity, technology and other current topics. The monthly *Ethan Allen Letter* and biweekly newspaper and public radio commentaries have brought free-market perspectives to many thousands of Vermonters who have little opportunity to get it from any other independent source in the state.

Evergreen Freedom Foundation

PO Box 552
Olympia
WA 98507
USA
Tel: +1 360 956 3482
Fax: +1 360 352 1874
Email: effwa@effwa.org
Web: www.effwa.org
President: Bob Williams

The EFF was founded in 1991 and after 18 months Atlas became a lifeline, providing funding and resources. The staff at Atlas also stressed the importance of producing quality work that could be well marketed.

The EFF is a non-profit, educational research organisation whose mission is to advance individual liberty, free enterprise and limited and responsible government. The foundation conducts research and publishes analyses and policy alternatives in the areas of state budgets, governance and citizenship, and health, education and welfare reform. Publications include *Medical Savings Accounts: A Building Block for Sound Health Care* (1995), *Reducing the Size and Cost of Government* (1996), *Faith-Based Welfare Reform: Church Training Manual* (1999), *Collective Bargaining in Public Schools: Turning the Focus to Students* (2000), and *Taking Employee Wages to Hijack Elections* (2000).

Projects include Teachers' Paycheque Protection, EFF's five-year battle to protect teachers (and other union workers) from compelled political speech through unauthorised union political payroll deductions.

The F. A. Hayek Foundation

Drienová 24

826 03 Bratislava

Slovak Republic

Tel: +421 2 4341 0148

Fax: +421 2 4341 0146

Email: hayek@changenet.sk

Web: www.hayek.sk

President: Dr Jan Oravec

The F. A. Hayek Foundation is an independent and non-partisan, non-profit organisation, established in 1991 with no direct involvement from either Antony Fisher or Atlas, although both the work of Antony Fisher and the IEA had been important influences in its founding.

It pursues the following liberal ideas and values: a market economy and an open society founded on the free choice of individuals and their personal accountability; a limited role for government with minimal interference in the economy so creating a favourable social and economic framework and a reduced tax burden; the rule of law with a clear legal framework for government activities and guarantees of contractual commitments, agreements and promises, and the rights of every individual to their life, liberty and property.

Since its establishment, the foundation has become a driving liberal force in the Slovak Republic and in September 2001 organised the first Mont Pélerin Society meeting of the millennium in Bratislava, in a country behind the former Iron Curtain. This is evidence of the esteem in which the foundation is held internationally.

Flint Hills Center for Public Policy

P.O. Box 1946

Topeka

KS 66601-1946

USA

Tel: +1 785 357 7709

Fax: +1 785 357 7524

Email: kppi@kppi.org

Web: www.kppi.org

President: Bob Corkins

Antony Fisher met with Charles Koch and George Pearson in Wichita in the early 80s, but it was after a meeting with John Blundell and with Atlas's support that Pearson and others founded the Kansas Public Policy Institute (now the Flint Hills Center for Public Policy) in 1996. Atlas provided critical seed money, ran a development workshop in Wichita and helped with fundraising.

The centre's mission is to preserve and enhance the principles of limited government, individual freedom, personal responsibility and open markets by serving as an independent source of information regarding public-policy issues. It accepts no government funding and produces studies, reports, conferences, seminars, commentaries on current events, media interviews and news conferences to influence the policy debate in Kansas.

The Flint Hills Center has broadened the policy debate in Kansas on income-tax reform by advocating the elimination of the individual and corporate state income tax; on reform in the state public-employment retirement system and on state-wide health insurance by advocating the replacement of the defined benefit approach with a defined contribution programme. The elimination of the cosmetology laws governing hairbraiding was the Flint Hills Center's most decisive victory, but its greatest influence to date has been on education spending in the state, and in 2001 legislators used its material to turn aside the ever-increasing demands of educators to spend more money on education.

Foundation for Economic Education

30 South Broadway

Irvington–on–Hudson

NY 10533

USA

Tel: +1 914 591 7230

Fax: +1 914 591 8910

Email: fee@fee.org

Web: www.cliches.org and www.fee.org

FEE was founded in March 1946 and was an inspiration to Antony Fisher in setting up the Institute of Economic Affairs. In turn, he inspired FEE leaders to continually improve.

The FEE publication *Ideas on Liberty* (formerly *The Freeman*) is the world's oldest continuously published magazine dedicated to individual liberty, private property and free trade. For nearly 50 years it has offered the best in economic theory, political philosophy and history. FEE encourages reprints of articles and regularly adapts them as op-ed columns for more than 150 newspapers.

Each summer FEE runs week-long sessions to explore the essentials of the free society and it sponsors seminars for students from colleges across the USA and the world. These offer concentrated exposure and full discussion of the principles underlying the free market and the free society. FEE also offers high-school-debate programmes and maintains two award-winning websites.

Foundation Francisco Marroquin

PO Box 1806

Santa Monica

CA 90406-1806

USA

Tel: +1 310 395 5047

Fax: +1 561 288 0670

Email: pvhffm@ix.netcom.com

Web: www.ffmnet.org

President: Paul V. Harberger

The Foundation Francisco Marroquin was founded in 1980 and has collaborated on many significant projects with Atlas and has been funded by them. We have co-sponsored several events, and our Foro Latino Americano (Latin-American Speakers Bureau) has provided speakers to many of the Atlas think tanks.

The Fraser Institute

4th Floor

1770 Burrard Street

Vancouver BC

V6J 3G7

Canada

Tel: +1 604 688 0221

Fax: +1 604 688 8539

Email: info@fraserinstitute.ca

Web: www.fraserinstitute.ca

Executive Director: Dr Michael A. Walker

The Fraser Institute was conceived by Mr T. P. Boyle and given realisation by John Raybould, Sally Pipes and Michael Walker. It was founded in 1974. Antony Fisher worked with the institute helping to raise funds, introducing it to international contacts and helping build the Editorial Advisory Board, as well as explaining the IEA approach which we had been in the process of reinventing. He provided a role model in how idea-warriors should behave, never treated anyone unkindly and treated most carefully those who did not believe the free-market model was the right one – and in Canada in 1975 that was most of the people we met!

The Fraser Institute has become Canada's largest public-policy institute independent of government financing and has a reputation for excellent public-policy research in more than 55 countries. Its 50 staff and senior fellows are constantly sought for their opinions on public policy. It has contributed to many of the central policy debates of the past quarter-century and its 200 books and thousands of articles have been published in more than 20 languages. Areas where the institute's work has been particularly important include wage and price controls, privatisation, agricultural marketing boards, the measurement of taxation (tax freedom day methodology), public sector unions, the service sector, the North American Free Trade Agreement, the measurement of economic freedom and many others.

Free Market Foundation of Southern Africa
2nd Floor, Export House
Cnr. West & Maude Streets
Sandown
Johannesburg
South Africa
or
P.O. Box 785121
Sandton 2146
South Africa
Tel: +27 11 884 0270
Fax: +27 11 884 5672
Email: fmf@mweb.co.za
Web: www.freemarketfoundation.com
Executive Director: Leon Louw

The FMF was founded in 1975 and the IEA was naturally an example. It has had great intellectual support from the publications of the 'Fisher' institutes and relations with Atlas and the other members of the network are of crucial importance. Great ideas change the world we live in if they fall on the receptive ears of people of great ability.

During the dark days of the apartheid years individual rights were being trampled on with impunity. In the early 1980s, the FMF persuaded the government to liberalise the economy and especially to relax trading restrictions on black people. It then concentrated on finding a political and constitutional dispensation that would allow a peaceful transition to democracy, work that culminated in the publication of the best-selling book *South Africa: The Solution* by Leon Louw and Frances Kendall. The ideas in the book were widely publicised through speeches, articles and media interviews. As a result, South Africa's final constitution is a great deal more protective of individual rights than it might otherwise have been.

More recently, the FMF has argued for economic freedom as the most effective means of rapidly overcoming many of the problems facing the country. Our foundation's efforts and economic reality have caused members of the government to temper their ideological leanings. The 'Economic Freedom of the World' reports have played a central role in the FMF's advocacy work.

The Frontier Centre for Public Policy
201–63 Albert Street
Winnipeg
Manitoba
R3B 1G4
Canada
Tel: +1 204 957 1567
Fax: +1 204 957 1570
Email: newideas@fcpp.org
Web: www.fcpp.org
President: Peter Holle

The Frontier Centre for Public Policy began operations in May 1997. The Atlas Foundation provided valuable and well-timed advice, assistance and networking at the beginning.

Our materials, events and topics have focused on policy innovators from around the globe, concentrating on the benefits of introducing competitive processes into the production of public services, narrowing the core business of government to policy-making and minimal regulation. We have shown how Phoenix and Indianapolis created excellent local government by requiring in-house suppliers to compete with external operators. We have shaken the health-care debate in Canada as well, by exploring Sweden's use of the purchaser-provider split in health-care delivery.

Our commentaries and analyses receive high exposure through a wide range of local and national publications.

Fundación DL (Development through Liberty)

Calle 25 Norte # 5 A 43 of 202
Cali oo
Colombia
Tel: +57 2 683 7237
Fax: +57 2 653 0260
Email: fdl@fundaciondl.org
Web: www.fundaciondl.org
President: Andrés Mejía-Vergnaud
The institute was founded in April 2000. Atlas was critical in its establishment as they provided some of our first funds and through attendance at their events we were able to participate in the free-market movement and make our young institute known.

Fundación DL was created to investigate and promote the economic and political ideas based on the principles of economic liberty and limited government, especially in the case of Colombia. We have managed to create high-impact programmes all levels and kinds of people in our society (students, businessmen and women, ordinary people). We are the first non-socialist organisation to run programmes in the highly socialist public universities of Colombia. Our email publications reach almost 650 people worldwide.

Fundación Libertad

Mitre 170

2000 – Rosario

Santa Fe

Argentina

Tel/Fax: +54 341 424 5000

Email: fundacion@libertad.org.ar

Web: www.libertad.org.ar

Director: Gerardo Bongiovanni

Fundación Libertad was founded in 1988 by a group of businessmen, professionals and intellectuals. Atlas introduced us to top intellectuals from all around the world, and helped in identifying and anticipating the important issues for debate.

Fundación Libertad is a private, non-profit institution working towards the research and diffusion of public-policy issues and the promotion of the concept of a free-market society. It produces courses, lectures, seminars, research, studies and publications on economic policies, education, regulations, public spending, etc. It also has a strong permanent presence in the media, through the columns and television and radio programmes it produces. Outstanding guest speakers have delivered lectures and conferences, including Peruvian writer Mario Vargas Llosa, and Nobel Laureates such as Gary Becker, Douglass North, Robert Lucas and James Buchanan, and Lech Walesa.

Fundación Libertad has also led to the creation of REFUN-DAR, a network of 10 leading Argentine foundations. This network has helped us spread our ideas throughout the country. It is also related to different worldwide networks of similar institutions.

Fundación Republica para una Nueva Generacion

Reconquista 609 8★

(1003) Buenos Aires

Argentina

Phone: +54 1 4314 6006

Fax: +54 1 4312 1903

President: Ponciano Vivanco

A group of young professionals who were deeply concerned about economic, political and social problems in Argentina and the future of freedom and free enterprise founded the institute in 1987. Since the beginning, Atlas played a fundamental role through sponsorship and as co-organiser of our activities in Buenos Aires. Some of our staff worked for Atlas in Washington DC and 50 per cent of our annual budget was from Atlas grants. The main purpose of the foundation, a non-profit organisation, is to create a greater public understanding of the principles of private property, individual rights and limited government order. It organises seminars and conferences and publishes essays and books on public-policy topics, including *The Economic Crisis and its Impact on Argentina*; *Interventionism in the Monetary Market*; *Tax Reform*; *Public Regulatory Agencies on Grain and Meat Markets*; *Deregulation of Ports* and *Pharmaceutical Patents and Property Rights*.

The Future of Freedom Foundation

11350 Random Hills Road, Suite 800

Fairfax

VA 22030

USA

Tel: +1 703 934 6101

Fax: +1 703 352 8678

Email: fff@fff.org

Web: www.fff.org

Atlas made a generous donation to enable the publication of *Separating School and State* by Sheldon Richman, which subsequently won one of Atlas's annual Antony Fisher Memorial Awards.

The Galen Institute

P.O. Box 19080
Alexandria
VA 22320-0080
USA
Tel: +1 703 299 8900
Fax: +1 703 299 0721
Email: gracemarie@galen.org
Web: www.galen.org
President: Grace-Marie Turner

The Galen Institute was founded in 1995 and Atlas provided valuable guidance and consultation on everything from development to communications technology. Galen is a free-market public-policy research organisation that promotes education on health and tax-policy issues.

It works to promote greater understanding of the dangers of government intervention, including price controls, on health care and pharmaceuticals. It believes the best way to facilitate continued medical progress is through a free and competitive marketplace. By demonstrating the destructiveness of centralised bureaucracies it works to liberate the health sector so tomorrow's medical miracles will be created.

The Hong Kong Centre for Economic Research

School of Economics and Finance
The University of Hong Kong
Pokfulam Road
Hong Kong
Tel: +852 2547 8313
Fax: +852 2548 6319
Email: hkcer@econ.hku.hk
Director: Y. C. Richard Wong
Executive Director: Alan K. F. Siu

John Greenwood founded the Hong Kong Centre in 1987 with the aim of replicating the IEA, following advice and assistance from Antony Fisher. Atlas paid for Prof. Hannes Gissurarson to go to Hong Kong to help with the start-up and scholars that were recruited through Atlas and its network wrote some early studies.

The centre is affiliated with the School of Economics and Finance at the University of Hong Kong but it is administratively and financially independent.

Its aim is to support research and publish and promote authoritative studies on important public-policy issues, which enhance public understanding of economic affairs and provide government with alternative policy choices. The centre has published over 30 research books in both English and Chinese on policy issues relevant to Hong Kong, and publishes the bimonthly policy report *The HKCER Letters*. It has contributed to changing policy decisions of the Hong Kong Government. Some examples are the liberalisation of telecommunications, privatisation of public housing, introduction of competition in air-cargo-terminal operations, preventing the introduction of a pay-as-you-go retirement scheme in favour of a mandatory, fully funded, private provident scheme, etc.

The Howard Center for Family, Religion and Society

934 North Main Street
Rockford
IL 61103
USA
Tel: +1 815 964 5819
Fax: +1 815 965 1826
Email: hwdctr@profam.org
Web: www.profam.org and www.worldcongress.org
President: Allan Carlson, Ph.D.

The centre was started in 1976 as the Rockford College Institute by John Howard, following encouragement by Antony Fisher, a Mont Pélerin colleague. It became the Howard Center in 1998 and has received considerable financial and intellectual support from Atlas.

The centre operates on the premise that free societies and

free economies depend on institutions that transmit values of responsibility across the generations. The centre sees the family as
the fundamental social unit, and defends its autonomy and fe-
cundity from centralising governments and other hostile forces.
It publishes books, monographs and monthly reports and organises conferences. The most important to date was the World
Congress of Families held in Geneva in 1999, with over 1,600
coming together from 65 nations to defend family autonomy
from national and international social engineering.

The Independent Institute
100 Swan Way
Oakland
CA 94621-1428
USA
Tel: +1 510 632 1366
Fax: +1 510 568 6040
Email: info@independent.org
Web: www.independent.org
Founder and President: David J. Theroux
The Independent Institute was founded in 1986. David Theroux
had previously worked closely with Antony Fisher at the Pacific
Research Institute, and as the founding Vice President of Acad-
emic Affairs for the Cato Institute he organised a series of
seminal monographs, the Cato Papers, which were based on the
IEA's approach to publications (two of them were reprints from
the IEA).

The Independent Institute sponsors comprehensive studies
of critical social and economic issues, with the results published
as books and other publications and publicly debated through
numerous conference and media programmes. It publishes the
quarterly journal *The Independent Review*, and numerous books
through Oxford University Press, University of Michigan Press,
New York University Press, etc. Student programmes include
the Olive Garvey Fellowships, Independent Scholarship Fund
and Summer Seminars in Political Economy.

The institute's series of lectures, seminars and debates, the Independent Policy Forum, regularly appears on the worldwide TV network C-SPAN, and the institute has hosted events honouring Nobel Laureate James Buchanan, Lord Bauer, Robert Conquest, Tom Peters and Sir John Templeton, awarding the Alexis de Tocqueville Memorial Award.

Institut Économique de Montréal/ Montreal Economic Institute

6418, St-Hubert Street
Montreal
H2S 2M2
Canada
Tel: +1 514 273 0969
Fax: +1 514 273 0967
Email: mkellygagnon@iedm.org
Web: www.iedm.org
President: Michel Kelly-Gagnon (Executive Director)
The institute was founded in 1998, with the Atlas Foundation providing financial support and management training. Its mission is to propose efficient and innovative solutions for public-policy problems, using successful reforms applied elsewhere as models. The MEI studies how markets function with the aim of identifying the mechanisms and institutions which foster the prosperity and long-term welfare of all individuals.

We organise public conferences in French or English and publish studies, either small-format 'Economic Notes', larger research papers or books. The publication with the greatest impact is our annual *Report Card on Quebec's Secondary Schools* (in collaboration with the Fraser Institute), which ranks the performance of public and private high schools in Quebec. The 2000 issue received a tremendous amount of media coverage for several weeks and established us as a major player in public-policy debates in Quebec. We get at least one media hit (TV, radio and print) every two days, and our columns and op-ed pieces appear regularly in major daily papers and magazines.

Institute for Children

University Place
124 Mt Auburn Street
Suite 2001 North
Cambridge
MA 02138
USA
Email: info@forchildren.org
Web: www.forchildren.org
President: Conna Craig

The Institute for Children was founded in March 1993. The Atlas Foundation provided the seed support, further funding and, just as important, advice and leadership.

The institute's mission is to reshape foster care and adoption so that every child will have the chance to grow up in a permanent, loving family. It brings essentially private solutions to deeply entrenched government bureaucracies in which federal/national-funding mechanisms have created incentives for states to keep children in state or local-authority care.

The IFC promotes a range of concrete policy reforms, advising legislators on how to streamline government regulation to make adoption work; demand accountability from public child-welfare agencies; and restructure the current reverse-incentive funding mechanisms that perpetuate the public child-welfare system. The IFC's greatest achievement has been to develop tangible, workable solutions for restructuring public-agency adoption and foster care, especially in the United States and United Kingdom.

The Institute for Economic Freedom

P.O. Box N 1688

Nassau

999999

Bahamas

Tel: +1 242 324 2035

Fax: +1 242 364 7838

Email: joanmt@coralwave.com

Web: iefbahamas.org

President: Joan Thompson

The institute was founded in 1995. Antony Fisher was its inspiration and Atlas has been encouraging, providing both money and intellectual support.

The IEF was founded to propose new directions in governance. The Bahamas has been described quite accurately as 'a highly regulated, central managed economy ... with a complex and contradictory set of entry restraints, targeted tax breaks and indirect subsidies'. A long period of pure state socialism was followed by limited privatisation of government enterprises and sharply increased business regulation.

In addition to seminars on privatisation, the budget and global warming, and appearances on radio shows, the institute publishes a booklet called *The Review*, a collection of essays providing brief but relevant analysis of political decision-making and its interaction with inevitable economic changes. We identified onerous labour legislation, and a series of 'Critical Issues' bulletins and surveys of business were factors in government deferring the labour bills in their original form.

Institute for Energy Research

6219 Olympia

Houston

Texas 77057

USA

Tel/Fax: +1 713 974 1918

Email: iertx@hern.org

Web: www.instituteforenergyresearch.org

President: Robert L. Bradley, JR

The Institute for Energy Research, founded in 1989 in conjunction with the Atlas Economic Research Foundation, is dedicated to advancing the theory and history of the market order with energy. IER president Robert L. Bradley JR. has published and lectured widely to educate policy-makers and the general public on the economic and environmental benefits of free-market energy. A summary of his writings and lectures can be found on the IER website.

Energy, as the late Julian Simon concluded, is the master resource. Advanced society needs abundant and affordable energy to sustain its populations and to improve living standards. Private property and voluntary exchange governed by the rule of law create the framework to sustain a growing and evolving energy economy. The historical record is replete with examples of both market-driven progress and government disorder. Energy mandates are inferior to market ordering of complexity, and energy is no exception.

Improving technology can not only make energy more plentiful but also environmentally benign if the market is simultaneously guided by sound science and consumer welfare.

Institute for Health Freedom

1155 Connecticut Avenue NW, Suite 300

Washington DC 20036

USA

Tel: +1 202 429 6610

Fax: +1 202 861 1973

Email: sblevins@ForHealthFreedom.org

Web: www.ForHealthFreedom.org

President: Sue A. Blevins

The Institute for Health Freedom was established in 1996, with Atlas playing a significant role.

Freedom is the foundation of civilised society and is viewed as a constitutional right. But when it comes to health care, the individual's freedom is often limited by regulations. Many citizens are not free to choose their own health-care providers and treatments without getting pre-approval from an insurance company or running up against government regulations. The IHF brings the issues of personal-health freedom to the forefront of policy debates. Our mission is to present the ethical and economic case for strengthening personal-health freedom. IHF does not endorse any health-care treatment, product, provider or organisation. Rather, IHF is a non-partisan, non-profit research centre.

Through research, publications and public-policy debates, IHF provides a forum for exchanging ideas about health freedom. Its research and analyses are published in policy briefings and disseminated through newspaper editorials, television appearances, professional conferences, public meetings and the IHF website.

The Institute for Justice

1717 Pennsylvania Avenue NW, Suite 200
Washington DC 20006
USA
Tel: +1 202 955 1300
Fax: +1 202 955 1329
Email: general@ij.org
Web:www.ij.org
President: Chip Mellor

The IJ was founded in September 1991. Antony Fisher hired Chip Mellor to run the Pacific Research Institute in 1986 and taught the importance of entrepreneurship in running policy institutes (see the publication *Carry the Torch*, http://www.ij. org/publications/torch/t_8_95.html).

The IJ is the first non-profit law centre dedicated to empowering individuals. By combining effective litigation with pioneering public-interest training, IJ secures greater protection for individual liberty, challenges the scope and ideology of the Regulatory Welfare State, and illustrates and extends the benefits of freedom.

Antony Fisher and Atlas taught that policy research and grassroots organising efforts could also enhance public-interest litigation. We recognised how highly efficient it would be to train grassroots activists and policy think tanks to recognise opportunities where public-interest law and tactics could enhance their respective missions. The IJ not only litigates, but runs training seminars for policy activists, lawyers and law students to advance our mutually held core beliefs in individual rights and limited government. Alumni of our training programmes become part of our Human Action Network (HAN) which seeks to connect talent with opportunities whenever the need arises. Today, HAN members are working actively in public-interest litigation, producing policy reports, serving as local counsel in lawsuits or providing much-needed research assistance.

Institute for Liberty and The Analysis of Public Policy

Apartado 329-4050

Alajuela

Costa Rica

Tel: +506 438 2464

Fax: +506 438 2444

Email: inlapp@racsa.co.cr

Web: www.inlap.com

President: Daniel Escalante

Executive Director: Dr Rigoberto Stewart

The Institute for Liberty and the Analysis of Public Policy began in 1995 and was officially launched in 1998. Atlas played a crucial and continuing role in the institute's development.

INLAP is a non-profit, non-partisan organisation, created to defend and promote all aspects of individual liberty through public-policy analysis and educational activities. Its specific objectives are: (1) To increase awareness of the moral foundations of liberty and to promote liberty as an individual right without which it is impossible to achieve the highest levels of economic and human development. (2) To foster changes in social organisation and public policies by influencing the thinking of policy-makers, community leaders and citizens at large.

INLAP produces timely analyses of proposed laws, decrees and regulations, and its specific recommendations provide insight and guidance for elected officials. Detailed studies of public policies that have adverse moral or economic effects are published as study material for academics and others interested in learning about the effects of well-meaning but harmful public policies.

Institute for the Study of the Russian Economy, Moscow

B. Nikitskaya 44-2

Suite 2–6

Moscow GSP–2

Russia

Tel: +7 095 290 5108

Fax: +7 095 292 6511

Email: economic@cicp.co.ru

President:Vitali Naishul

The institute was founded in 1992 and Atlas played a very special role in the development of the liberal community in Russia in general and my institute in particular.

In spring 1990, I was invited to speak at Atlas when I was on my first trip to the USA – and to the West as well. It was recognised that Russia and Latin America have common institutional problems and as a result, I went to a Liberty Fund seminar on liberalism in Latin America (I was the only non-Latin American participant) and to the Mont Pélerin Society meeting, both in Munich in 1990. There I established extensive long-term contacts with foreign economists, especially those from Latin America. As a result, in 1991 twenty Russian economists visited Santiago, at the invitation of Institudo Libertado y Desarollo and Universitado's Adolfo Ibanez, to study the Chilean process of economic reforms. Many members of the Russian group later played important roles in the economic transformation in Russia: the future Deputy Director of the Russian Central Bank, the Deputy Finance Minister of Russia and the Russian Director of the IMF were from this group.

Most foreign contacts of my Institute are direct results of my meeting with Alex Chafuen in Atlas in spring 1990.

The Institute of Economic Affairs

2 Lord North Street

London SW1P 3LB

UK

Tel: +44 (0)20 7799 8900

Fax: +44 (0)20 7799 2137

Email: iea@iea.org.uk

Web: www.iea.org.uk

General Director: John Blundell

The IEA was founded in 1955 by Antony Fisher and its history and achievements are covered in this book. Its mission is to improve public understanding of the fundamental institutions of a free society, with particular reference to the role of markets in solving economic and social problems. It achieves this by a high-quality publishing programme, conferences, seminars and other events.

IEA publications are sold throughout the world, reprinted and translated into over 25 languages. It has subscribers from over 55 countries and sales in over 65 countries, with many titles becoming required reading in universities and classrooms.

Institute of Economic Affairs, Ghana

28 Independence Avenue

Accra

Ghana

or

P.O. Box OS1936

Christianborg

Accra

Ghana

Tel: +233 21 776 641

Fax: +233 21 222 313

Email: iea@ncs.com.gh

President: Dr Charles Mensa

IEA Ghana was founded in 1989. I met Sir Antony Fisher, Lord Harris and John Blundell at a Mont Pélerin conference and discussed a possible institute in Ghana. Alex Chafuen and John Blundell were very much involved. Initial travel and equipment costs were borne by Atlas and Ralph Harris's counsel was greatly valued. Atlas workshops are learning experiences for us and we look for the successful activities of others so that we can replicate them here.

In 1989 there was no public-policy institute in Ghana as no civil-society organisations were tolerated under the military regime of Lt Jerry John Rawlings. However, the IEA continued working with the newly created parliament to identify key laws that constrained individual freedom and limited the development of a free-market economy. We sent detailed studies and proposals for the repeal of such laws to Parliament and several of these laws have been repealed. One about to be repealed is the Criminal Libel Code that has sent several journalists to prison for doing absolutely nothing wrong.

Institute of Public Policy Analysis

P.O. Box 6434
Shomolu
Lagos
Nigeria
Tel: +234 1 823 093
Email: Thompsondele@onebox.com
Web: www.ippanigeria.org
Director: Thompson Ayodele

IPPA was incorporated in December 2000. It is a private, non-profit organisation involved in research, education, and publication on matters affecting the freedom of individuals. Its objective is to provide market-oriented analysis of current and emerging policy issues, with a view to influencing the public debate. IPPA does not accept government funds, relying instead entirely on the financial support of individuals, foundations and other private organisations. It has received support from Atlas and IPN.

Rising ethnic nationalism and endemic corruption are the

greatest threats to the freedom of Nigerians and have their origins in the centralisation of power and economic resources in the hands of the state. Nigeria's economy can only achieve sustained growth if there is an increase in foreign investment but this will not take place in the current over-regulated economy. IPPA will research the costs of centralisation and regulation and it will make the results public in publications and conferences.

Instituto Acton

Piazza del Gesù
46 Roma
Italy
Tel. +39 335 625 8804/338 176 6148
Email: flfelic@tin.it; pollini@cdu.it
Web: www.actonitalia.org
President: Prof. Pierluigi Pollini
Honorary President: Prof. Michael Novak, Fr Robert Sirico
Director: Prof. Flavio Felice

The Instituto Acton was founded in 2000. Its mission is to foster dialogue among those who want to build a new synthesis between the free-market culture and a communitarian culture of solidarity in the modern Western democracies. It deals with the fundamental principles of human societies; the law, state and economy in order to identify directives for action that create, maintain or foster the development of life worthy to be called human. The foundation will be the meeting point of diverse traditions.

Non-clerical Catholic culture fully assimilated the methods of freedom and can be identified with the second Vatican Council and with the post-council Catholic social teaching. Christian social thought in recent years, from Laborem Exercens to Centesimus Annus, has undergone a process of radical renovation that makes it perhaps the most ductile and concrete tool available for those who want to defend humanity and its dignity in post-industrial societies.

Instituto Cultural Ludwig von Mises (Mexico City and Queretaro)

Calle 27 de abril No. 5

Col. Avila Camacho

53910 Naucalpan

Estado de México

Mexico

Tel: +52 5 294 5309

Fax: +52 5 294 9253

or

San Isidro 107

76230 Juriquilla

Queretaro

Mexico

Tel: +52 42 34 06 85/34 13 48

Fax: +52 42 34 06 85

Email: icumi@infosel.net.mx

Web: www.icumi.org.mx

President: Carolina Romero de Bolivar

The Instituto was founded in 1983 in Mexico City. Its mission is the defence and promotion of liberty and it covers the economic, educational, social and political arenas.

Antony Fisher sowed the first seeds in Carolina Bolivar's mind at the Mont Pélerin Society meeting in Chile in 1981. Two years later, when socialism became almost a political dogma in the main institutions in Mexico, she and her husband followed Antony's example and started their own institute. Antony's goal was to develop a sound methodology, almost non-existent at that time, which would help us to defend and promote liberty in a professional and effective way. And so it was.

The Instituto started to influence the universities through bright academics, new economic and philosophical theories, seminars and books. It proposed new alternatives and policies. Little by little other journalists and commentators joined this effort. Public-policy proposals were written and sent to different levels of government and to natural leaders in society. Some years later, Ronald Reagan, Margaret Thatcher, the Pope and other personalities of the world embraced the same ideas. Finally socialism collapsed. Antony's model proved to be right in turning the world around. After 19 years of hard work, Mexico is today a free and democratic country.

The Instituto Cultural Ludwig von Mises is proud of having contributed to this significant change although there is still much to be done.

Instituto Ecuatoriano de Economia Politica

Higueras 106 y Costanera
Guayaquil
Ecuador
Tel: +593 488 1011
Fax: +593 488 5991
Email: dampuero@ecua.net.ec
Web: www.his.com/~ieep
President: Dora de Ampuero

The institute was founded in 1991. Its mission is to promote individual freedom, the free market, the importance of property rights and a limited government. Atlas provided seed money and assistance. As part of Atlas's network of institutes, IEEP actively exchanges information and experiences with others think tanks around the world.

Political leaders, academicians, journalists, students and prominent leaders of Ecuadorian society participate in our seminars, workshops and conferences and receive our publications. IEEP has the only library in Ecuador with books and publications of the most important liberal thinkers, which attracts intellectuals and students from all over the country.

IEEP has played an important role in bringing dollarisation to the country thereby reducing inflation and so the government's ability to plunder people's property. It campaigns for a healthier economy through studies on taxation reform to the social security system and defence of property rights.

Instituto de Libertad y Democracia (ILD)

Av. Del Parque Norte 829
San Isidro
Lima 27
Peru
Tel: +51 1 225 4131/225 4132 (switchboard)
Fax: +51 1 224 9825
Email: hds@ild.org.pe
Web: www.ild.org.pe
President: Hernando de Soto

The Instituto de Libertad y Democracia was founded in January 1980 following a meeting with Antony Fisher in San Francisco. He then came to Lima to discuss how to structure the statutes, plan the goals, raise funding and what to expect in the short and long term. It became operational in 1984.

The ILD is a private, non-profit organisation. Its purpose is to help Peru create the legal underpinnings of a market economy that would benefit the poor. Within ten years, the organisation had drafted or initiated and then implemented some 400 laws and regulations for three succeeding governments that modernised Peru's economic and political systems and opened them up to greater participation. The ILD has also successfully created and managed legal property systems that have moved hundreds of thousands of businesses and real-estate holdings from the underground economy into the economic mainstream.

The ILD, which began as an organisation with a broad economic and political agenda, is today focused totally on creating modern legal frameworks that help the poor of the developing and ex-communist world access property rights and turn their assets into leveragable capital. The ILD has discovered not only how to locate extra-legal businesses and assets, but also how to redesign and put into operation legal and administrative property systems so that the owners of those businesses and assets will voluntarily move them from the extra-legal to the legal economy.

Since 1996, at the request of more than a dozen heads of state from Asia, the Middle East and Latin America, the ILD broadened its operations from Peru to the world.

Instituto de Libre Empresa (ILE)

Calle Barajas 522

Lima 41

Peru

Tel: +51 1 475 9752/346 0884/224 5645

Fax: +51 1 475 9752/423 9727/346 2762

Email: info@ileperu.net

President: Jose Luis Tapia

The institute was founded in December 1998 and follows the Fisher rule of independence from any vested political interests as well as benefiting from advice on publications available on the Atlas website. ILE is a non-profit, educational and research organisation, which promotes and defends individual and entrepreneurial freedom, following the tradition of the Austrian School, especially of Israel M. Kirzner, to build a prosperous and free society in Peru.

ILE scholars and professionals promote our institutional philosophy on current issues through workshops, forays and seminars directed to businessmen and university students. We publish on international trade, the environment, the Austrian School, economic policy and education. We distribute our ideas in newspapers and on our website and edit working papers and bulletins under our well-known trade mark 'Propiedad Privada'. The ILE has grown from 3 staff in 1998 to 9 in 2001 and is respected by businesses and students due to its strong academic record. An ILE television programme was watched by 500,000 people, and our weekly newspaper column has a readership of 10,000. Since 1998, the institute has taught Economics of the Austrian School to 180 students and delivered more than 2,500 bulletins to congressmen, students, media, professors and businessmen. The website has 465 requests a day.

Instituto Liberal

Rua Professor Alfredo Gomes, 28
Rio de Janeiro 22251-080
Brazil
Tel: +55 21 2539 1115
Fax: +55 21 2537 7206
Email: ilrj@gbl.com.br
Web: www.institutoliberal.org.br
President: Arthur Chagas Diniz

Antony Fisher passed the advice that Hayek had given him to Donald Stewart Jr, a Brazilian entrepreneur, and as a result he founded the Instituto in 1983. It was based on the IEA and greatly benefited from Atlas. As there were a very limited number of pro-liberalism publications in Portuguese in the country, a high priority was given to the translation, editing and publishing of books and booklets. Other activities were also initiated: lectures, seminars, the writing of articles for the Brazilian press, and an active exchange with analogous institutions in Brazil and abroad. One of the most important projects was a series of policy papers on education, health, social security, energy, the financial system, industrial policy, etc. Another relevant project was the bi-monthly publication of NOTAS, an analytical and critical examination of important bills under discussion in the Brazilian Congress.

The Liberal Institute of Rio is in charge of editing and publishing *Think Tank*, a quarterly review sponsored by the National Council of the Brazilian Liberal Institutes.

The International Policy Network

2 Lord North Street
London SW1P 3LB
UK
Tel: +44 (0)20 7799 8900
Fax: +44 (0)20 7799 2137
Email: julian@policynetwork.net
Web: www.policynetwork.net
Directors: Dr Roger Bate and Julian Morris

The International Policy Network (formerly the Atlas Economic Research Foundation UK, founded by Antony Fisher) began work in 2001. It promotes the advancement of learning by research and seeks to encourage the sharing of ideas by intellectuals and others interested in public-policy issues that have international implications. It also provides advice, materials and small amounts of funding to assist in the creation of research and educational charities in developing countries.

Current research topics include globalisation, biotechnology, agriculture, land degradation, water quality, malnutrition, food safety, public health, disease, technology, energy, privatisation, labour standards, resource use, environmental protection, international trade and intellectual property.

Inter Region Economic Network (IREN), Kenya

Box 135 Code 00100 GPO
Nairobi
Kenya
Tel: +254 733 823 062
Email: info@irenkenya.org and jshikuku@yahoo.com
Web: www.irenkenya.org
Director: Shikuku James Shikwati

IREN was founded in 1997 and registered in 2001 through the efforts of Atlas and other institutes that share Antony Fisher's vision.

IREN is founded on the basis of intellectual entrepreneurship. It is a private, non-political organisation and exists to improve accessibility to policies that will enable and encourage the development of Kenya, East Africa and Africa in general, through academic research.

Our mission is 'To free the human mind which is the main spring of all development'. Our vision is to contribute towards the creation of a free society, where the market is informed, choice-driven and fewer and fewer people turn to government to solve problems they can solve on their own.

The Israel Center for Social and Economic Progress
P.O. 84124
Mevasseret-Zion 90805
Israel
Tel: +972 2 534 6463
Fax: +972 2 533 0122
Email: dorondun@012.net.il
Web: www.icsep.org.il
Director and Founder: Daniel Doron

After 5 years of planning the centre was officially launched in 1984. Antony Fisher provided inspiration through his intellectual integrity and ICSEP received sporadic help from him and Atlas.

Only prosperity can enable Israel to pursue peace with strength, to absorb massive immigration and to offer its young opportunities to develop their talents. Many of Israel's social problems and its laggard growth derive from its inefficient state-dominated economic system which needs much more liberalisation before market forces can express the enormous potential of the Israeli worker and entrepreneur. Prosperity has also proven to be the most effective means of mitigating the Arab-Israeli conflict, and offers the best hope for liberating the Arab masses from their misery and endemic poverty.

ICSEP plays a critical role in providing the knowledge needed to implement change and overcome resistance to it and is a leader in shaping a consensus for liberalisation and deregulation of markets, a major educator and spokesman for market economics, a catalyst and facilitator of reform.

James Madison Institute

2017 Delta Boulevard, Suite 102

P.O. Box 37460

Tallahassee

FL 32315

USA

Tel: +1 850 386 3131

Fax: +1 850 386 1807

Email: jmi@jamesmadison.org

Web: www.JamesMadison.org

President: Edwin H. Moore

The James Madison Institute was founded in April 1987 following Dr J. Stanley Marshall's attendance at an Atlas conference in Jamaica to encourage and assist people in the Americas to establish institutes. He persuaded Antony Fisher to stop in Tallahassee on his return and, although there for only a day, he exerted a profound influence on everyone's thinking and Dr Marshall determined to found a public policy institute. Atlas then played a key role.

The James Madison Institute provides research and publications on issues affecting Florida. It interacts with policy-makers from across the state with an emphasis on providing the practical, conservative public-policy solutions required for a fast growing state. It was recently selected by the Florida House to provide 10 days of training for newly elected members, where, due to term limits, there were 63 new members out of 120, and has used the relationships gained by this training to continue to expand its role as an information resource for policy-makers.

John Locke Foundation
200 W. Morgan Street, Suite 200
Raleigh
NC 27601
USA
Tel: +1 919 828 3876
Fax: +1 919 821 5117
Email: kswanson@johnlocke.org
Web: www.johnlocke.org
Chairman and President: John M. Hood

The Atlas Foundation was instrumental in helping the John Locke Foundation in its founding in 1990. It assisted with initial funding and provided valuable counsel on the nature and operation of a dynamic, state-based public-policy think tank.

The mission of the John Locke Foundation (JLF) is to develop and promote solutions to North Carolina's most critical challenges. An independent think tank based in Raleigh, JLF seeks to transform state and local government through the principles of competition, innovation, personal freedom and personal responsibility in order to strike a better balance between the public sector and private institutions of family, faith, community and enterprise. JLF is a source of cutting-edge research, a publisher of news and commentary, and a catalyst for change.

Jon Thorlaksson Institute
P.O. Box 1577
Reykjavik
Iceland
Tel: +354 525 4502
Email: Hannesgi@rhi.hi.is
President: Hannes Gissurarson

Hannes Gissurarson first met Antony Fisher at the Mont Pélerin Society meeting in Stanford in 1980, and admired Antony's ability to distinguish the essential from the non-essential and his all-consuming interest in the liberalisation of society. He also remembers his favourite toast: To peace and low taxes!

In 1983, Antony and Dorian visited Hannes in Iceland when Antony spoke to businessmen with whom he was very effective as he spoke their language and shared their concerns, although he had a much wider horizon than most of them. The same year the Jon Thorlaksson Institute was set up and, with others, was responsible for the visits of James M. Buchanan, Milton Friedman and other leading speakers.

The institute arranged the translation of books by Hayek and Friedman amongst others into Icelandic and held many meetings. The impact was great. Iceland is one of the countries which has liberalised the most over the last 10–15 years, according to the Freedom Index. Since 1991, many members of government, including the prime minister (the longest serving leader in Europe at present), have fully participated in the work of the Libertarian Association and in the Jon Thorlaksson Institute. Antony Fisher acted as one of the catalysts of this great change in the fortunes of the Icelanders. Having deregulated, liberalised, privatised and stabilised the economy, the next step in Iceland should be radically to lower taxes, and to engage in fierce tax competition with other countries.

The Josiah Bartlett Center for Public Policy

7 South State Street
P.O. Box 897
Concord
NH 03302-0987
USA
Tel: +1 603 224 4450
Fax: +1 603 224 4329
Email: jbartlett@conknet.com
Web: www.jbartlett.org
President: Daphne A. Kenyon

Emily and Edgar Mead founded the centre in 1993 after Edgar attended a meeting at the Heritage Foundation. Atlas provided critical general funding from 1995 through 1999.

The centre has as its core beliefs individual freedom and

responsibility, limited and accountable government, and an appreciation of the role of the free-enterprise system. It is a non-profit, non-partisan, independent think tank focused on state and local public-policy issues that affect the quality of life for New Hampshire citizens. To improve economic prosperity and the general welfare, the centre provides information, research and analysis to decision-makers. It runs an annual Better Government Competition to help locate and publicise ideas for making state and local government more effective. It publishes a newsletter, *Ideas*, and runs the Charter Resource Centre.

The Liberal Conservative Institute
(The ILK Foundation)

UL Judyma 8
20–716 Lublin
Poland
Tel: +48 81 526 7244
Fax: +48 81 533 8577
Email: ilk@platon.man.lublin.pl
Web: www.ilk.lublin.pl
President: Jan Jacek Szymona, Ph.D.

The ILK Foundation was founded in 1990 and although Antony Fisher played no part in it he played a great role in the development of Jacek Szymona's political and economic views. In about 1980 he read a Polish translation of *Must History Repeat Itself?* In fact he read it several times. Atlas supports ILK financially, translating, editing and printing the books published by the ILK Foundation. ILK is financed exclusively by donations from private individuals and companies from within as well as from outside Poland.

The purpose of the institute is to disseminate ideas of classical liberalism and conservatism by various educational, informative and popularising activities. It maintains a library and runs a mail-order bookstore of classical-liberal, libertarian and conservative literature with English editions and some Polish translations. The institute has published 14 books, and runs conferences and funds scholarships.

Liberales Institut Zurich

Vogelsangstrass 52
Zurich CH-8006
Switzerland
Tel: +41 1 364 1666
Fax: +41 1 364 1669
Email: Libinst@bluewin.ch
Web: www.libinst.ch
President: Prof. Daniel Thurer
Executive Vice-President: Robert Nef

The Liberales Institut was founded in 1979 and although it had no input from Antony Fisher it has found inspiration from Atlas's workshops and meetings, when people who are in favour of liberty and free markets get together.

It is a forum where the basic values and concepts of a free society can be discussed and questioned. Its aim is the establishment of free markets as the best way towards openness, diversity and autonomy. It is not associated with any political party and seeks to disseminate classical liberal ideas through publications, discussion forums and seminars. It organises lunchtime discussions with an introductory speaker, public lectures for larger audiences and lecture series on political, social, economic and cultural subjects. It has a library of over 3,000 books at its offices.

Libertad y Desarrollo

San Crescente 551
Las Condes
Santiago
CP 6760461
Chile
Tel: +56 2 377 4800
Fax: +56 2 234 1893
Email: lyd@lyd.com
Web: www.lyd.com
Executive Director: Christian Larroulet

Libertad y Desarrollo was founded in 1990 and has had the sus-

tained support of the Atlas Foundation, which has enthusiastically assisted in establishing international contacts, provided
high-quality specialists for numerous visits to Chile, promoted
operative links to similar institutions and backed several projects
such as the web page.

It is a private research think tank, independent of any political, religious, business or government affiliations. It focuses on
public policies promoting the values and principles of a free
society, organising economic, social, political, legislative and environmental programmes as well as the Center of International
Economics. It has published 14 books and issues 7 regular publications. All its studies, analyses and proposals are distributed to
government authorities, congressmen, academic researchers,
businessmen, the media and the general public.

Libertad y Desarrollo works closely with congressmen and
produces *Legislative Summary*, a weekly publication providing
the reader with a systematic format to explain the technical, legal
and economic implications of each bill being discussed in Congress, including a description of each bill's content and status.

Liberální Institut

Spalena 51
Prague 1
11000 Czech Republic
Tel: +420 2 2491 2199/2493 0796
Fax: +420 2 2493 0203
Email: info@libinst.cz
Web: www.libinst.cz
President: Dr Jiri Schwarz

The Liberální Institut was founded in 1989 and registered in
1990. Atlas provided funding during the first two years as well as
know-how and books. It is an independent, non-governmental,
non-profit organisation aimed at the development and application of classical liberal ideas and programmes. It undertakes specific research projects, as listed below, and presentations in the
form of discussion-fora, colloquia and conferences.

Its educational projects include: Financial Economics for Future Leaders and their Teachers; The Liberalni Institut Summer University; The Road to a Free Society (a seminar on the transformation of former totalitarian societies); The Gary Becker Prize for the best student paper in economics.

Regular monthly discussions are held on public-policy affairs and there is an annual presentation of the most significant book published by the Liberální Institut. Current research projects include Deregulation and Competition within Electricity Market, Competition in the Czech Gas Industry, Energy Markets Cohesion, Railroads as a Part of the Transportation Market, Water Industry Privatisation, Privatisation of Postal Services, Deregulation and Competition within Telecommunications, Tax Burden and Its Acceptance by Voters, Health Care Reform, Education as a Private Good, Free Market Approach to Environmental Protection, Negative Impacts of Advertisement (on Tobacco Products) Limitation; Index of Economic Freedom – Structure, Trend Analysis, International Comparison; Theory of Spontaneous Order.

The Liberální Institut has for the last two years been one of the three most quoted institutions in the Czech Republic.

Liberty Institute

Julian L. Simon Centre
J-259, Saket (2nd floor)
New Delhi 110 017
India
Tel: +91 11 651 2441/652 8244
Fax: +91 11 685 6992
Email: info@libertyindia.org
Web: www.libertyindia.org
President: Barun S. Mitra

Liberty Institute was formally launched in December 1995 with the motto 'where the mind is without fear'. It believes that political and economic freedoms are indivisible, and together form the core of man's rights. The institute is constrained neither by the politically correct, nor current fashion. It does not accept funding from governmental organisations, and is completely dependent on private contributions so as to retain its integrity and independence.

The late Julian L. Simon introduced us to Atlas and as a tribute to Professor Simon's unending spirit of inquiry, and his everlasting belief in the unlimited potential of man, the institute named its policy-research section after him. Atlas's contribution has been fourfold: it welcomed us into its global network and invited us to international gatherings, introducing us to people and ideas, it encouraged and exposed us to the range of work being undertaken internationally to preserve liberty, it provided our initial funding to enable us to initiate a few activities and to learn hands-on the basic functioning of an independent think tank; and it then provided seed capital to help us establish the institute, build our credentials and attract the attention of opinion-makers, media and the public at large.

Liberty Institute is a non-profit, independent policy-research and educational organisation. It has a growing publications programme, conducts seminars and conferences and has a range of activities aimed at youth. Its activities are primarily geared to provide market-based responses to contemporary social, economic and environmental issues with the aim of preserving individual liberty and expanding freedom of choice. Currently, the institute is hosting on average one public event a month. An increasing number of independent scholars are expressing interest in working with the institute on a range of issues. We have so far brought out 10 books and monographs, and hosted dozens of seminars on topics such as rent control, broadcasting, education, biotechnology, agriculture, environment, health, intellectual property and many others.

Love of individual liberty unites all the friends of freedom to the Atlas network.

Lithuanian Free Market Institute

56 Birutes St
Vilnius 2004
Lithuania
Tel: +370 2 72 25 84
Fax: +370 2 72 12 79
Email: lfmi@lrinka.lt
Web: www.freema.org
President: Elena Leontjeva

LFMI was founded in 1990 and its close relationship with Atlas has given it involvement and visibility in the international think-tank community.

LFMI is an independent non-profit organisation established to advance the ideas of individual freedom and responsibility, free markets and limited government. Since its inception it has been at the forefront of economic thought and reform in Lithuania. It helped frame policy debates by conducting research and creating reform packages on key issues, and played a key behind-the-scenes role in helping to craft and refine legislative proposals. It was involved in the Law on Litas Credibility, the creation of the legal and institutional framework for the securities market, the privatisation legislation and private, fully-funded pension insurance. LFMI's recommendations were adopted in legislation on commercial banks, the Bank of Lithuania, credit unions, and insurance and foreign investment, and it provided a valuable input to tax and budgetary policy amongst other things.

The Locke Institute

Suite 103
4084 University Drive
Fairfax 22030
USA
Tel: +1 703 934 6934
Fax: +1 703 934 6927
Email: locke@thelockeinstitute.org
Web: www.TheLockeInstitute.org
President: Professor Charles K. Rowley

Inspired by the IEA, the Locke Institute was founded in 1989. Atlas provided funding and other help.

The Locke Institute is dedicated to the preservation of private property rights, individual freedom, limited government and the rule of law. The institute pursues this mission through a programme of publications, lectures and workshops as well as by interacting with other like-minded institutes and centres. The greatest achievement of the institute is the John Locke Series of books, three of which won the Sir Antony Fisher International Memorial Awards for 1994, 1995 and 1996, a unique achievement.

The institute is proud of its Distinguished Lecture Series in Law and Economics (in association with the James M. Buchanan Centre). It also publishes a bi-annual journal *The Locke Luminary*, and monographs which provide scholarly and serious-minded treatises on important issues of classical liberalism, clearly written for a wide readership.

The Mackinac Center for Public Policy

P.O. Box 568

140 W. Main Street

Midland

Michigan 48640

USA

Tel: +1 989 631 0900

Fax: +1 989 631 0964

Email: reed@mackinac.org

Web: www.mackinac.org

President: Lawrence W. Reed

The centre was founded in 1987, with Antony Fisher's work and influence shaping and motivating the thinking of the founding board. There has been collaboration with Lawrence Reed's fellow Grove City College alum, Alex Chafuen and Atlas on joint projects, and Atlas is a real assistant to the movement as a whole and of our individual groups in particular.

The Mackinac Center for Public Policy has a full-time staff of 30, plus a summer intern staff of 14, and an annual budget of approximately $3 million. It has been influential in shaping Michigan public policy, especially on issues pertaining to education, labour, privatisation, economic development and government spending. The combined circulation of two of its quarterly publications, *The Michigan Education Report* and *The Michigan Privatisation Report*, exceeds 140,000.

Its expertise in management, communications, marketing, development and strategic planning has been sought after, leading to a bi-annual 'leadership conference' at its headquarters where executives and staff from like-minded groups from around the world are trained.

The Mackinac Center prides itself on its many efforts to strengthen the entire movement of state-based free-market think tanks. It mentors and advises other organisations on a regular basis.

Making Our Economy Right (MOER)

Apt # 201

NE(G) 2–A

Road # 84

Gulshan-2

Dhaka

Bangladesh

Tel: +880 2 882 9070

Fax: +880 2 882 9070

Email: nizam@bdmail.net

Web: www.moer.org

President: Nizam Ahmad

MOER was founded in 1991 and is the only free-market organisation in Bangladesh, where speaking about free-market economics is dangerous and fundraising is difficult because our corporate world does not see government interference as a problem but a blessing for mutual profit.

John Blundell introduced MOER to Atlas, which has given financial and moral support and opened the free-market academic world to MOER. Through them, it is a member of the Economic Freedom Network. MOER feels strong in their beliefs because they know a huge academic storehouse exists to back up our views.

MOER has had articles published and articles and books translated into Bangla. It would like to put on a series of seminars to challenge the role of government and of development economists who are the chief reason for our poverty and our distorted economy. It suits the ultra-rich and the so-called industrialists whose fortunes were created with massive government support and protection at the great cost of our personal freedom.

The Maryland Public Policy Institute

P.O. Box 195
Germantown
Maryland 20875-0195
USA
Tel: +1 240 686 3510
Fax: +1 240 686 3511
Email: csummers@mdpolicy.org
Web: www.mdpolicy.org
President: Christopher B. Summers

Atlas played an important role in the institute's founding in January 2001 with regards to advice, encouragement and the basic funding needed to move the idea off paper. The institute's first op-ed, 'Don't Throw Money at Schools', was published in Maryland's leading newspaper, the *Baltimore Sun*, and a keynote address by Dr Ron Utt, 'The Result of Playing In-Bounds', discussed the implications of administering smart growth policies and the adverse effects of these policies on housing costs and home-ownership rates. Over 400 Maryland builders, realtors and state legislators attended the event.

The institute has already published three policy papers. The first was a legislative wrap-up of the 2001 Maryland General Assembly session, followed by a piece on smart growth and home-ownership, and the third addressed the lack of local telephone service competition.

Minaret of Freedom Foundation

4323 Rosedale Avenue
Bethesda
MD 20814
USA
Tel: +1 301 907 0947
Fax: +1 301 656 4714
Email: mfi@minaret.org
Web: www.minaret.org
President: Imad-ad-Dean Ahmad

Atlas played an indispensable role in the founding of the institute in 1993, as Dean Ahmad met the founders of Muslim libertarian think tanks at an Atlas workshop and conceived the idea of an Islamic think tank centred on the importance of liberty, including free markets, to Islamic thought and Muslim life. Atlas then provided funding, invaluable information on structure and other guidance.

In fulfilment of the obligations laid upon Muslims by the Qur'an and the Sunnah, the mission of the foundation is to discover and publish the politico-economic policy implications of Islamic law (shari'ah) and their consequences on the economic well-being of the community; to promote the establishment of free trade and justice (an essential common interest of Islam and the West); to educate Islamic religious and community leaders in economics and in the fact that liberty is a necessary, though not sufficient, condition for the achievement of a good society; and to wage unending holy struggle (jihâd) against every form of tyranny over the mind of man.

These goals shall be implemented by independent scholarly research (ijtihâd) into policy issues of concern to Muslim countries and/or to Muslims in America, through publication of scholarly and popular expositions of such research; translation of appropriate works on the free market into the languages of the Muslim world with introductions and commentaries by Muslim scholars; and the operation of a scholars exchange programme.

Manhattan Institute for Policy Research

52 Vanderbilt Avenue
New York 10017
USA
Tel: +1 212 599 7000
Fax: +1 212 599 3494
Email: lmone@manhattan-institute.org
Web: www.manhattan-institute.org
Director: Dr Lawrence J. Mone

The history and work of the Manhattan Institute are described in the main text of this book and can be studied in detail on their website.

The Mount Hood Philosophical Society

P.O. Box 17576
Portland
OR 97217
USA
Tel: +1 503 282 3260/541 753 7271
Email: deckerf@ucs.orst.edu
President: Dr Fred W. Decker

Antony Fisher's role in support of the IEA stimulated our efforts to develop knowledge and leadership for freedom and the founding of the Mount Hood Philosophical Society in 1972.

As a public forum sponsor, the society has worked to bring to the Pacific Northwest advocates in various disciplines to appear at seminars, conferences and lectures so that students, teachers and community leaders were exposed to the key ideas underlying free societies. It also co-sponsored a ten-year series of Global Affairs Seminars and co-sponsored ROBIS (Role of Business in Society) conferences. MHS also initiated development of ROGIS (Role of Government in Society) events and began an ongoing investigation of the omission of freedom classics from many college and university curricula for which those works appear uniquely appropriate.

The National Center for Policy Analysis

12655 N. Central Expressway

Suite 720

Dallas

Texas 75243

USA

Tel: +1 972 386 0672

Fax: +1 972 386 0924

Email: ncpa@ncpa.org

Web: www.ncpa.org

President: John C. Goodman

Antony Fisher encouraged John Goodman to set up the NCPA in 1983. He helped him form a board (on which he served) and supplied a grant and good counsel. Atlas's annual workshops were invaluable in providing the opportunity to learn from others.

Everything anyone wants to know about the NCPA and its achievements can be found at www.ncpa.org/about/profile2001.html.

The National Wilderness Institute

P.O. Box 25766

Georgetown Station

Washington

DC 20007

USA

Tel: +1 703 836 7404

Fax: +1 703 836 7404

Email: nwi@nwi.org

Web: www.nwi.org

President and Executive Director: Robert E. Gordon, Jr

The NWI was founded in 1989 and Atlas provided financial support, promoted its projects in its publications, introduced it to individuals interested in its work, helped it network in the international community and assisted in the establishment of its website.

The NWI is dedicated to using science to guide the wise

management of natural resources for the benefit and enjoyment of people. It recognises the direct, positive relationship between freedom, progress and environmental quality, and champions private stewardship, which enhances nature's bounty while encouraging economic growth. NWI recognises that renewable resources such as wildlife, fish, wetlands, wilderness, forest, range, air, water and soil are dynamic, resilient and respond positively to wise management. It supports site- and situation-specific practices which unleash the creative forces of the free market, protect or extend private-property rights, and reduce the inefficient and counter-productive effect of government regulations.

We have conducted exhaustive peer-review studies on endangered species; regularly testified before the US Congress and exposed mismanagement of US environmental agencies that resulted in laws reforming important national conservation programmes.

Open Republic
54 Shelbourne Road
Dublin 4
Ireland
Tel: +353 1 660 8012
Fax: +353 1 660 8012
Email: pmacdonnell@openrepublic.org
Web: www.openrepublic.org
President: Paul MacDonnell

Antony Fisher was the inspiration and Atlas the guide to the Open Republic's founding in January 2001 to provide a platform for discussing market and individual-oriented alternatives to state intervention in social and economic matters.

The core philosophy is that individuals have key rights such as freedom of expression, freedom of conscience and freedom to provide for their welfare and the welfare of their families through economic activity. We believe that these rights need to be understood and upheld in the context of a complex economic and social system. However, today in Ireland, our basic rights and freedoms are often the direct or indirect casualties of regulation and legislation from both Dublin and Brussels.

We have achieved publicity and recognition in the Irish and international media (WSJ Europe) since we were founded, and are the Irish publishers for the Fraser Institute's *Economic Freedom Network*. However most of our work is ahead of us.

Pacific Research Institute for Public Policy

755 Sansome St
Suite 450
San Francisco
CA 94111
USA
Tel: +1 415 989 0833
Fax: +1 415 989 2411
Web: www.pacificresearch.org
Email: spipes@pacificresearch.org
President: Sally C. Pipes

Antony Fisher founded PRI with the assistance of its first chairman, James North, in 1979. Atlas was founded shortly after and was one of the key organisations that helped PRI over a transition to Sally Pipes's leadership in 1991–2. Without that generous support, PRI may not have survived.

PRI promotes individual freedom and personal responsibility – the cornerstones of a civil society. It believes these principles are fostered through a free economy, limited government and private initiative. In order to put these ideas into action, PRI publishes books and studies, provides commentary to leading media, hosts public events, and conducts comprehensive grassroots and community outreach.

Its 'outside the beltway' independence, coupled with California's influence as a national trendsetter, gives PRI a unique role in the public debate. It is often able to address important issues before they reach national prominence, and it also leads the way in anticipating future threats to liberty.

PRI has become a highly respected resource for prominent

mainstream media and its website receives on average 55,000 hits per month. Much of PRI's research is presented as a template or blueprint for reform that can be easily implemented and readily adapted by other free-market organisations at the state level. It collaborates with hundreds of like-minded groups nationwide, leveraging its analysis to the widest possible audience.

Pioneer Institute for Public Policy Research

85 Devonshire Street
Boston
MA 02109
USA
Tel: +1 617 723 2277
Email: cchieppo@pioneerinstitute.org
Executive Director: Stephen J. Adams

Lovett C. Peters had been on the Foundation for Economic Education board for many years and met Antony Fisher through Leonard Read at FEE in the mid-50s and then at Mont Pélerin Society meetings after 1975. He sold his oil business in the mid-80s and replicated the IEA in Massachusetts, launching Pioneer in December 1987 with a lunch for 50 business leaders which Antony Fisher was to have addressed. Unfortunately he was by then too ill and John Blundell came instead.

Pioneer now has a $2m annual budget, all private money, 14 paid employees (three who pay to keep their jobs), and some part-time researchers, and it is having a substantial impact in probably the most left-leaning state in the USA. From the beginning it concentrated on improving education and Massachusetts now has excellent charter school law, 14,000 children in charter schools, half of which are producing exemplary results and the other half somewhat better than average.

Now in our 11th year, the Better Government Competition seeks ideas from the public to downsize, privatise or improve governmental functions. This has been a major success and has been copied in eight states, Canada and the UK, and is soon to be initiated in Argentina.

The Science & Environmental Policy Project

1600 South Eads Street
Suite 712–S
Arlington
VA 22202-2097
USA
Tel: +1 703 920 2744
Email: singer@sepp.org
Web: www.sepp.org
President: S. Fred Singer

SEPP was founded in 1992, receiving early support from Atlas at a crucial stage. The 'perspectives' offered by SEPP are simply those of sound science. We are a strictly non-partisan organisation and undertake no lobbying, but respond when requested by Congress or administration officials.

SEPP benefits from an extensive network of prominent scientists who volunteer their time and expertise and conduct independent analyses of the scientific evidence that underpin government environmental policy. They are brought together by a common desire to see such policy based on facts, observable results and reproducible research rather than emotional and political opportunism. The Project provides objective policy analyses and scientific assessment untainted by activist agendas. Aside from our major interests in global warming and ozone depletion, SEPP has also studied and continues to deal with problems of asbestos, radon, health effects of arsenic and technological means of reducing urban air pollution.

Professor Frederick Seitz, a former president of the US National Academy of Sciences, chairs our international Board of Scientific Advisors.

For more details, look at the website.

The Smith Center for Private Enterprise Studies

California State University
Hayward
CA 94542
USA
Tel: +1 510 885 2640
Fax: +1 510 885 4222
Email: cbaird@bay.csuhayward.edu
Web: www.sbe.csuhayward.edu/~sbesc
President: Dr Charles W. Baird

Antony Fisher and Atlas helped inspire the creation of the Smith Center in 1991. Its mission is the restoration and promulgation of the principles of classical liberalism in the US and around the world.

We sponsor campus speakers, visit high-school classrooms, award scholarships and sponsor sessions at such conferences as the Southern Economic Association. We train high-school teachers during the summer, run essay and business-planning contests for high-school students, award the annual Smith Prize in Austrian economics, teach a university course in new-venture financing, and publish occasional pamphlets. Our greatest achievement consists of the classical-liberal events that we bring to this campus, which otherwise is a redoubt for democratic socialists.

Social Affairs Unit

314–322 Regent Street
Suite 5/6
London W1R 5AB
UK
Tel: +44 (0)20 7637 4356
Fax: +44 (0)20 7436 8530
Email: digbyanderson@compuserve.com
Web: www.socialaffairsunit.org.uk
Director: Dr Digby Anderson
Deputy Director: Michael Mosbacher

The Social Affairs Unit was founded in 1980. As its name suggests, it is primarily interested in social affairs, and in practice this has meant cultural affairs, such as the role of morality and manners in maintaining a free but responsible and orderly society; the extent to which social policy in health, housing and education should involve the state; and the regulation of hazard and risk in commercial affairs. Several of these are obviously 'Fisher affairs', but the SAU's real debt to Antony and Atlas is organisational as it was modelled on the IEA in the way it works by publishing, in its fundraising and so on. In this sense it is a Fisher think tank and Fisher's Atlas Foundation has been important in helping the SAU's message reach beyond UK shores, especially in the USA. The unit has won two Antony Fisher Memorial Prizes.

The South Carolina Policy Council

1323 Pendleton Street

Columbia

SC 29201

USA

Tel: +1 803 779 5022

Fax: +1 803 779 4953

Email: etm@scpolicycouncil.co,

President: Edward T. McMullen Jr

The SCPC was the first state-based think tank in the USA and was founded in 1986 by Thomas A. Roe, an admirer of Antony Fisher's work and briefly a trustee of Atlas before his death. As a Heritage Foundation trustee, he used Fisher's vision and applied it to the USA. Atlas has provided educational and financial support and has helped on several of our school-choice projects as well as through conferences and in providing intellectual ammunition.

The St Lawrence Institute

P.O. Box 307
NDG Station
Montreal QC
H4A 3P6
Canada
Tel: +1 514 233 8321
Fax: +1 514 489 0312
Email: sid@stlawrenceinstitute.org
Web: www.stlawrenceinstitute.org
Executive Director: Sid Parkinson

The St Lawrence Institute was founded in 1980 with help from the Fraser Institute, Antony Fisher and Atlas. It is an educational think tank to study market-oriented solutions to important social issues. Its programmes have been aimed towards educating general or specific audiences rather than putting forward suggestions for public policy. Its approach is influenced by its members – historians, educators and journalists – and by their inclinations concerning the traditional liberal arts (as opposed to the social-science approach of economists). Areas of concern include education policy and curricula, ethics and philosophy, culture, foreign affairs and international relations, and a proper understanding of our civilisation based upon a comprehension of its history and how it evolved.

The Sutherland Institute

111 E. 5600 South
Suite 202
Salt Lake City
Utah 84070
USA
Tel: +1 801 281 2081
Fax: +1 801 281 2414
Email: si@sutherlandinstitute.org
Web: www.sutherlandinstitute.org
President: Paul T. Mero

Atlas provided seed money, introductions and advice for the Sutherland Institute's founding in 1996 and Antony Fisher's ideas shape its intellectual progress.

The institute is a public-policy research organisation that focuses on policy issues in Utah. It is named after the only Utahn ever appointed to the US Supreme Court, one of the 'four old men' derided by Franklin Roosevelt because they thwarted his most egregious socialist projects.

Amongst other things, the institute has brought the ideas of limited government, liberty and self-reliance to the fore in Utah. School choice has become a viable legislative option, our consumer's guide to Utah public and private schools has given tens of thousands of parents the information necessary to choose their schools wisely for the first time. Privatisation, as well as the problem of public agencies competing with private companies, is now a valid topic of debate due in part to our efforts.

Thomas Jefferson Institute for Public Policy

9035 Golden Sunset Lane
Springfield
VA 22153
USA
Tel: +1 703 440 9447
Fax: +1 703 455 1531
Email: mikethompson@erols.com
Web: www.thomasjeffersoninst.org
President: Michael Thompson

The TJI was founded in 1996 and Atlas was one of Michael Thompson's first stops on his journey to found it. Atlas is the foundation's 'favourite uncle' – always there to talk with, to seek advice from – and it provided financial assistance.

The TJI is a state-focused public-policy foundation based on the principles of limited government, free enterprise and individual responsibility. It has a highly respected bi-partisan board of directors and its greatest achievements have been bi-partisan respect and endorsements from leading Republicans and Democrats; the development of and major state support for a new bioinformatics research institute at Virginia Tech University; the broad-based support for the proposed 'Virginia Investment Act' which was drawn from a TJI idea that would limit the growth of state government to the rate of inflation and population growth, with the 'extra money' going toward transportation and education needs; and because of our K-12 education studies, one county has begun an in-depth analysis of its current teaching methods.

Virginia Institute for Public Policy

20461 Tappahannock Place
Potomac Falls
20165-4791
USA
Tel: +1 703 421 8635
Fax: +1 703 421 8631
Email: JTaylor@VirginiaInstitute.org
Web: www.VirginiaInstitute.org
President: John Taylor

The Atlas Foundation provided the seed capital for the Virginia Institute soon after its incorporation in 1996, and Leonard Liggio, Atlas vice-president, sits on the board. Both he and Alex Chafuen have provided encouragement, information and advice.

The Virginia Institute for Public Policy is an independent, non-partisan, education and research organisation committed to the goals of individual opportunity and economic growth. Through research, policy recommendations and symposia, it works ahead of the political process to lay the intellectual foundation for a society dedicated to individual liberty, dynamic entrepreneurial capitalism, private property, the rule of law and constitutionally limited government.

The vision of the institute is that the people of Virginia understand and practise the fundamentals of a free society, including the inextricable link between political and economic freedom; personal accountability for one's actions; and respect for the time, labour, income and property of others.

Index

Egg Marketing Board 57–8
Egg Reorganisation Committee 58
Ehrenfield, David 128
Endangered Species Act (1973) 129, 130
Erpro 210 2
Esso 141
Eton College 14–16, 21
exchange controls 43, 107, 108–9

Fabian Society 44
Fabians 40, 66, 81, 82, 104, 135
Fairfax, Virginia 163
Farmers' and Smallholders' Association 37
Feulner, Dr Edwin J. 146, 147, 150
Field, Frank 152
Financial Times 94, 101
Fisher, Sir Antony George Anson: appearance
    xvii, 18, 37, 43, 46, 143; personality xix, 5, 7,
    23–4, 28, 30, 35, 37, 43, 52–3, 55, 75, 76, 143,
    165, 169, 170; birth (28 June 1915) 6;
    childhood 7, 11, 13; Christian Science 13–14,
    17, 35, 163, 164, 165, 170; education 3–4,
    14–17, 52; Deroy Car Company 18, 19; Close
    Brothers 19–20, 36, 40; car rental company
    21, 35; war record xv, xvii, 2–5, 23–31, 33, 87,
    139–40; marries Eve Naylor 23; effect of
    Basil's death 4, 25–6, 43; buys Newplace
    33–4; farming 33, 45, 46, 47; forms views on
    economics 34–5; visits Hayek xvi, 39–40, 41,
    43, 59, 109; chicken-breeding xvi, xviii, 46,
    48–51, 54–7, 60, 75, 109, 169, 170; as
    chairman of Buxted 50–51, 115, 122;
    relationship with his children 51–2; view of
    politicians xvii, 5, 54; founds the Institute of
    Economic Affairs xvi, xvii–xviii, 18, 59, 72,
    109–12, 115; Joseph praises 103–4;
    'contretemps' with the Directors 111–13;
    collapse of first marriage 115, 117; turtle-
    breeding xvi, 118–32; run of business failures
    130–33; creation of IEA-like bodies abroad
    133, 137–62; marries Dorian 143–4;
    establishes Atlas Economic Research
    Foundation xvi, 153, 154; terminal illness
    xvii, 162, 163, 164; knighthood (1988) xvii,
    113, 164; death (8 July 1988) xvi, xvii, 145,
    164; memorial service xvii, 165; Harris's
    tribute 165, 168; estate 165; legacy of
    xvii–xviii, 165, 167–72; *The Case for Freedom*
    41–2, 87; *Must History Repeat Itself?* 41, 86–9
Fisher, Basil (AF's brother) 20, 86; childhood 7,
    11, 13; education 3–4, 15, 16–17; war record
    2, 23, 31; death 3–6, 24–7, 43; obituary 26
Fisher, Basil Mark (known as Mark; AF's son)
    15, 34, 46, 52, 115–21, 127, 130, 132

Fisher, Dorian (née Crocker; AF's second wife)
    xvi, xvii, 35–6, 56, 112, 135, 136, 143–5, 156,
    161, 163, 164
Fisher, Eve Lilian (née Naylor; AF's first wife)
    4, 20, 23, 24, 34, 52–5, 115, 116–17, 121
Fisher, Bishop George Carnac (AF's paternal
    grandfather) 8, 14
Fisher, George Kenneth Thompson (AF's
    father) 3, 6, 8–13, 14, 23
Fisher, Giles (AF's grandson) 120
Fisher, Janet Katherine Mary (née Anson; AF's
    mother) 4, 6, 8, 9–10, 13, 14
Fisher, Lucinda (AF's granddaughter) 120
Fisher, Lucy (AF's daughter) 34, 115, 117
Fisher, Mark (AF's son) *see* Fisher, Basil Mark
Fisher, Mary (AF's paternal grandmother) 8
Fisher, Michael (AF's cousin) 4, 24
Fisher, Mike (AF's son) 19, 34, 52, 115, 121, 161
Fisher, Rosie (AF's daughter-in-law) 117, 120
Fisher, William (AF's uncle) 17
Fisher Memorial Prize 153
'Fisher Trainer' 28–9, 30
Flair Plastics 132
Forest Row 8
Fosdick, Peggy and Fosdick, Sam: *Last Chance
    Lost?* 124, 125, 126, 130
Foundation for Economic Education (FEE),
    Irvington-on-Hudson 47
Fourth Norfolk Regiment 6
Framfield, Sussex 33, 49, 53; parish church 53
Fraser Institute, Vancouver 138–43, 154, 171;
    Rent Control: A Popular Paradox 140–41
Freedom Association 79
Friedman, Milton 74, 79, 82–6, 92, 93, 95, 106,
    107, 109, 137, 144; 'The Counter-Revolution
    in Monetary Policy' 84
Friedman, Rose 106, 144
Fripp, Rex 15, 21
Fujimori, Alberto 159

Gardyne, Jock Bruce 95
Gaza, Palestine 3, 6; Military Cemetery 12
General Management Services 62
General Metal Utilisation Company 36
Geoffrey Gunther Memorial prize 14
German air force 1–2
Gilder, George 148; *Wealth and Poverty* 148
Gingrich, Newt 160
Giuliani, Mayor Rudolph 148
Glasgow Herald 65
globalisation xviii, 171
Goldsmith, Sir James xviii
Goodier, Mike 124–5
Goodman, John 160, 161